Social Reproduction Theory

Social Reproduction Theory

Remapping Class, Recentering Oppression

Edited by Tithi Bhattacharya

Foreword by Lise Vogel

First published 2017 by Pluto Press
345 Archway Road, London N6 5AA

www.plutobooks.com

British Library Cataloguing in Publication Data
A catalogue record for this book is available from the British Library

ISBN 978 0 7453 9989 8 Hardback
ISBN 978 0 7453 9988 1 Paperback
ISBN 978 1 7868 0157 9 PDF eBook
ISBN 978 1 7868 0159 3 Kindle eBook
ISBN 978 1 7868 0158 6 EPUB eBook

This book is printed on paper suitable for recycling and made from fully managed and sustained forest sources. Logging, pulping and manufacturing processes are expected to conform to the environmental standards of the country of origin.

Typeset by Stanford DTP Services, Northampton, England

Simultaneously printed in the United Kingdom and United States of America

For Shayari and Bill.

And for every woman who has been patronised
while trying to change the world.

Contents

Acknowledgements

This volume came together through ongoing conversations, explorations and engagements among the contributors. It is such collaborations that made this volume possible.

I am grateful for a grant from the College of Liberal Arts at Purdue University and generous contributions from the Founders College at York University that allowed us to host a workshop on social reproduction theory in May 2016. Kole Kilibarda ensured the success of that workshop with his unstinting hard work and thoughtful comments at sessions.

David Shulman at Pluto Press is not only one of the best but also perhaps the most patient of editors I have worked with. Sarah Grey's wonderful work proved that it makes a great difference when even the copyeditor for a book is a Social Reproduction feminist!

Thanks are due to the Historical Materialism conference, which has, over the years, allowed many of us to explore Marxist ideas without fear of heresy hunting. Many of the ideas and essays in this volume were presented and/or seeded at the conference.

The editors at *Viewpoint* magazine helped me clarify my own thoughts regarding class formation. I am thankful to them for letting me reproduce my essay for this volume. Thanks are also due to *New Left Review* (100: July–August 2016), where Nancy Fraser's essay in this volume was first published.

Several friends have read drafts of these essays and/or patiently answered my questions regarding several aspects of social reproduction theory. Colin Barker and Charlie Post have always been there to read and comment, whenever asked, usually at unreasonably short notice. Hester Eisenstein is someone I continue to learn from; her friendship and support have sustained both the volume and its editor. Nancy Holmstrom, Cindi Katz, Sara Farris, and Kevin Floyd are friends and comrades to whom I owe much. Their work provides much of the analytical scaffolding on which this volume stands. Mike McCarthy was very generous with his time and insights.

I have been talking to Gareth Dale for over two decades, sometimes about social reproduction theory and sometimes not, both to my benefit.

Also, 2017 marks 150 years from the first publication of Volume 1 of *Capital*, the one text to which this volume perhaps owes the greatest debt. Chris Harman helped me understand parts of that text in my twenties. I still miss being able to pick up the phone to ask Chris how to make sense of a difficult passage.

I *could* not write this book without Bill and I *would* not write it without Shayari. Every day they re-enchant the world for me.

And because of them, every day, I recapitulate to hopes about its future.

Foreword

Lise Vogel

What a pleasure it is for me to welcome this important and timely collection of essays. *Social Reproduction Theory* is probably the first book to draw on the past decade's resurgent interest in developing a coherent Marxist-feminist understanding of everyday life under capitalism. And who better to edit it than Tithi Bhattacharya, herself operating on the cutting edge of recent work on social reproduction theory.

The ten essays in *Social Reproduction Theory* address a range of questions. But one way or another, each contributor tackles the thorny problem of explaining just what social reproduction theory is. Not surprisingly, they do not always agree. Having myself had a go at this demanding task 35 years ago—in *Marxism and the Oppression of Women*, originally published in 1983[1]—I'm sympathetic with their difficulties. At the same time, I have to recognize that the context in which this work is being developed has markedly changed, and in ways I find very exciting. First, people interested in these questions today benefit from a more developed understanding of Marxism and of history than what was available to us decades ago. And second, they appear to be connected to one another and to the nascent social movements of the twenty-first century, again in contrast to the relative isolation many of us felt in the late 1970s and after.

As proponents of social reproduction theory, the authors are wrestling with both new and old challenges. One of the oldest debates among women's liberationists concerned dualism, or dual-systems theory. By the early 1980s, the verdict was in, at least among Marxist feminists, who shared a desire to replace the dualism of earlier analyses with what they called a "unitary" account. To put it another way, instead of conceptualizing social reproduction as having two component aspects (for example, production of commodities and reproduction of labor power), they sought to develop an approach that would enclose both production and reproduction within a unitary framework. This is still easier said than done, as several of the essays in *Social Reproduction Theory* show. The pull of dual-systems thinking remains powerful, something that requires constant vigilance.

Several contributors explicitly link social reproduction theory to their understanding of "intersectionality." Like social reproduction theory, intersectionality is one of several theoretical frameworks deployed over the past eighty-plus years to represent social heterogeneity as consisting of the interaction of multiple "categories of social difference," for example, race, class, gender, etc.[2] To some extent the two theoretical stances have been taken as antagonistic—as a confrontation between Marxist (social reproduction theory) and non-Marxist (intersectionality) approaches. In contrast, these authors argue that it is possible to embrace social reproduction theory without discarding the strengths of intersectionality thinking, especially its ability to develop nuanced descriptive and historical accounts of various "categories of social difference." This strikes me as a promising direction in which to go.

In the long run, however, I think we must jettison two dearly-held assumptions. First, the assumption that the various dimensions of difference—for example, race, class, and gender—are comparable. Second, the implication that the various categories are equal in causal weight. Willy-nilly, these two assumptions lead to an interest in identifying parallels and similarities among the categories of difference, and a downplaying of their particularities. With these assumptions gone, we can break out of the tight little circle of supposedly similar categories. Our theoretical task would then be to focus on the specificities of each dimension and to develop an understanding of how it all fits—or does not fit—together. Out of this process could come a lens, or perhaps several lenses, with which to analyze empirical data.[3]

Some of the most interesting essays in *Social Reproduction Theory* explore the strategic or policy implications of social reproduction theorizing. Among the topics considered are: childhood; sexuality; pensions; migration; paid domestic service; and the International Women's Strike on March 8, 2017. Here we see the power of the social reproduction framework to shape our understanding of practical concerns. Or, as Bhattacharya puts it in the introduction to this book (page 19):

> [Social reproduction theory] reveals the essence-category of capitalism, its animating force, to be human labor and not commodities. In doing so, it exposes to critical scrutiny the superficiality of what we

> commonly understand to be "economic" processes and restores to the economic process its messy, sensuous, gendered, raced, and unruly component: living human beings, capable of following orders as well as of flouting them.

Readers new to the issues covered in *Social Reproduction Theory* will have much to learn from this collection. And those who lived through the frustrations of the various early women's liberation debates will find novel answers to old questions. Tithi Bhattacharya and Pluto Press are to be congratulated for bringing this thought-provoking collection to us.

NOTES

1. Lise Vogel, *Marxism and the Oppression of Women: Toward a Unitary Theory* (New Brunswick, NJ: Rutgers University Press, 1983). Although the book's official publication date was 1983, I view it as in fact a product of the hopes, discussions, and activism of the 1970s and before.
2. For this analysis of intersectionality, see Lise Vogel, "Beyond Intersectionality," *Science & Society*, in press.
3. For the metaphor of theory as a lens, see Lise Vogel, "Domestic Labor Revisited," *Science & Society*, 64, no. 2 (2000): 151–70; reprinted in Vogel, *Marxism and the Oppression of Women* (Chicago: Haymarket Books, 2013 [1983]), 183–98. For the view of theory as necessarily abstract, and disjunct from empirical investigation, see *ibid.*, esp. 184–95.

1
Introduction: Mapping Social Reproduction Theory

Tithi Bhattacharya

> Life itself appears only as a means to life.
>
> —Karl Marx, *Economic and Philosophical Manuscripts of 1844*

> A working woman comes home from work after an eight hour day, eats dinner in 8 to 10 minutes, and once again faces a load of physical work: washing linens, cleaning up, etc.
>
> There are no limits to housework . . . [a woman is] charwoman, cook, dressmaker, launderer, nurse, caring mother, and attentive wife. And how much time it takes to go to the store and drag home dinner!
>
> —testimonies of factory women in Moscow, 1926

> This [unpaid care work] is the type of work where we do not earn money but do not have free time either. Our work is not seen but we are not free as well.
>
> —woman in Patharkot, Nepal, 2013

> If our kitchens are outside of capital, our struggle to destroy them will never succeed in causing capital to fall.
>
> —Silvia Federici, *Revolution at Point Zero: Housework, Reproduction and Feminist Struggle*

Let us slightly modify the question "who teaches the teacher?" and ask this of Marxism: If workers' labor produces all the wealth in society, who then produces the worker? Put another way: What kinds of processes enable the worker to arrive at the doors of her place of work every day so that she can produce the wealth of society? What role did breakfast play in her work-readiness? What about a good night's sleep? We get into even murkier waters if we extend the questions to include processes lying outside this worker's household. Does the education she received at school also not "produce" her, in that it makes her employable? What about the public transportation system that helped bring her to work, or the public parks and libraries that provide recreation so that she can be regenerated, again, to be able to come to work?

The goal of social reproduction theory (SRT) is to explore and provide answers to questions such as these. In doing so, SRT displays an analytical irreverence to "visible facts" and privileges "process" instead. It is an approach that is not content to accept what seems like a visible, finished entity—in this case, our worker at the gates of her workplace—but interrogates the complex network of social processes and human relations that produces the conditions of existence for that entity. As in much of critical theory, here too we "build from Marx," for both this approach and the critical interrogation mirror the method by which Marx studies the commodity.

The fundamental insight of SRT is, simply put, that human labor is at the heart of creating or reproducing society as a whole. The notion of labor is conceived here in the original sense in which Karl Marx meant it, as "the first premise of all human history"—one that, ironically, he himself failed to develop fully. Capitalism, however, acknowledges productive labor for the market as the sole form of legitimate "work," while the tremendous amount of familial as well as communitarian work that goes on to sustain and reproduce the worker, or more specifically her labor power, is naturalized into nonexistence. Against this, social reproduction theorists perceive the relation between labor dispensed to produce commodities and labor dispensed to produce people as part of the systemic totality of capitalism. The framework thus seeks to make visible labor and work that are analytically hidden by classical economists and politically denied by policy makers.

SRT develops upon the traditional understanding of both Marxism and capitalism in two transformative ways.

First, it proposes a commodious but more specific reading of the "economy." SRT, as Susan Ferguson has recently pointed out,

> insists that our understanding of capitalism is incomplete if we treat it as simply an economic system involving workers and owners, and fail to examine the ways in which wider social reproduction of the system—that is the daily and generational reproductive labor that occurs in households, schools, hospitals, prisons, and so on—sustains the drive for accumulation.[1]

Marx clearly marks for us the pivotal role played by labor power, for it is that which in effect sets the capitalist production process in motion. He also indicates how, unlike all other commodities under capitalism, the "unique" commodity labor power is *singular* in the sense that it is not produced capitalistically. The implications of this insight are, however, underdeveloped in Marx. Social reproduction theorists begin with these silences in Marxism and show how the "production of goods and services and the production of life are part of one integrated process," as Meg Luxton has put it.[2] If the formal economy is the production site for goods and services, the people who produce such things are themselves produced outside the ambit of the formal economy, in a "kin-based" site called the family.

Second, and following from above, SRT treats questions of oppression (gender, race, sexuality) in distinctly nonfunctionalist ways precisely because oppression is theorized as structurally relational to, and hence shaped by, capitalist production rather than on the margins of analysis or as add-ons to a deeper and more vital economic process.

The essays in this volume thus explore questions of who constitutes the global working class today in all its chaotic, multiethnic, multigendered, differently abled subjectivity: what it means to bind class struggle theoretically to the point of production alone, without considering the myriad social relations extending between workplaces, homes, schools, hospitals—a wider social whole, sustained and coproduced by human labor in contradictory yet constitutive ways. Most importantly, they address the relationship between *exploitation* (normally tethered to class) and *oppression* (normally understood through gender, race, etc.) and reflect on whether this division adequately expresses the complications of an *abstract level* of analysis where we forge our conceptual equipment, and a *concrete level* of analysis, i.e., the historical reality where we apply those tools.

RENEWING SOCIAL REPRODUCTION THEORY IN THE SHADOW OF NEOLIBERALISM

Since the financial crisis of 2008 and 2009 and exacerbated by the government bailouts of those who perpetrated the crisis, there has emerged a renewed interest in Marx and Marxism. Major news sources of the Global North, from the *New York Times* to the *Guardian* and even to the conservative *Foreign Policy* have declared that Marx, without a doubt, "is back."[3]

Within this generalized interest, there has been a revival of more specific attention to Marx's *Capital*. Even aside from Thomas Piketty's 700-page *Capital in the Twenty-First Century* becoming a runaway bestseller, the period following 2008 has seen an unprecedented rise in scholarly publications on Marx's seminal text.[4]

While this is an unqualifiedly welcome development, there remains room—indeed, an urgency—to redraw the contours of some of these conversations about *Capital* in particular and its object of study, capitalism, in general. This book is an attempt to begin that process by highlighting the critical contribution of SRT to an understanding of capitalist social relations.

There is a limited but rich literature by Marxists and feminists across disciplinary boundaries which has, since the 1980s, developed the insights of the social reproduction framework in very productive directions.[5] The republication in 2014 of Lise Vogel's classic work *Marxism and the Oppression of Women: Toward a Unitary Theory* has given a new lease of life to this growing body of scholarship. While this literature embodies *instantiations* of SRT in a range of critical areas, there remains a need for a text that can act as a map and guide to this vivid and resonant body of work. Indeed, it is precisely because social reproduction scholars have so effectively applied and extended its theoretical insights to a diverse set of concerns in such creative ways that it is useful to compile and outline its key *theoretical* components along with its most significant *historical* applications.

That said, this volume stands in a very specific relationship to the recent literature on oppression. We see our work as furthering the theoretical conversation with this existing body of scholarship in two kinds of ways: (a) as a conversation between Marxism and the study of specific oppressions such as gender and race, and (b) as developing a richer way of understanding how Marxism, as a body of thought, can address the relationship between theory and empirical studies of oppression.

Let me elaborate. We make two central proposals in this volume about SRT: first, that it is a *methodology* to explore labor and labor power under capitalism and is best suited to offer a rich and variegated map of capital as a social relation; further, that this is a methodology that privileges process, or, to use Lukács's words, we believe that the "developing tendencies of history constitute a higher reality than the empirical 'facts.'"[6]

Many recent studies similarly grapple with elaborating on these. Cinzia Arruzza, in her book *Dangerous Liaisons* (2013), offers a summary of the historic relationship between Marxism and feminism and tries to plot precisely where the tributaries of analysis about the system as a whole (capitalism) meet or diverge from analyses of categories produced by the system (gender and/or race). Arruzza's work refuses the reduction of this complex dynamic to a simple question of "whether class comes before gender or gender before class," but points the way toward thinking about how "gender and class intertwine in capitalist production."[7]

Similarly, Shahrzad Mojab, in her recently edited volume *Marxism and Feminism* (2015), alerts us to the actual dangers of theoretically severing the integrated relationship between class and gender. Contributors to Mojab's volume show how decoupling feminism from capitalism carries the twin perils of emptying out the revolutionary content of feminism which "reduces gender to questions of culture" and of "reduc[ing] gender to class relations."[8]

A slightly older edited volume by Nancy Holmstrom (2002) likewise takes a integrative approach to the relationship between the oppression and the source of oppressions: capitalism. Holmstrom clarifies that although Marxism's "basic theory" does not require "significant revision," it does need to be "supplemented." The volume thus seeks to champion a specific deployment of historical materialism that "gives a fuller picture of production and reproduction than Marx's political economic theory does, that extends questions of democracy not only to the economy but to personal relations."[9]

Kate Benzanson and Meg Luxton's edited collection *Social Reproduction* (2006) is perhaps the closest theoretical kin to our project. This is not solely because Benzanson and Luxton deal explicitly with SRT, but because they restore to it a "thick" description of the "economy" and "political process." The volume is premised upon the understanding that "in capitalist societies the majority of people subsist by combining paid employment and unpaid domestic labor to maintain themselves . . . [hence] this version of social reproduction analyzes the ways in which both labors are part of the *same socio-economic process.*"[10]

While Benzanson and Luxton problematize the concept of labor and the role it plays in the constitution and disruption of capitalism, Kathi Weeks (2011) has usefully drawn our attention to the most common articulation of labor under capitalism, namely, work. Weeks's approach coincides with our own in that it is dissatisfied with efforts to align "work" with "a more equitable distribution of its rewards"—in other words, to think about how our working lives might be improved. Instead, Weeks points to the fundamental incommensurability of capitalism with any productive or creative sense of work. Hence her volume urges us to think about how the right to work and the right of refusal to work can be reimagined under the sign of an anticapitalist political theory.

This brings us to how this volume, while in conversation with the above scholarship, is nonetheless about developing a set of theoretical concerns that are related but different. The contributing essays of the volume can be said, broadly, to do three kinds of work: determining the definitional contours of SRT, using SRT to develop and deepen Marxist theory, and exploring the strategic implications of applying SRT to our current conjuncture. It is to an elaboration of those themes that we now turn.

MAPPING SOCIAL REPRODUCTION THEORY: THE WORK OF DEFINITIONS

All the essays in this volume are in some way engaged in the task of sketching out the contours of what exactly social reproduction theory is and what kinds of questions it seeks to answer.

In Marx's own writing, the term *social reproduction* is most often deployed to refer to the reproduction of the capitalist system as a whole. Johanna Brenner and Barbara Laslett therefore suggest a useful distinction between societal and social reproduction, with the former retaining the original meaning as Marx has used it, and the latter referring to

> the activities and attitudes, behaviors and emotions, and responsibilities and relationships directly involved in maintaining life, on a daily basis and intergenerationally. It involves various kinds of socially necessary work—mental, physical, and emotional—aimed at providing the historically and socially, as well as biologically, defined means for maintaining and reproducing population. Among other things, social reproduction includes how food, clothing, and shelter are made available for immediate consumption, how the maintenance

> and socialization of children is accomplished, how care of the elderly and infirm is provided, and how sexuality is socially constructed.[11]

The primary problematic of what is meant by the social reproduction of labor power is, however, only a preliminary start to this definitional project. Simply put, while labor puts the system of capitalist production in motion, SRT points out that labor power itself is the *sole* commodity—the "unique commodity," as Marx calls it—that is produced outside of the circuit of commodity production. But this status of labor power as a commodity that is simultaneously produced outside the "normal" productive cycle of other commodities raises more questions than it answers. For instance, Marx is very clear that every commodity under capitalism has two manifestations: one as use value, the other as exchange value. Indeed, when the commodity appears in its *social form* we only encounter it in its second manifestation because the capitalist circulation process, through an act of "necromancy," turns use value into its direct opposite. But labor power becomes a "commodity" (that is, it becomes something that is not simply endowed with use value) without going through the same process of "necromancy" as other commodities, which raises a question about the very ontology of labor power beyond the simple questions of its "production" and "reproduction." If the totality of the capitalist system is shot through with this "commodity" that is not produced in the manner of other commodities, what then are the points of determination and/or contradictions that must necessarily be constitutive of the system, yet must be overcome within it?

One way of resolving this problem is through a spatial understanding: that there are two separate but conjoined spaces—spaces of production of value (points of production) and spaces for reproduction of labor power. But then, as we gestured above, labor power is not simply replenished at home, nor is it always reproduced generationally. The family may form the site of individual renewal of labor power, but that alone does not explain "the conditions under which, and . . . the habits and degree of comfort in which" the working class of any particular society has been produced.[12] Public education and health care systems, leisure facilities in the community, and pensions and benefits for the elderly all compose together those historically determined "habits." Similarly, generational replacement through childbirth in the kin-based family unit, although predominant, is not the only way a labor force may be replaced. Slavery and immigration are two of the most common ways capital has replaced labor in a bounded society.

The complex concatenation of social relations making up the reproduction of labor power has led some theorists to define social reproduction to include "the processes necessary for the reproduction of the workforce, both biologically and as compliant wage workers."[13]

How can labor be made "compliant"? Relatedly, if labor power is a "unique" commodity in the sense of being produced noncapitalistically, then does that countervailing fact work against the manufacture of compliance? Susan Ferguson's essay in this volume seeks to explore the dynamic, often contested relationship between capital and childhood. Ferguson takes us beyond the trope of consumerism under which capitalist childhoods are most often studied. Instead, she asks a more difficult question: "What exactly are capitalist *productive* relations? And how are children implicated in them?" (Emphasis mine.) While she argues that "capitalist productive relations determine the terrain upon which children and childhoods are produced and reproduced," Ferguson avoids any functionalist correlation between capital's vision of/need for children as pre-workers and the actual historical delineation of childhood. Instead, the essay illuminates the "deeply contradictory relationship between the social reproduction of children and childhoods, on the one hand, and the continued thriving and expansion of capital, on the other." Like Walter Benjamin in his *Berlin Childhood*, Ferguson urges us to reconsider the child as a liminal, ambiguous figure, one capable of both compliance with capital and collusion with chthonic revolutionary energies.

If under capitalism the child will always be a figuration of what could be, then the retired worker is perhaps, in capitalist terms, the termination of all possibilities. But a social reproduction framework that extends analysis beyond both wage labor and spaces of production suggests a more robust understanding of human labor. Serap Saritas Oran's essay in this volume hence theorizes pensions as "not simply deferred wages or individual savings" but "from a political economy perspective." Oran's essay reframes the question of what constitutes labor power: is it composed of a set of use values represented by the labor time necessary for its production, or can we determine its value through its exchange value, or wage? She locates a lacuna in both approaches, for they fail to adequately theorize those goods and services that have "use value but not exchange value, such as reproductive household activities or state services" such as pensions. Since pensions are not necessarily commodities, nor do they correspond neatly with labor time; they cannot be considered the direct equivalent of an individual worker's labor power during the worker's work life. Oran thus urges us to look at pensions as "a component of the broader understanding of the value of labor power as a standard of living for the working class that consists of the payments and benefits necessary for generational social reproduction."

Theorizing pensions is one way to reveal the superficial nature of the neat spatial divisions between production (public) and reproduction (private), for the two separate spaces—spaces of production of value (point of production) and spaces for reproduction of labor power—while they may be separate in a strictly spatial sense are actually united in both the theoretical and operational senses. They are *particular historical forms of appearance* in which capitalism as a process posits itself.

The question of separate spheres and why they are historical forms of appearance is an important one, and we will reflect upon it at length in this volume. One understanding of social reproduction is that it is about two separate spaces and two separate processes of production: the economic and the social—often understood as the workplace and home. In this understanding, the worker produces surplus value at work and hence is part of the *production* of the total wealth of society. At the end of the workday, because the worker is "free" under capitalism, capital must relinquish control over the process of regeneration of the worker and hence the *reproduction* of the workforce. The corpus of social relations involving regeneration—birth, death, social communication, and so on—is most commonly referred to in scholarly as well as policy literature as *care* or *social care*.

If, as we propose, the spatial separation between production (public) and reproduction (private) is a historical form of appearance, then the labor that is dispensed in both spheres must also be theorized integratively.

The classical Marxist example that outlines the relationship between the two forms of labor is Marx's discussion of the working day. The reduction of the working day (time of production), for Marx, is the first step toward humanity developing any rudimentary notion of freedom or its own potential. In the third volume of *Capital* he argues that "the realm of freedom really begins only where labor determined by necessity and external expediency ends.... . . the reduction of the working day is the basic prerequisite."[14] Thus Marx famously describes the effects of alienation in the productive sphere, as "the worker . . . only feels himself outside his work, and in his work feels outside himself. He is at home when he is not working, and when he is working he is not at home."

Some scholars have gone as far as to claim that concrete labor, as opposed to abstract labor, is nonalienated labor, as it is not producing for profit or exchange.[15] This sort of interpretation conflates the relationship between "work" and "leisure" in commonsensical terms with abstract and concrete labor in Marxist terms. For example, I may garden in my own yard during the weekend (concrete labor) and work at Starbucks during the week (abstract labor). Is this gardening then nonalienated? A strong reading of Marx may suggest otherwise.

In my reading, along with the useful distinction between concrete and abstract labor, Marx is also proposing that our performance of concrete labor, too, is saturated/overdetermined by alienated social relations within whose overall matrix such labor must exist. Hence even my concrete labor (gardening) is not performed during and for a time of my own choosing or in forms that I can determine, but has to "fit in" with the temporal and objective necessities of other social relations. Indeed, if we go back to the epigraphs with which this essay begins, then it seems that the time after work (time of reproduction) is equally tedious. Lenin, usually not one to mince words, refers to the woman worker as a "domestic slave" precisely because "petty housework crushes, strangles, stultifies, and degrades her, chains her to the kitchen and the nursery, and she wastes her labor on barbarously unproductive, petty, nerve-wracking, stultifying and crushing drudgery."[16] Was Marx then wrong, or simply sexist, to indicate this sphere as a point of departure for freedom?

It is certainly true that Marx reserves both his developed theorization and his rage against the form that labor assumes in the sphere of production.[17] But since under capitalism the wage-labor relation "suffuses the spaces of nonwaged everyday life," the time of reproduction must necessarily respond to the structuring impulses of the time of production. Structuring impulse, however, is not simple correspondence, and it is important to highlight this point—for, while capitalism limits our horizon of possibilities in both spheres, it simultaneously does have to relinquish *absolute* control over the time of reproduction.

Marx recognizes this weak link of capitalism but, like many analytical categories of social reproduction, leaves it undertheorized. Consider his oft quoted statement about the bestiality of capitalist social relations. The worker, says Marx,

> no longer feels himself to be freely active in any but his animal functions—eating, drinking, procreating, or at most in his dwelling and in dressing-up, etc.; and in his human functions he no longer feels himself to be anything but an animal.[18]

Certainly, Marx recognizes that "eating, drinking, procreating, etc., are also genuine human functions." But "in the abstraction which separates them from the sphere of all other human activity" these activities are turned into their "sole and ultimate ends": that is, they come to seem purely biological and, in that, they can be likened to animal functions. That abstraction is the conditioning impulse of wage labor. But there is more to this passage, for note how Marx states that the worker does feel "freely active" in her time away from production. From this Bertell Ollman correctly summarizes:

> Eating, drinking and procreating are occasions when all man's powers may be fulfilled together; yet, in capitalism, they only serve their direct and most obvious functions as do their equivalents in the animal kingdom. *Despite their depraved state, however, the individual exercises more choice in these activities than he does in those others, work in particular, which distinguish him as a human being.* As unsatisfactory as eating and drinking are from a human point of view, the worker feels at least he is doing something he wants to do. The same cannot be said of his productive activity.[19] [Emphasis mine]

Capitalism, then, generates a set of two distinct relations that are nevertheless unified: the particular relations that adhere to production and to reproduction. Ollman's description of Marx's method is of use to us in addressing this contradictory unity. Marx's practice, says Ollman, "of seeing the whole in the part links all particular relations together as aspects in the full unfolding of any one of them."[20]

Much more theoretical attention needs to be paid to the relationship between the physical body in all its acts (such as "eating, drinking and procreating") and the social relationships of capital that such a body finds itself in. Insights from queer theory are useful in this regard to draw out how far the social implicates the physical and vice versa. Alan Sears's essay in this volume grapples with a particular aspect of the physical-social question. Sears perceptively imbricates the horizons of sexual freedom with freedom from capitalism, thus making one the condition of possibility for the other. The essay shows why sexuality under capitalism is always-already organized as a "paradoxical double freedom, in which control over one's own body is always combined with forms of compulsion." Contradictory impulses of the capital-labor relation shape and mirror body-consciousness expressions, such as sexuality. Sears roots the paradoxes of capitalist sexuality, the constant shadow dance between freedom and repression in a systemic contradiction:

> Members of the working class are free in that they own their own bodies, yet are subjected to systemic compulsion because they must sell their capacity to work in order to gain access to the basic requirement for subsistence. The combination of consent and compulsion that underlies basic labor relations under capitalism also shapes the realities of sexual freedom within the bounds of that system.

Nancy Fraser's essay similarly theorizes this constitutive and contradictory impulse that is indicative of capitalism as a system. While the neoliberal moment is marked by a crisis of social provisioning, Fraser challenges the notion that this is simply a "crisis of care" or a crisis of "the capacities available for birthing and raising children, caring for friends and family members, maintaining households and broader communities, and sustaining connections more generally." Instead Fraser offers a much darker thesis that this is a generalized crisis of the system's ability to reproduce itself, brought on by the depletion and decimation of social reproductive functions. The crises evidenced in care work, then, is "not accidental but have deep systemic roots in the structure of our social order." They have been generated and accelerated by "unlimited accumulation" that "tends to destabilize the very processes of social reproduction on which it relies." Fraser, like many other contributors to the volume, offers us a deeply gendered vision of capital, one in which the resolution to the crisis of care can only proceed by way of a resolution of the inherent injustice of the system as a whole and "requires reinventing the production/reproduction distinction and reimagining the gender order."

This line of theorization about the nature of waged and unwaged labor also touches upon critical branches of feminist thought and activism, the most prominent of course being the wages-for-housework movement. Carmen Teeple Hopkins's essay discusses the important contributions of scholar-activists such as Mariarosa Dalla Costa, Selma James, and Silvia Federici and addresses the theoretical challenge that autonomist feminists posed to the Marxist schema of social reproduction.[21]

Teeple Hopkins's study of immigrant domestic workers in Montreal adds another layer of theoretical questions to the complex issue of domestic labor. She argues that while we owe the autonomist feminists "a debt of gratitude" for their serious consideration of housework, we need to have a renewed conversation about the very category of "care" in an age where care is increasingly becoming commodified and sold on the market for a price. Here, Teeple Hopkins denaturalizes paid care work in two important ways. The first is by reminding us that such work takes very specific forms under the current conjuncture, in that it is mostly performed by "working-class women of color and migrant workers," a fact that rightly locates "race and citizenship status" as central determinants of both societal and social reproduction. Second, her essay places the racialization process in its historical context of "unpaid labor of enslaved African American women during US slavery" and the "paid domestic labor that many African American women performed in the post-slavery period," thereby putting the "recognized social reproduction canon" in a productive dialogue with Black feminist writing.

One challenge to defining SRT is a more literal one. The content of this volume deals with issues (such as domestic labor and the informal economy) that have been addressed under theoretical rubrics other than social reproduction, such as anthropology, labor studies, and certain historiographic traditions, such as subaltern history. Should we continue to think of this tradition specifically as a social reproduction framework or should we think more broadly? This raises an important question that goes to the heart of what this theoretical tradition stands for as well as its scope.

Social reproduction theorists, who by no means represent a unified political or theoretical tradition, are generally concerned with *one* particular aspect of the reproduction of the capitalist production cycle as a whole. Marx famously concentrates on the cycle of *production of commodities* to show how surplus value is produced through this process of production ($M - C (M_p, L_p) - P - C' - M'$).[22] He leaves undeveloped or undertheorized the production and reproduction of labor power. It is this part of the total reproduction of the system that is of concern to social reproduction theorists. In this sense, it is perhaps more accurate to think of this theoretical tradition as a series of reflections on the political economy of labor power, a recasting of the labor theory of value from the point of view of wage labor (as opposed to from the side of capital).

Nevertheless, I believe, *social reproduction theory*, as a term, still carries an important analytical charge to which we should be attentive. First, it is not simply an attempt to explore the relationship between social relations established *through* the market and extramarket social relations. It represents an effort to develop Marx's labor theory of value in a specific direction. SRT is primarily concerned with understanding how categories of oppression (such as gender, race, and ableism) are coproduced in simultaneity with the production of surplus value. In this aspect, it seeks to overcome reductionist or deterministic representations of Marxism while at the same time creatively exposing the organic totality of capitalism as a system. It is important thus to retain the term *social reproduction theory*, as it declares its heritage to be within the Marxist tradition. Second, several new terms have been in circulation among social theorists to describe the sphere of extramarket relations. *Moral economy*, *shadow economy*, *the social factory*, and *the unwaged work sector* are among some of the terms employed.[23] SRT is unique in the sense that it theorizes the *relationship* between the market and extramarket relations rather than simply gesturing toward their distinction.

MAPPING SOCIAL REPRODUCTION THEORY: DEFENDING A THEORY OF TOTALITY

Following from above, a basic element that troubles the relationship between market and nonmarket categories is surely the thorny problem of reality itself. For instance, the reality I can see tells me that the worker and her boss are fundamentally and juridically equal, and the difference in their wages or life situations are the consequence of personal choices. Similarly, a slightly darker version of the same reality tells me that, because white workers in the Global North typically earn more than workers of color, there can never be common grounds of struggle uniting them, as the very real, material, empirically documented difference between them will always fuel white racism. The same can be said about the real material differences between men and women. What is interesting about these very real situations is that to try to challenge them *within the context set by capitalism*—or capitalist reality—would have two consequences:

either failure (for example, as in the numerous historical instances where sexism and/or racism overwhelm or choke the workers' movement) or a political strategy that seeks to overcome such differences of race/gender between workers by moral appeals, asking people to "do the right thing" even if it is not in their immediate interest to do so: Even though the male worker earns more than his female counterpart, he ought to join in a struggle on her behalf because it is the right thing to do, even if it does not further his own interests.

In contrast to this vision of the world and politics, Marx argues that to try to act upon our world on the basis of an empirical or factual knowledge of reality, *as it is perceived*, involves a category mistake. Instead, he presents us with a more disconcerting idea: that the reality we perceive is only the partial truth, and that it appears to us in a particular, historically specific form. *Capital* concerns itself with demonstrating this "difference between everyday experience of the surface phenomena determined by the prevailing mode of production and a scientific analysis of which goes beneath this surface to grasp an essence."[24] We thus need "science" to fully grasp the phenomena that remain hidden behind this appearance of the real. But as Ben Fine and Laurence Harris have reminded us, the hidden phenomena are not "simply there waiting to be found." Indeed, it is the task of science to forge tools so as to produce "concepts appropriate to these hidden phenomena" and knowledge that explains how such phenomena give rise to and determine the specific appearance of reality.[25] To develop this further: What is the logic of the relationship between us (subjects) and empirically apprehended facts (objects)?

Empirical appearances, then, do not simply shroud some unspoiled "truth" or essence. There is, rather, a relationship between hidden phenomena and empirical appearance. "The question then becomes," as Lukács puts it,

> are the empirical facts—(it is immaterial whether they are purely "sensuous" or whether their sensuousness is only the ultimate material substratum of their "factual" essence)—to be taken as "given" or can this "givenness" be dissolved further into rational forms, i.e. can it be conceived as the product of "our" reason?

As far as SRT is concerned, we can draw two important conclusions from this discussion: first, that the way reality appears in all its racialized and gendered form is neither accidental nor complete; and second, that our tools to understand that reality can neither consist of a rejection of said empirical facts nor a simple aggregation of them. Instead, following Marx, we ought to think of reality or the "concrete" as "concrete because it is the concentration of many determinations, hence unity of the diverse."

David McNally's essay approaches intersectionality theory from this understanding of a concrete totality to explore whether intersectionality is an adequate tool, or the science we need, to expose the hidden phenomena that shape our apprehension of reality and whether such a theory can explain the relationship between the diverse "real" elements that form a unified "concentration of many determinations." While McNally acknowledges at the outset the "deep theoretical flaws" of intersectionality theory, his essay is particularly notable for its rejection of dualist (often pugilist) approaches to the problem. While many recent debates around the efficacy of intersectionality as a theoretical tool pit it against Marxism or SRT, this essay *situates* it analytically as a body of critical thought. For instance, to take just one example out of many, a left that ignores Patricia Hill Collins's detailed study of postwar racism in the United States does so at the risk of its own impoverishment; Hill Collins draws a masterful picture of "globalization, transnationalism, and the growth of hegemonic ideologies within mass media [that] provide the context for a new racism that has catalyzed changes within African, Black American, and African-Diasporic societies."[26] McNally thus begins by acknowledging the rich empirical work done by scholars of intersectionality that arose in response to inadequate scholarly attention to race as a central dynamic of capitalism.

But how should we situate these empirical data in our understanding of reality?

Martha Gimenez points out that Marx, in one of his rare methodological propositions, argues that if we started our investigations from aspects of social reality that seem to us the most concrete and real, like say, the family, then we would in fact be beginning with "a very vague notion of a complex whole." Instead, Marx suggests that we produce knowledge about reality when we advance from such "imaginary concrete concepts" (the family, childcare, etc.) to "increasingly simple concepts" or abstractions (such as, for example, domestic labor). Such abstractions then have to be investigated at an empirical level, keeping in mind their historic conditions of production and thereby their limits. But then a reverse theoretical movement must take place. We must return to the phenomena we started out with, but now they can be understood as "a totality comprising many determinations and relations." The concept is now a "real concrete" because it is "a synthesis of many definitions, thus representing the unity of diverse aspects."[27]

Intersectionality theory, however, shows us a world where race, gender, and other oppressions "intersect," thereby producing a reality that is latticed—a sum total of different parts. At first glance this "whole," as an aggregate of different parts, may appear to be the same as the Hegelian-Marxist concept of totality. An elementary question about the nature of intersections, however, reveals the distinction between the two concepts. If, as intersectionality theory tells us, race and gender intersect like two streets, then surely they are two separate streets, each with its own specificities? What, then, is the *logic* of their intersection?

I suggest that the insights or conclusions of intersectional theorists actually contradict their methodology. Instead of race and gender being separate systems of oppression or even separate oppressions with only externally related trajectories, the findings of Black feminist scholars show how race and gender are actually co-constitutive. Intersectionality theory's methodology belies its own findings, for its theoretical model, as McNally shows, is a social Newtonian one—of discrete parts colliding, intersecting, or interlocking to produce a combined, an externally related whole. In contrast, McNally's essay is a powerful discussion of how SRT offers us a way to "retain and reposition" the insights of intersectionality, yet reject its theoretical premise of an aggregative reality.

The understanding of totality as an organic whole rather than an aggregate of parts is important precisely because it has real material implications for how we must choose to act upon that world. Are struggles against racism and sexism internally or externally related? Does the white worker have a material, not moral, interest in challenging racism? The next section is about how and why, in a praxis-predicated philosophy such as Marxism, what we theoretically determine has strategic import in the lived experience of our world.

MAPPING SOCIAL REPRODUCTION THEORY: STRATEGY AS A HEURISTIC PRINCIPLE

How can our theoretical understanding about whether production and reproduction belong to separate processes impinge upon our ways of grasping the nature of labor as well as its organizational impulses?

The materials necessary to produce the worker in the image of her own needs and goals—be they food, housing, "time for education, for intellectual development" or the "free play of his [or her] own physical and mental powers"—cannot be realized within the capitalist production process, for the process as a whole exists for the valorization of capital and not the social development of labor.[28] Thus the worker, due to the very nature of the process, is always-already reproduced as *lacking* in what she needs. Hence the struggle for higher wages (or, to call it by its more agentive name, *class struggle*) is built into the fabric of wage labor as a form.

Here we arrive at the strategic implications of SRT, or how an integrative sense of capitalism is central to our actual battles against capital. In this volume we approach the question of class struggle from this standpoint in order to address the conceptual and strategic totality of workplace struggle, along with struggle that erupts away from the point of production. My own essay theoretically explores the analytical category and historical processes of "class formation." While it is easy to state that workers have an existence outside of the circuit of commodity production or point of production, the challenge the essay takes up is to clarify "the relationship between this existence and that of their productive lives under the direct domination" of capital, for that relation between spheres has the potential to chart the path of class struggle.

Similarly, Salar Mohandesi and Emma Teitelman's essay is based on a *longue durée* approach to class struggle upon what they call the "terrain of social reproduction" in the United States. Tracing a counterintuitive history of labor struggles in the early twentieth century, Mohandesi and Teitelman show how the work of life-production—"household budgeting, food shopping, managing household needs"—acquired a new political charge in this period in response to earnings from wage labor emerging as the dominant component of total household income. Whereas, in previous decades, keeping animals in the backyard or growing vegetables in family plots had always supplemented wage earnings for families, the expansion and consolidation of the social relations of capital undermined or even outlawed such practices, eventually forcing households to become primarily dependent on wage labor. As the activities to reproduce life (unwaged) and the activities to produce commodities (waged) grew to be strictly separated and the latter began to determine the former, "rent, food, and cost of living" developed as "key points of contestation that inspired a variety of actions, such as boycotts, rent strikes, and the organization of cooperatives." Mohandesi and Teitelman's rich account of the past allows us to review our current political conjuncture through the framework of SRT, for the present moment is a map of political protest that is united in its extreme unevenness, where militant workplace strikes (China and India) are combined with political struggles against various forms of dispossession (water rights in Ireland, land rights in Latin America) and forms of oppression (the Black Lives Matter movement in the United States).

Cinzia Arruzza's contribution to the volume is a vibrant instantiation of SRT in practice. As one of the national organizers of International Women's Strike on March 8, 2017, Arruzza brings to the volume a productive urgency. Her essay, on the one hand, outlines the theoretical framework that informed the national mobilization for the strike; on the other, it boldly rejects what Engels once called "specific tactics of hushing up the class struggle." Indeed, the political methods of the Women's Strike, Arruzza shows, could be one of our lineaments of hope.

SRT, then, offers us an opportunity to reflect upon the manifold ways that the neoliberal moment has forced us to reassess the potency and efficacy of certain previously uncontested terms in the Marxist tradition. Conceptual categories such as "class," the "economy," or even the "working class" can no longer be filled with the historical data of the nineteenth century that were available to Marx. This does not invalidate them as categories. Instead, our own historical moment demands that we engage rigorously with these categories and make them represent our own politico-historic totality.

SRT is especially useful in this regard because it reveals the essence-category of capitalism, its animating force, to be human labor and not commodities. In doing so, it exposes to critical scrutiny the superficiality of what we commonly understand to be "economic" processes and restores to the economic process its messy, sensuous, gendered, raced, and unruly component: living human beings, capable of following orders as well as of flouting them.

Like all worthwhile Marxist projects, it is important to state that this project to develop SRT is both ongoing and collective. It is ongoing in the sense that our understanding of Marxism ought to be paradigmatic rather than prescriptive, where we see Marxism as a framework or tool to understand social relations and thereby change them. This means, necessarily, that such a tool will sometimes need to be sharpened and honed to fit new, emerging social realities. The revolutionary Marxist tradition has always used Marxism in this manner, which has allowed it to rejuvenate and add to itself in new moments of crises. Lenin's theory of imperialism, Luxemburg's understanding of the mass strike, and Trotsky's thesis on the permanent revolution are all examples of this constant revivification of Marxism in different epochs because these thinkers employed the Marxist method to understand the social reality of their own time.

The present volume is similarly animated by this sense of the historical materialist approach as, essentially, a method of analysis that applies itself to concrete historical situations. As the global neoliberal economy continues to foreclose real living alternatives for the vast majority and centers of resistance start developing from within its matrix, we hope SRT will continue to develop Marxism as a real tool for understanding our world in order to change it.

Such a project must also, of necessity, be collaborative. So we see this as the start of a conversation about SRT, one that will contribute to and continue that tradition of practicing critical thinking in open and exploratory ways to combat the challenges of our sly and dangerous times.

While this book is very much about excavating and recuperating the revolutionary Marxist tradition from the past, like Ernst Bloch, we reserve our greatest excitement for the "not yet."

2

Crisis of Care? On the Social-Reproductive Contradictions of Contemporary Capitalism

Nancy Fraser

We hear a lot of talk today about "the crisis of care."[1] Often linked to such phrases as "time poverty," "family/work balance," and "social depletion,"[2] this expression refers to the pressures from several directions that are currently squeezing a key set of social capacities: the capacities available for birthing and raising children, caring for friends and family members, maintaining households and broader communities, and sustaining connections more generally. Historically, this work of "social reproduction" has been cast as women's work, although men have always done some of it too. Comprising both affective and material labor and often performed without pay, it is indispensable to society. Without it there could be no culture, no economy, no political organization. No society that systematically undermines social reproduction can endure for long. Today, however, a new form of *capitalist* society is doing just that. The result, as I shall explain, is a major crisis—not simply of care, but of social reproduction in this broader sense.

I understand this crisis as one strand of a general crisis that also encompasses other strands—economic, ecological, and political, all of which intersect with and exacerbate one another. The social reproduction strand forms an important dimension of this general crisis, but it is often neglected in current discussions, which focus chiefly on the economic or ecological strands. This "critical separatism" is problematic. The social strand is so central to the broader crisis that none of the others can be properly understood in abstraction from it. However, the converse is also true. The crisis of social reproduction is not freestanding and cannot be adequately grasped on its own.

How, then, should it be understood? My claim is that what some call "the crisis of care" is best interpreted as a more or less acute expression of *the social-reproductive contradictions of financialized capitalism.* This formulation suggests two ideas. First, the present strains on care are not accidental but have deep systemic roots in the structure of our social order, which I characterize here as financialized capitalism. Nevertheless, and this is the second point, the present crisis of social reproduction indicates something rotten not only in capitalism's current, financialized form but in capitalist society per se.

These are the theses I shall elaborate here. My claim, to begin with the last point, is that *every* form of capitalist society harbors a deep-seated *social-reproductive* "crisis tendency" or "contradiction." On the one hand, social reproduction is a condition of possibility for sustained capital accumulation; on the other hand, capitalism's orientation to unlimited accumulation tends to destabilize the very processes of social reproduction on which it relies. This "social-reproductive contradiction of capitalism" lies at the root, I claim, of our so-called crisis of care. Although inherent in capitalism as such, it assumes a different and distinctive guise in every historically specific form of capitalist society—for example, in the liberal, competitive capitalism of the nineteenth century, the state-managed capitalism of the postwar era, and the financialized neoliberal capitalism of our time. The care deficits we experience today are the form this contradiction takes in that third, most recent phase of capitalist development.

To develop this thesis, I first propose an account of the social contradiction of capitalism *as such*, without reference to any specific historical form. Second, I shall sketch an account of the unfolding of this contradiction in the two earlier phases of capitalist development I just mentioned. Finally, I shall propose a reading of today's so-called "care deficits" as expressions of capitalism's social contradiction in its current, financialized phase.

SOCIAL CONTRADICTIONS OF CAPITALISM "AS SUCH"

Most analysts of the contemporary crisis focus on contradictions internal to the capitalist economy. At its heart, they claim, lies a built-in tendency to self-destabilization, which expresses itself periodically in economic crises. This view is right, as far as it goes, but it fails to provide a full picture of capitalism's inherent crisis tendencies. Adopting an economistic perspective, it understands capitalism too narrowly, as an economic system *simpliciter.* In contrast, I shall assume an expanded understanding of capitalism, encompassing both its official economy and the latter's "noneconomic" background conditions.[3] Such a view permits us to conceptualize and to criticize capitalism's full range of crisis tendencies, including those centered on social reproduction.

My argument is that capitalism's economic subsystem depends on social-reproductive activities external to it, which form one of its background conditions of possibility. Other background conditions include the governance functions performed by public powers and the availability of nature as a source of "productive inputs" and a "sink" for production's waste.[4] Here, however, I will focus on the way that the capitalist economy relies on—one might say, free-rides on—activities of provisioning, caregiving, and interaction that produce and maintain social bonds, although it accords them no monetized value and treats them as if they were free. Variously called *care*, *affective labor*, or *subjectivation*, this activity forms capitalism's human subjects, sustaining them as embodied natural beings while also constituting them as social beings, forming their *habitus* and the cultural ethos in which they move. The work of birthing and socializing the young is central to this process, as is caring for the old, maintaining households and family members, building communities, and sustaining the shared meanings, affective dispositions, and horizons of value that underpin social cooperation. In capitalist societies, much, though not all, of this activity goes on outside the market—in households, neighborhoods, civil-society associations, informal networks, and public institutions such as schools; relatively little of it takes the form of wage labor. Unwaged social reproductive activity is necessary to the existence of waged work, the accumulation of surplus value, and the functioning of capitalism as such. None of those things could exist in the absence of housework, child-raising, schooling, affective care, and a host of other activities that serve to produce new generations of workers and replenish existing ones, as well as to maintain social bonds and shared understandings. Social reproduction is an indispensable background condition for the possibility of economic production in a capitalist society.[5]

Since at least the industrial era, however, capitalist societies have separated the work of social reproduction from that of economic production. Associating the first with women and the second with men, they have remunerated "reproductive" activities in the coin of "love" and "virtue," while compensating "productive work" in that of money. In this way, capitalist societies created an institutional basis for new, modern forms of women's subordination. Splitting off reproductive labor from the larger universe of human activities, in which women's work previously held a recognized place, they relegated it to a newly institutionalized "domestic sphere," where its social importance was obscured. In this new world, where money became a primary medium of power, the fact of this work being unpaid sealed the matter: those who do it are structurally subordinate to those who earn cash wages, even as their work supplies a necessary precondition for wage labor—and even as it also becomes saturated with and mystified by new, domestic ideals of femininity.

In general, then, capitalist societies separate social reproduction from economic production, associating the first with women and obscuring its importance and value. Paradoxically, however, they make their official economies dependent on the very same processes of social reproduction whose value they disavow. This peculiar relation of separation-*cum*-dependence-*cum*-disavowal is a built-in source of potential instability. Capitalist economic production is not self-sustaining, but relies on social reproduction. However, its drive to unlimited accumulation threatens to destabilize the very reproductive processes and capacities that capital—and the rest of us—need. The effect over time, as we shall see, can be to jeopardize the necessary social conditions of the capitalist economy.

Here, in effect, is a "social contradiction" inherent in the deep structure of capitalist society. Like the economic contradiction(s) that Marxists have stressed, this one, too, grounds a crisis tendency. In this case, however, the contradiction is not located inside the capitalist economy but at the border that simultaneously separates and connects production and reproduction. Neither intra-economic nor intra-domestic, it is a contradiction *between* those two constitutive elements of capitalist society.

Often, of course, this contradiction is muted, and the associated crisis tendency remains obscured. It becomes acute, however, when capital's drive to expanded accumulation becomes unmoored from its social bases and turns against them. In that case, the logic of economic production overrides that of social reproduction, destabilizing the very social processes on which capital depends—compromising the social capacities, both domestic and public, that are needed to sustain accumulation over the long term. Destroying its own conditions of possibility, capital's accumulation dynamic effectively eats its own tail.

HISTORICAL REGIMES OF REPRODUCTION-CUM-PRODUCTION

This is the general social-crisis tendency of capitalism as such. However, capitalist society does not exist "as such," but only in historically specific forms or regimes of accumulation. In fact, the capitalist organization of social reproduction has undergone major historical shifts—often as a result of political contestation. Especially in periods of crisis, social actors struggle over the boundaries delimiting economy from society, production from reproduction, and work from family—and sometimes succeed in redrawing them. Such *boundary struggles*, as I have called them, are as central to capitalist societies as the class struggles analyzed by Marx.[6] The shifts they produce mark epochal transformations. If we adopt a perspective that foregrounds these shifts, we can distinguish (at least) three regimes of social reproduction-*cum*-economic production in capitalism's history.

The first is the nineteenth-century regime of liberal competitive capitalism. Combining industrial exploitation in the European core with colonial expropriation in the periphery, this regime tended to leave workers to reproduce themselves "autonomously," outside the circuits of monetized value, as states looked on from the sidelines. But it also created a new bourgeois imaginary of domesticity. Casting social reproduction as the province of women within the private family, this regime elaborated the ideal of "separate spheres" even as it deprived most people of the conditions needed to realize it.

The second regime is the state-managed capitalism of the twentieth century. Premised on large-scale industrial production and domestic consumerism in the core, underpinned by ongoing colonial and postcolonial expropriation in the periphery, this regime internalized social reproduction through state and corporate provision of social welfare. Modifying the Victorian model of separate spheres, it promoted the seemingly more modern ideal of "the family wage"—even though, once again, relatively few families were permitted to achieve it.

The third regime is the globalizing financialized capitalism of the present era. This regime has relocated manufacturing to low-wage regions, recruited women into the paid workforce, and promoted state and corporate disinvestment from social welfare. Externalizing care work onto families and communities, it has simultaneously diminished their capacity to perform it. The result, amid rising inequality, is a dualized organization of social reproduction, commodified for those who can pay for it, privatized for those who cannot—all glossed by the even more modern ideal of the "two-earner family."

In each regime, therefore, the social reproductive conditions for capitalist production have assumed a different institutional form and embodied a different normative order: first "separate spheres," then "the family wage," now the "two-earner family." In each case, too, the social contradiction of capitalist society has assumed a different guise and found expression in a different set of crisis phenomena. In each regime, finally, capitalism's social contradiction has incited different forms of social struggle—class struggles, to be sure, but also boundary struggles, both of which were entwined not only with one another but also with other struggles aimed at emancipating women, slaves, and colonized peoples.

SOCIAL CONTRADICTIONS OF LIBERAL CAPITALISM

Consider, first, the liberal competitive capitalism of the nineteenth century. In this era, the imperatives of production and reproduction appeared to stand in direct contradiction to each other. Certainly that was the case in the early manufacturing centers of the capitalist core, where industrialists dragooned women and children into factories and mines, eager for their cheap labor and reputed docility. Paid a pittance and working long hours in unhealthy conditions, these workers became icons of capital's disregard for the social relations and social capacities that underpinned its productivity.[7] The result was a crisis on at least two levels: a crisis of social reproduction among the poor and working classes, whose capacities for sustenance and replenishment were stretched to the breaking point, and a moral panic among the middle classes, who were scandalized by what they understood as the "destruction of the family" and the "de-sexing" of proletarian women. So dire was this situation that even such astute critics as Marx and Engels mistook this early head-on conflict between economic production and social reproduction for the final word. Imagining that capitalism had entered its terminal crisis, they believed that, as it eviscerated the working-class family, the system was also eradicating the basis of women's oppression.[8] But what actually happened was just the reverse: over time, capitalist societies found resources for managing this contradiction—in part by creating "the family" in its modern, restricted form; by inventing new, intensified meanings of gender difference; and by modernizing male domination.

The process of adjustment began, in the European core, with protective legislation. The idea was to stabilize social reproduction by limiting the exploitation of women and children in factory labor.[9] Spearheaded by middle-class reformers in alliance with nascent workers' organizations, this "solution" reflected a complex amalgam of different motives. One aim, famously characterized by Karl Polanyi, was to defend "society" against "economy."[10] Another was to allay anxiety over "gender leveling." But these motives were also entwined with something else: an insistence on masculine authority over women and children, especially within the family.[11] As a result, the struggle to ensure the integrity of social reproduction became entangled with the defense of male domination.

Its intended effect, however, was to soften the social contradiction in the capitalist core—even as slavery and colonialism raised it to an extreme pitch in the periphery. Creating what Maria Mies called "housewifization" as the flip side of colonization,[12] liberal competitive capitalism elaborated a new gender imaginary centered on "separate spheres." Figuring woman as "the angel in the home," its proponents sought to create stabilizing ballast for the volatility of the economy. The cutthroat world of production was to be flanked by a "haven in the heartless world."[13] As long as each side kept to its own designated sphere and served as the other's complement, the potential conflict between them would remain under wraps.

In reality, this "solution" proved rather shaky. Protective legislation could not ensure labor's reproduction when wages remained below the level needed to support a family, when crowded, polluted tenements foreclosed privacy and damaged lungs, and when employment itself (when available at all) was subject to wild fluctuations due to bankruptcies, market crashes, and financial panics. Nor did such arrangements satisfy workers. Agitating for higher wages and better conditions, they formed trade unions, went out on strike, and joined labor and socialist parties. Riven by increasingly sharp, broad-based class conflict, capitalism's future seemed anything but assured.

Separate spheres proved equally problematic. Poor, racialized, and working-class women were in no position to satisfy Victorian ideals of domesticity; if protective legislation mitigated their direct exploitation, it provided no material support or compensation for lost wages. Nor were those middle-class women who *could* conform to Victorian ideals always content with their situation, which combined material comfort and moral prestige with legal minority and institutionalized dependency. For both groups, the separate-spheres "solution" came largely at women's expense. But it also pitted them against one another—witness nineteenth-century struggles over prostitution, which aligned the philanthropic concerns of Victorian middle-class women against the material interests of their "fallen sisters."[14]

A different dynamic unfolded in the periphery. There, as extractive colonialism ravaged subjugated populations, neither separate spheres nor social protection enjoyed any currency. Far from seeking to protect indigenous relations of social reproduction, metropolitan powers actively promoted their destruction. Peasantries were looted, their communities wrecked, to supply the cheap food, textiles, mineral ore, and energy without which the exploitation of metropolitan industrial workers would not have been profitable. In the Americas, meanwhile, enslaved women's reproductive capacities were instrumentalized to the profit calculations of planters, who routinely tore apart families by selling their members off separately to different slaveowners.[15] Native children, too, were ripped from their communities, conscripted into missionary schools, and subjected to coercive disciplines of assimilation.[16] When rationalizations were needed, the "backward, patriarchal" state of pre-capitalist indigenous kinship arrangements served quite well. Here, too, among the colonialists, philanthropic women found a public platform, urging, in the words of Gayatri Spivak, "white men to save brown women from brown men."[17]

In both settings, periphery and core, feminist movements found themselves negotiating a political minefield. Rejecting coverture and separate spheres while demanding the right to vote, refuse sex, own property, enter into contracts, practice professions, and control their own wages, liberal feminists appeared to valorize the "masculine" aspiration to autonomy over "feminine" ideals of nurture. On this point, if not on much else, their socialist-feminist counterparts effectively agreed. Conceiving women's entry into wage labor as the route to emancipation, they too preferred the "male" values associated with production to those associated with reproduction. These associations were ideological, to be sure. But behind them lay a deep intuition: despite the new forms of domination it brought, capitalism's erosion of traditional kinship relations contained an emancipatory moment.

Caught in a double bind, many feminists found scant comfort on either side of Polanyi's double movement, neither on the side of social protection, with its attachment to male domination, nor on the side of marketization, with its disregard for social reproduction. Able to neither reject nor embrace the liberal order, they needed a third alternative, which they called *emancipation*. To the extent that feminists could credibly embody that term, they effectively exploded the dualistic Polanyian figure and replaced it with what we might call a *triple movement*. In this three-sided conflict scenario, proponents of protection and marketization collided not only with one another but also with partisans of emancipation: with feminists, to be sure, but also with socialists, abolitionists, and anticolonialists, all of whom endeavored to play the two Polanyian forces off against each other, even while clashing among themselves.[18]

However promising in theory, such a strategy was hard to implement. As long as efforts to "protect society from economy" were identified with the defense of gender hierarchy, feminist opposition to male domination could easily be read as endorsing the economic forces that were ravaging working-class and peripheral communities. These associations would prove surprisingly durable long after liberal competitive capitalism collapsed under the weight of its (multiple) contradictions in the throes of inter-imperialist wars, economic depressions, and international financial chaos—giving way in the mid-twentieth century to a new regime, that of state-managed capitalism.

SOCIAL CONTRADICTIONS OF STATE-MANAGED CAPITALISM

Emerging from the ashes of the Great Depression and World War II, this regime tried to defuse the contradiction between economic production and social reproduction in a different way—by enlisting state power on the side of reproduction. Assuming some public responsibility for "social welfare," the states of this era sought to counter the corrosive effects on social reproduction not only of exploitation but also of mass unemployment. This aim was embraced by the democratic welfare states of the capitalist core and the newly independent developmental states of the periphery alike—despite their unequal capacities for realizing it.

Once again, the motives were mixed. A stratum of enlightened elites had come to believe that capital's short-term interest in squeezing out maximum profits needed to be subordinated to the longer-term requirements for sustaining accumulation over time. For these actors, the creation of the state-managed regime was a matter of saving the capitalist system from its own self-destabilizing propensities—as well as from the specter of revolution in an era of mass mobilization. Productivity and profitability required the "biopolitical" cultivation of a healthy, educated workforce with a stake in the system, as opposed to a ragged revolutionary rabble.[19] Public investment in health care, schooling, child care, old-age pensions, supplemented by corporate provision, was perceived as a necessity in an era in which capitalist relations had penetrated social life to such an extent that the working classes no longer possessed the means to reproduce themselves on their own. In this situation, social reproduction had to be internalized, brought within the officially managed domain of the capitalist order.

That project dovetailed with the new problematic of economic "demand." Seeking to smooth out capitalism's endemic boom/bust cycles, economic reformers sought to ensure continuous growth by enabling workers in the capitalist core to do double duty as consumers. Accepting unionization, which brought higher wages, and public-sector spending, which created jobs, these actors reinvented the household as a private space for the domestic consumption of mass-produced objects of daily use.[20] Linking the assembly line with working-class familial consumerism, on the one hand, and with state-supported reproduction, on the other, this "Fordist" model forged a novel synthesis of marketization and social protection, projects Polanyi had considered antithetical.

But it was above all the working classes—both women and men—who spearheaded the struggle for public provision, acting for reasons of their own. For them, the issue was full membership in society as democratic citizens—hence dignity, rights, respectability, and material well-being, all of which were understood to require a stable family life. In embracing social democracy, then, working classes were also valorizing social reproduction against the all-consuming dynamism of economic production. In effect, they were voting for family, country, and lifeworld against factory, system, and machine.

Unlike the protective legislation of the liberal regime, the state-capitalist settlement resulted from a class compromise and represented a democratic advance. Unlike its predecessor, too, the new arrangements served (at least for some and for a while) to stabilize social reproduction. For majority-ethnicity workers in the capitalist core, they eased material pressures on family life and fostered political incorporation. But before we rush to proclaim a golden age, we should register the constitutive exclusions that made these achievements possible.

Here, as before, the defense of social reproduction in the core was entangled with imperialism. Fordist regimes financed social entitlements in part by ongoing expropriation from the periphery (including the periphery within the core), which persisted in forms old and new, even after decolonization.[21] Meanwhile, postcolonial states caught in the crosshairs of the Cold War directed the bulk of their resources, already depleted by imperial predation, to large-scale development projects, which often entailed expropriating "their own" indigenous peoples. Social reproduction, for the vast majority in the periphery, remained external, as rural populations were left to fend for themselves. Like its predecessor, too, the state-managed regime was entangled with racial hierarchy. US social insurance excluded domestic and agricultural workers, effectively cutting many African Americans off from social entitlements.[22] The racial division of reproductive labor, begun during slavery, assumed a new guise under Jim Crow, as women of color found low-waged work raising the children and cleaning the homes of "white" families at the expense of their own.[23]

Nor was gender hierarchy absent from these arrangements, as feminist voices were relatively muted throughout the process of their construction. In a period (roughly from the 1930s through the 1950s) when feminist movements did not enjoy much public visibility, hardly anyone contested the view that working-class dignity required "the family wage," male authority in the household, and a robust sense of gender difference. As a result, the broad tendency of state-managed capitalism in the countries of the core was to valorize the heteronormative male-breadwinner/female-homemaker model of the gendered family. Public investment in social reproduction reinforced these norms. In the US, the welfare system took a dualized form, divided into stigmatized poor relief for ("white") women and children lacking access to a male wage and respectable social insurance for those constructed as "workers."[24] By contrast, European arrangements entrenched androcentric hierarchy differently, in the division between mothers' pensions and entitlements tied to waged work—driven in many cases by pronatalist agendas born of interstate competition.[25] Both models validated, assumed, and encouraged the family wage. Institutionalizing androcentric understandings of family and work, both of them naturalized heteronormativity and gender hierarchy and largely removed them from political contestation.

In all these respects, social democracy sacrificed emancipation to an alliance of social protection and marketization, even as it mitigated capitalism's social contradiction for several decades. But the state-capitalist regime began unraveling, first, politically, in the 1960s, when the global New Left erupted to challenge its imperial, gender, and racial exclusions, as well as its bureaucratic paternalism, all in the name of *emancipation*; then, economically, in the 1970s, when "stagflation," the "productivity crisis," and declining profit rates in manufacturing galvanized efforts by neoliberals to unshackle *marketization*. What would be sacrificed, were those two parties to join forces, would be *social protection*.

SOCIAL CONTRADICTIONS OF FINANCIALIZED CAPITALISM

Like the liberal regime before it, the state-managed capitalist order dissolved in the course of a protracted crisis. By the 1980s, prescient observers could discern the emerging outlines of a new regime which would become the financialized capitalism of the present era. Globalizing and neoliberal, this new regime is now promoting state and corporate disinvestment from social welfare while recruiting women into the paid workforce. Thus, it is externalizing care work onto families and communities while diminishing their capacity to perform it. The result is a new, *dualized* organization of social reproduction, commodified for those who can pay for it and privatized for those who cannot, as some in the second category provide care work in return for (low) wages for those in the first. Meanwhile, the one-two punch of feminist critique and deindustrialization has definitively stripped "the family wage" of all credibility. That ideal has given way to today's more modern norm of the "two-earner family."

The major driver of these developments, and the defining feature of this regime, is the new centrality of debt. Debt is the instrument by which global financial institutions pressure states to slash social spending, enforce austerity, and generally collude with investors in extracting value from defenseless populations. It is largely through debt, too, that peasants in the Global South are dispossessed by a new round of corporate land grabs, aimed at cornering supplies of energy, water, arable land, and "carbon offsets." It is increasingly via debt that accumulation proceeds in the historic core as well. As low-waged, precarious service work replaces unionized industrial labor, wages fall below the socially necessary costs of reproduction; in this "gig economy," continued consumer spending requires expanded consumer debt, which grows exponentially.[26] It is increasingly through debt, in other words, that capital now cannibalizes labor, disciplines states, transfers wealth from periphery to core, and sucks value from households, families, communities, and nature.

The effect is to intensify capitalism's inherent contradiction between economic production and social reproduction. Whereas the previous regime empowered states to subordinate the short-term interests of private firms to the long-term objective of sustained accumulation, in part by stabilizing reproduction through public provision, this one authorizes finance capital to discipline states and publics in the immediate interests of private investors, not least by requiring public disinvestment from social reproduction. And whereas the previous regime allied marketization with social protection against emancipation, this one generates an even more perverse configuration in which emancipation joins with marketization to undermine social protection.

The new regime emerged from the fateful intersection of two sets of struggles. One set pitted an ascending party of free-marketeers bent on liberalizing and globalizing the capitalist economy against declining labor movements in the countries of the core, once the most powerful base of support for social democracy but now on the defensive, if not wholly defeated. The other set of struggles pitted progressive "new social movements" opposed to hierarchies of gender, sex, "race"/ethnicity, and religion against populations seeking to defend established lifeworlds and privileges, now threatened by the "cosmopolitanism" of the new economy. Out of the collision of these two sets of struggles there emerged a surprising result: a "progressive" neoliberalism that celebrates "diversity," meritocracy, and "emancipation" while dismantling social protections and re-externalizing social reproduction. The result is not only to abandon defenseless populations to capital's predations, but also to redefine emancipation in market terms.[27]

Emancipatory movements participated in this process. All of them, including antiracism, multiculturalism, LGBTQ liberation, and ecology, spawned market-friendly neoliberal currents. But the feminist trajectory proved especially fateful, given capitalism's longstanding entanglement of gender and social reproduction.[28] Like each of its predecessor regimes, financialized capitalism institutionalizes the production/reproduction division on a gendered basis. Unlike its predecessors, however, its dominant imaginary is liberal-individualist and gender-egalitarian—women are considered the equals of men in every sphere, deserving of equal opportunities to realize their talents, including—perhaps especially—in the sphere of production. Reproduction, by contrast, appears as a backward residue, an obstacle to advancement that must be sloughed off one way or another en route to liberation.

Despite, or perhaps because of, its feminist aura, this conception epitomizes the current form of capitalism's social contradiction, which assumes a new intensity. As well as diminishing public provision and recruiting women into waged work, financialized capitalism has reduced real wages, thus raising the number of hours of paid work per household needed to support a family and prompting a desperate scramble to transfer care work to others.[29] To fill the "care gap," the regime imports migrant workers from poorer to richer countries. Typically, it is racialized and/or rural women from poor regions who take on reproductive and caring labor previously performed by more privileged women. But to do this, the migrants must transfer their own familial and community responsibilities to other, still poorer caregivers, who must in turn do the same—and on and on, in ever longer "global care chains." Far from filling the care gap, the net effect is to displace it—from richer to poorer families, from the Global North to the Global South.[30]

This scenario fits the gendered strategies of cash-strapped, indebted postcolonial states subjected to International Monetary Fund structural adjustment programs. Desperate for hard currency, some of them have actively promoted women's emigration to perform paid care work abroad for the sake of remittances, while others have courted foreign direct investment by creating export-processing zones, often in industries (such as textiles and electronics assembly) that prefer to employ women workers.[31] In both cases, social-reproductive capacities are further squeezed.

Two recent developments in the United States epitomize the severity of the situation. The first is the rising popularity of egg-freezing, normally a ten-thousand-dollar procedure but now offered free by IT firms as a fringe benefit to highly qualified female employees. Eager to attract and retain these workers, firms like Apple and Facebook provide them a strong incentive to postpone childbearing, saying, in effect, "Wait and have your kids in your forties, fifties, or even sixties; devote your high-energy, productive years to us."[32]

A second US development equally symptomatizes the contradiction between reproduction and production: the proliferation of expensive, high-tech mechanical pumps for expressing breast milk. This is the "fix" of choice in a country with a high rate of female labor-force participation, no mandated paid maternity or parental leave, and a love affair with technology. This is a country, too, in which breastfeeding is *de rigueur* but has changed beyond all recognition. No longer a matter of suckling a child at one's breast, one "breastfeeds" now by expressing one's milk mechanically and storing it for feeding by bottle later by one's nanny. In a context of severe time poverty, double-cup, hands-free pumps are considered the most desirable, as they permit one to express milk from both breasts at once while driving to work on the freeway.[33]

Given pressures like these, is it any wonder that struggles over social reproduction have exploded over recent years? Northern feminists often describe their focus as the "balance between family and work."[34] But struggles over social reproduction encompass much more—including grassroots community movements for housing, health care, food security, and an unconditional basic income; struggles for the rights of migrants, domestic workers, and public employees; campaigns to unionize those who perform social service work in for-profit nursing homes, hospitals, and child-care centers; struggles for public services such as daycare and eldercare, for a shorter work week, and for generous paid maternity and parental leave. Taken together, these claims are tantamount to the demand for a massive reorganization of the relation between production and reproduction: for social arrangements that could enable people of every class, gender, sexuality, and color to combine social reproductive activities with safe, interesting, and well-remunerated work.

Boundary struggles over social reproduction are as central to the present conjuncture as are class struggles over economic production. They respond, above all, to a crisis of care that is rooted in the structural dynamics of financialized capitalism. Globalizing and propelled by debt, this capitalism is systematically expropriating the capacities available for sustaining social connections. Proclaiming its ideal as "the two-earner family," it recuperates movements for emancipation, who join with proponents of marketization to oppose the partisans of social protection, now turned increasingly resentful and chauvinistic.

What might emerge from this crisis?

ANOTHER MUTATION?

Capitalist society has reinvented itself several times in the course of its history. Especially in moments of general crisis, when multiple contradictions—political, economic, ecological, and social-reproductive—intertwine and exacerbate one another, boundary struggles have erupted at the sites of capitalism's constitutive institutional divisions: where economy meets polity, where society meets nature, and where production meets reproduction. At those boundaries, social actors have mobilized to redraw the institutional map of capitalist society. Their efforts propelled the shift, first, from the liberal competitive capitalism of the nineteenth century to the state-managed capitalism of the twentieth, and then to the financialized capitalism of the present era. Historically, too, capitalism's social contradiction has formed an important strand of the precipitating crisis, as the boundary dividing social reproduction from economic production has emerged as a major site and central stake of social struggle. In each case, the gender order of capitalist society has been contested and the outcome has depended on alliances forged among the principal poles of a triple movement: marketization, social protection, and emancipation. Those dynamics propelled the shift from separate spheres to the family wage, and then to the two-earner family.

What follows for the current conjuncture? Are the present contradictions of financialized capitalism severe enough to qualify as a general crisis, and should we anticipate another mutation of capitalist society? Will the current crisis galvanize struggles of sufficient breadth and vision to transform the present regime? Might a new form of socialist-feminism succeed in breaking up the mainstream movement's love affair with marketization while forging a new alliance between emancipation and social protection—and, if so, to what end? How might the reproduction/production division be reinvented today, and what can replace the two-earner family?

Nothing I have said here serves to answer these questions directly. But in laying the groundwork that permits us to pose them, I have tried to shed some light on the current conjuncture. I have suggested, specifically, that the roots of today's crisis of care lie in capitalism's inherent social contradiction—or, rather, in the acute form this contradiction assumes today, in financialized capitalism. If that is right, then this crisis will not be resolved by tinkering with social policy. The path to its resolution can only go through deep structural transformation of this social order. What is required, above all, is to overcome financialized capitalism's rapacious subjugation of reproduction to production—but this time without sacrificing either emancipation or social protection. This, in turn, requires reinventing the production/reproduction distinction and reimagining the gender order. Whether the result will be compatible with capitalism at all remains to be seen.

3

Without Reserves

Salar Mohandesi and Emma Teitelman

> The historical experience is not one of staying in the present and looking back. Rather it is one of going back into the past and returning to the present with a wider and more intense consciousness of the restrictions of our former outlook. We return with a broader awareness of the alternatives open to us and armed with a sharper perceptiveness with which to make our choices. In this manner it is possible to loosen the clutch of the dead hand of the past and transform it into a living tool for the present and future.
>
> —William Appleman Williams, *The Contours of American History* (1961)

Since the 1970s, when feminists first developed Karl Marx's cursory reflections on the concept, social reproduction has assumed a central place in our theoretical arsenal. The concept has helped us refine how to think about the relationship between gender, sexuality, race, and class; better understand the sources of women's oppression; recognize capitalism's dependence on unpaid domestic labor; and highlight the diversity of class struggle, among many other things. Unfortunately, when it comes to dominant narratives of capitalism, the discoveries of social reproduction theory have only added more epicycles to the received model, not fundamentally transformed it. The story is still essentially one about the eventual decline of the peasantry, the rise of factories, struggles of brawny wageworkers, and deindustrialization—even if one now adds a few more sections here and there about women.

What's so tragic about this is not only that the story is exclusionary and in many respects wrong, but that feminist scholars have already created the necessary elements for a completely revised, more inclusive, and nuanced history of capitalism. Not only have they generated numerous localized studies, some have written lengthy histories of women's labor, social reproduction, care work, and the welfare state. Yet this work too often goes unrecognized or is categorized exclusively as women's history. What follows, therefore, is a modest attempt to draw on those rich insights to begin the long process of rewriting a general narrative of capitalism, class composition, and state formation in the United States from the perspective of social reproduction. To be sure, we are not attempting to write the definitive counterhistory here. Space has constrained us to chart major tendencies rather than chronicle exact historical phenomena. While this means a great deal has unfortunately been left out, this approach allows us to synthesize a number of trends that better illuminate our present conjuncture.

Shifting our perspective from the point of production to that of social reproduction does not merely add to the narrative: it has the potential to transform that story. It allows us a far more nuanced approach to class formation, one that focuses not simply on waged factory workers but on the articulation of different kinds of struggles—those of the waged and unwaged, men and women, whites and nonwhites, and citizens and immigrants. It allows us to deepen our understanding of the capitalist mode of production by showing how its rise was partly based on the manifold subsumption of socially reproductive activities under capitalist relations. Last, it allows us to approach the state in a more complex manner, revealing the crucial role that contests over social reproduction played in the historical formation of the state and its relationship to capitalists.

There is a particular urgency to revisiting the history of capitalism today, for new debates about the present moment have been grounded in comparisons to the past. Some have argued that we are in fact witnessing a return to an era before the social democratic compromise of the mid-twentieth century, with unregulated capitalism, unprotected workers, and an absence of substantive social welfare.[1] Others have suggested that we have entered an entirely distinct moment, one marked by rising precarity, soaring surplus populations, and an imperiled wage system.[2] This is not just an academic debate. How we understand our own place within the arc of capitalism's history sheds light on the field of political strategies available today. If the present resembles the past in crucial ways, then perhaps inherited strategies, organizations, and forms of struggle are still appropriate. But if capitalist accumulation, the composition of the working classes, and the role of the state have completely changed, then strategies must be rethought.

Despite disagreements over today's relationship to the past, there seems to be general consensus in the overarching historical narrative: both sides begin and end at the point of production. In challenging this narrative, we intend to move beyond that impasse. Viewing the history of capitalism in the United States through the lens of social reproduction compels us to confront, in the words of William Appleman Williams, the "restrictions of our former outlook," facilitating new ways of thinking about a politics of the present.[3]

THE FUNCTIONS OF THE HOUSEHOLD

Under the capitalist mode of production, social reproduction, whether waged or unwaged, refers to the totality of those activities required to create, maintain, and restore the commodity labor power.[4] Although this kind of work has historically unfolded in a variety of sites, such as camps, schools, orphanages, churches, civic associations, and communes, for most of American history socially reproductive activities have overwhelmingly taken place in and around households, making the home one of the most vital institutions in the reproduction of capitalist relations as a whole.[5]

The household, of course, has always had a contradictory existence. On the one hand, capitalism depends heavily on the household to replenish labor power and reproduce gendered hierarchies. On the other hand, as a site of mutual aid, income pooling, and the accumulation of vital reserves, the household, though always changing, has proven vital to the survival of the working class. In short, the household has been essential to the reproduction of both sides of the equation—capital and labor.

While social reproduction creates and recreates labor power, it does not do so from nothing. Like all kinds of work, socially reproductive labor draws a range of materials, which are themselves historical. In the nineteenth century, cooking required not only food but firewood and cookware. To make clothing, one needed cotton, thread, and needles. Washing required soap, water, a basin, and a washboard, and to heal, one needed herbs and medicine. To maintain morale, one needed toys, alcohol, musical instruments. Where did these raw materials come from? In most cases, they were directly produced or acquired: tomatoes growing in the garden or pigs in the shed. Sometimes they were salvaged or scavenged, acquired through barter, or received as gifts.

Over the course of the nineteenth century, these materials increasingly came indirectly, through money, which was then used to purchase necessary commodities. Some households generated money income by renting a spare room. In other cases, households received an inheritance—clothes, furniture, coins. The members of a household may have engaged in petty commodity production, selling the surplus. The household was—and continues to be—that place where members who may not have been biologically related and who perhaps lived in different places each contributed their various incomes, significantly increasing their individual chances of survival.[6] In this way, we may speak of the household as an income-pooling unit, among its many other functions. Thus, households have historically served as bulwarks against capitalism and even as organizational nodes in class struggles. Yet, at the same time, proletarian households have nearly always been sites of oppression, particularly between adults and children and above all between men and women.

VARIETIES OF ENCLOSURE

By the turn of the century, money from wage labor had come to occupy a much greater component of total household income for most working-class people in the United States. Several related, though distinct, historical pressures produced this greater dependence on waged income. First and most simply, despite recessions and panics, there were more waged jobs to be had. For some, the opportunity to work for wages was a welcome break from traditional household labors and hierarchies.

However, the mere availability of waged jobs did not automatically translate to more wage workers. For many, dependence on the wage was coerced, directly or indirectly. Rural tenants in the Northeast, for example, struggled fiercely to maintain their modes of subsistence farming and challenged their uprooting with anti-rent strikes in the mid-nineteenth century. This upheaval met armed suppression at the hands of local militiamen. Meanwhile, many rural people held out hope that the Western frontier would provide opportunities to reproduce traditional household economies. But Western imperialism was predicated on the colonial dispossession of indigenous peoples. Furthermore, migrants had to compete with land speculators, railroad developers, and industrialists, many of whom were subsidized by government policies. These rural people were much more likely to end up in towns and cities in search of employment.[7]

As capitalism expanded throughout the nineteenth century, it became more and more difficult to sustain alternative forms of life. To be sure of this, the US government mounted violent campaigns against communities that were not dependent exclusively on capitalist relations, such as Indian peoples and Mormons, and struggled to reorganize their living arrangements. Persecuting polygamy, chipping away at the Mormon church's property, and opening Utah to transcontinental railroads precipitated the failure of Mormons' nineteenth-century economies, which had strived to maintain independence by pooling land and labor.[8] To take another example, the Dawes Severalty Act of 1887 subdivided indigenous peoples' reserved lands into forty-acre plots, each distributed to a male-headed nuclear household. This land allotment marked a culmination of colonial policies, undermining Native Americans' sovereignties and dispossessing them of more than half of their reservation lands.[9]

The enclosure of common lands proceeded well into the late nineteenth century, particularly in the South and the West. In the post–Civil War South, for example, formerly enslaved people's desires for economic independence were thwarted by the planter class's movement to limit their access to common lands. These policies not only ensured that black Southerners remained an agricultural workforce, but also transformed the household economies of white yeoman farmers, who had relied on those unenclosed lands for hunting, fishing, and foraging for livestock. By the end of the century, the majority of white and black Southerners were landless and dependent on capitalist relations for their subsistence.[10] In the same period in the formerly Mexican regions of the Southwest, Congress and the courts denied many Spanish-speaking New Mexicans, Texans, and Californians traditional rights to communal holdings and grazing lands. Cattle corporations and commercial agriculture replaced herding economies and ranchos, displacing the villages and communities that had subsisted on those resources. These processes created a workforce of agricultural, mining, and migrant laborers.[11]

Although the most encompassing enclosure movements took place in the countryside, urban dwellers were not immune to similar processes. For example, beginning in the early nineteenth century and continuing until the twentieth, municipal authorities in urban centers throughout the country banned livestock from roaming city streets. Pigs, in particular, became targets of public health regulations, particularly in the wake of yellow fever and cholera epidemics. Not coincidentally, pigs were often the most accessible farm animals for working-class people, because they could survive on garbage and in limited space (rather than unenclosed fields for pasture). In New York City, it took many decades—and significant policing—for municipal pig laws to replace social custom.[12]

As these enclosure movements suggest, the growing dependence on wages was a highly uneven process that reflected the vast and heterogeneous political geography of the United States. As dispossessed populations grew, labor relations did not simply homogenize but remained regionally specific. In the late-nineteenth-century South, for example, sharecropping, a particular form of agricultural labor, emerged out of struggles between landowning planters and formerly enslaved people. Under this system, sharecroppers were legally defined as wage workers, and most landowners explicitly refused to pay for reproductive work in order to force all household members to engage directly in production. Like wage workers, sharecroppers were compelled to purchase their own subsistence goods, usually from country stores, landowners, or merchants. But as so little cash circulated in the South during this period, sharecropping functioned almost entirely on credit, a pattern that "locked" workers into repressive cycles of debt. Thus sharecroppers lived on and worked someone else's land not for cash wages but for a percentage of the future cotton crop, which they pledged as collateral to purchase necessities from creditors. In many places in the South, money did not directly mediate labor relations, but workers were nevertheless dependent on some form of compensation to purchase the means of their reproduction.[13]

THE CAPITALIZATION OF SOCIAL REPRODUCTION

As many scholars have shown, the fitful expansion of waged labor thoroughly transformed the composition of proletarian households, as well as the relationship between production and social reproduction. In early US history, a strict separation between "production" and what is now called "social reproduction" did not exist, and despite a gendered division of labor, men and women did not perform categorically distinct kinds of activity. Historian Jeanne Boydston has shown that both men and women "brought raw materials into the household, both spent long hours processing raw materials into usable goods, and both conducted the exchanges necessary to supplement the family's own resources."[14] Over time, however, industrialization tended to physically separate the workplace from the site of social reproduction, a division which contributed to the belief that there existed two separate spheres of activity. Households' growing dependence on the wage gave greater social power to men, who came to believe that they were the major providers for the family. This encouraged a further division of social life between the world of work, dominated by men, and that of the home, the domain of women. Thus, as men's work increasingly took them outside of the household, their value as wage-earners was legitimized by the cultural and ideological devaluing of women's domestic labor within the household. The domestic tasks of wives and mothers became invisible as work, while women who worked for wages were considered the exception, not the rule. In this way, dependence on the wage not only integrated men and women into capitalist relations, but worked to formalize a rigid and hierarchical gendered division of labor within working-class households.[15]

The ideological separation between production in the workplace and social reproduction in the household obscured the fact that capital accumulation depended on transforming socially reproductive activities into work that was directly productive of surplus value. Industrial manufacturing of textiles and other consumer goods, the sine qua non of early American capitalism, benefited directly from women and children's "outwork." Through this "putting-out" system, manufacturers distributed raw materials or semi-finished commodities to individual households, and paid women to spin yarn, sew textiles, bind soles, braid straw, and so on. Thousands of women in towns, cities, and rural hinterlands were thus engaged in waged socially reproductive work, even if they remained atomized within their own homes. The rise of outwork coincided with the decline of households' self-sufficiency, even though this labor often resembled traditional domestic tasks.[16]

Eventually, many of these activities moved into workplaces outside of individual homes. The textile industry, for example, relied less and less on the putting-out system as new technologies became available. Instead, production became organized around large-scale, integrated mills, replete with closely supervised boarding houses for workers—usually young women. The formerly unwaged work of sewing, once constitutive of households' reproduction, first became waged, and then physically separated from its social context. Clothes became commodities produced in factories, sold on the market, and purchased with money.

Another form of remunerated socially reproductive work was domestic service, easily one of the largest paid occupations in the nineteenth century. In some major cities in the 1880s, for example, there was one domestic servant for every four American families.[17] Some homes employed an entire fleet of servants. The centrality of domestic labor suggests that the distinction between waged and unwaged socially reproductive work was not as sharp as sometimes suggested.[18] After all, domestics performed the same kinds of work they did in their own households, the only difference was that it was now in someone else's home and for a wage.

It is significant that this kind of waged social reproduction still tended to be performed by women. As the ideological distinction between production and reproduction hardened, an entire category of "women's work" firmly took root, encompassing labors that most clearly resembled those of the household. Wage-earning women were clustered in the textile and garment industries, laundering, nursing, service work, and, especially, domestic work in someone else's home—in 1870, for example, 50 percent of all employed women worked as domestics.[19] Of course, there was nothing "natural" about women performing this category of socially reproductive work. Rather, ideologies of separate spheres were reinforced by notions that men and women's social roles were biologically rather than culturally assigned. Femininity became associated with domesticity, caregiving, physical weakness, and dependence, and this ideology shaped both the jobs women could access and the wage rates they were paid. Employers and wage-earning men could reason that women were only temporary members of the labor force, that they were not responsible for supporting their own households, and that they were physically and mentally incapable of certain types of work. Women were thus relegated to working in low-paying and so-called "unskilled" jobs.[20]

For many women, working for wages was, indeed, temporary. There were many women who worked until they were married: by 1900, upwards of 40 percent of single women on average worked for wages, while an average of 6 percent of married women did. However, these numbers were much higher among non-white and immigrant women, for whom wage work was often necessary well into adulthood.[21] Black married women, for example, were five times more likely to work for wages than white wives. Whether a married woman worked for wages correlated directly to her husband's employment status; in a racially segmented labor market, black men's earnings were usually insufficient to fully subsist a household, or men were driven to other towns and cities altogether in search of employment. This greater relative dependence on the wage meant that black and immigrant households were more precarious when incomes fluctuated. For married women who relied on waged work, jobs that allowed for versions of "outwork"—like laundering—were often most attractive. Although pay was low, taking in laundry meant that married women could perform waged and unwaged reproductive work simultaneously, even integrating the labor of children or other household members into the process.[22]

Within the category of "women's work," then, there were significant stratifications along the lines of race and class, and poor, black, or foreign-born women often found non-agricultural jobs of the lowest status and wage rates. Whereas many native-born, white single women at the turn of the century might find opportunities in teaching, clerical, or sales work, immigrant women were more likely to work in garment factories or as hired help in middle-class households. Black women found non-agricultural work almost exclusively in domestic service and laundering. This racial segmentation was so stark that in some major cities, as many as 90 percent of wage-earning black women were domestic workers.[23] In this way, social reproduction was not only gendered, but racialized.

THE TERRAIN OF SOCIAL REPRODUCTION

Social reproduction, whether waged or unwaged, became a crucial, though often neglected, site of working-class struggle in the United States. With the expansion of capitalist relations, the unwaged work of consumption—household budgeting, food shopping, managing household needs—became politicized in new ways, especially in response to inflation and price increases in the early twentieth century. Rent, food, and cost of living were key points of contestation that inspired a variety of actions, such as boycotts, rent strikes, and the organization of cooperatives. Conflicts over consumption—inextricably linked to the growing dependence on wages—were also reflected in the labor movement's growing emphasis on a "living wage," which rejected older ideas about the economic determination of wage rates and insisted instead that wages should sustain a standard of living above subsistence levels.[24]

One of the better-known struggles over rent and food took place in New York City's Lower East Side, where working-class Jewish women organized powerful tenant strikes and consumer boycotts in the early twentieth century. In 1902, thousands of women, the majority of them housewives, organized a three-week boycott of the "Meat Trust" and kosher meat retailers. They rioted, picketed, coordinated with labor unions, and planned cooperatives, pooling resources to subsidize not only food but also arrest funds. Their organizing model inspired a wave of tenant organizing just a few years later, initiating a round of rent strikes beginning in 1907. These autonomous worker actions soon came under the aegis of the Socialist Party, which organized a massive, coordinated rent strike in 1908. Workers confronted the police, hung their landlords in effigy, and waved petticoats died in red from their windows.[25] Less than a decade later, as wartime inflation reached all-time highs, women in Brooklyn once more responded to price increases with riots, overturning pushcarts, setting produce ablaze, and battling police. These soon spread to other cities, such as Washington, D.C., Boston, and Philadelphia.[26]

Thus it was the politics of consumption that often linked struggles of the unwaged to a broader labor movement. Dana Frank's work on the general strike of 1919 offers a clear example. The general strike involved a great deal of consumer coordination, with food cooperatives that fed some 30,000 people each day. Consumers' cooperatives endured after the strike's close, cultivating the power of workers' purchasing activities and challenging exploitation at the "point of consumption," as some put it at the time. Although they were hardly free from internal tensions and contradictions, these movements were built by men and women, waged and unwaged. Indeed, working-class housewives were particularly active, for their work of household budgeting was deeply affected by the high inflation of the era.[27]

But if struggles over social reproduction linked unwaged workers at the "point of consumption," they also played an interesting articulating function among waged workers, linking different kinds of struggles together. This was powerfully demonstrated by a southern washerwomen's strike in 1881. Demanding higher pay, respect, and greater control over their work, twenty black washerwomen formed a trade union in Atlanta, Georgia, calling a strike in July 1881.[28] Building on the communal nature of laundry work, leaning on support from the black community, and canvassing door to door, the washerwomen's strike developed into a major struggle. Within three weeks the Washing Society had not only grown to 3,000 strikers and sympathizers, but even succeeded in involving a few white washerwomen—and this in a time of racial segregation. The strike not only weathered fierce repression, but spread to other socially reproductive industries. Nurses, cooks, and maids all began to agitate for higher wages, and even male workers in other service industries went on strike. As the washerwomen's strike revealed, workers could use the terrain of social reproduction as a powerful site of working-class self-activity. As historian Tera W. Hunter concludes:

> Through the use of formal and informal community networks in which they shared work routines, work sites, living space, and social activity, the strikers organized thousands of women and men. The importance of these everyday networks and sequestered social spaces was thrown into relief by the strike: they not only promoted quotidian survival, but also built a base for political action. The areas of everyday survival, on the one hand, and resistance and large-scale political protests, on the other, were mutually reinforcing; both were necessary parts of a collective cultural whole of working-class self-activity.[29]

Although highly uneven, bifurcated between waged and waged work, divided by gender, and oftentimes invisible, the patchy terrain of social reproduction was not only a site of struggle, but a potential site of class formation. Rent strikes, boycotts, and demonstrations all involved a great deal of self-organization. Self-reliance and mutual aid had the potential to build solidarity. Actions over social reproduction could not only trigger struggles elsewhere, but fuse them together. Acknowledging this changes our understanding of the history of working-class formation in this country. Rather than a history confined to the male factory worker, we see that every step of the way proletarian struggles developed over social reproduction, oftentimes sparking great social upheavals.

RELIEF

Although collective action often proved central to workers' material well-being, many workers also looked to some form of outside relief. Reliance on the wage bred precarity. Full-time employment was far from the norm; many jobs were seasonal, and contracts were often part-time. When economic panics hit, as they did with greater frequency, working people's insecurity became all the more stark.[30] Throughout the nineteenth century, many precariously employed people found relief from poorhouses, as well as public outdoor relief, which provided material aid without forcing its recipients into institutions and almshouses. However, as panics hit and a permanent working class grew, traditional poor laws and local relief institutions became overwhelmed by the growing demand. At the same time, elite social thought became increasingly hostile to traditional forms of public assistance, which many in the middle classes believed to encourage "idleness" among working people.[31]

By the 1870s and 1880s, this strain on public relief had inspired innovations—and retrenchments—in social welfare services. Middle-class advocates of so-called "scientific charity" led campaigns to curtail public outdoor relief.[32] Rooted in assumptions about poor people's own failings, these policies attempted to get the able-bodied off of public relief rolls, transform traditional poorhouses into institutions for the elderly and mentally ill, and transfer the children of impoverished parents to orphanages. If some non-laboring individuals received care in public institutions, these policies nonetheless proved disastrous to working people's families and their abilities to sustain themselves. Relief for laboring men and women was increasingly privatized to charitable organizations, which were themselves being reorganized to achieve maximum efficiency and bureaucratic rationality. These private, "scientific" charities made judgments about who was deserving of relief, and excluded those who were physically able to labor. The goal was to instill working-class discipline, deter dependence, and disabuse working people of notions that public relief was a right. The effect was to institutionalize ideas about the deserving and undeserving poor that remain embedded in public policy to this day.[33]

Yet the growing militancy and frequency of working-class actions, the explosive growth of cities and immigration, the spread of socialism and farmers' insurgencies, and the depression of 1893 all revealed the inadequacies of this model of relief. Indeed, as Michael Katz has written, "the 1890s mark the start of a new era in the history of social welfare."[34] This wave of reform involved a spectrum of activities and groups, which were heterogeneous in their goals but coalesced around the belief that this form of capitalism was unsustainable. Among corporate elites emerged a movement for "welfare capitalism," which recognized that workers' insufficient abilities to reproduce themselves was bad for business: happier and healthier workers, they argued, would help to mitigate high turnover rates. Thus organizations like the National Civic Federation made tentative alliances with the most conservative segments of the labor movement, and advocated policies to subsidize workers' health, recreation, and housing.

Not coincidentally, the movement for company welfare programs also aimed to undercut the power of unions, which in some sectors had begun to organize their own insurance initiatives. The United Mine Workers of America, for example, not only bargained for better wages and working conditions, but also provided hospitals, as well as health, disability, and death insurance to protect workers from the considerable dangers of mining. Union locals waged significant struggles to protect these programs from being coopted by company welfare initiatives, and to maintain control over the domain of workers' health.[35] As this example suggests, contests between capital and organized labor unfolded not only on the shop floor, but also on the terrain of social reproduction.

This desire among capitalists to control the social lives of workers was exemplified by Henry Ford. Indeed, Ford's experiments with rationalizing production in his factory went hand in hand with rationalizing socially reproductive work at home, again highlighting the inextricable link between the two. Ford expected men to keep themselves in good moral standing, their children in school, and their wives at home. For their part, wives were expected to budget the wage, keep the house tidy, and raise the next generation. To assist with this work, the company provided loans to buy furniture and kept a team of doctors and nurses to offer health advice. And to ensure maximum discipline, Ford's sociology department eventually hired nearly two hundred inspectors to interrogate workers, enter their homes unannounced, check on the work of wives, and even investigate how they managed the household budget. If workers failed to conform to Ford's model of social reproduction, they risked being fired. Ford framed this rationalization as a nationalist project, subjectifying his workers, many of whom were immigrants, as specifically *American* workers.[36]

In subjecting workers' domestic routines to inspection and discipline, Ford contributed to a broad and heterogeneous movement of middle class reformers, many of them women, who took interest in the moral and physical "uplift" of the working class. In private philanthropic organizations and professionalizing social work associations, middle-class women's "maternalist" politics projected the ideals of domesticity to transform society. They prioritized a number of causes (safe food, for example), but focused their energies especially on regulating the lives and labors of working-class women and children. Horrified by the living conditions of wage-earning women, middle-class reformers pushed for labor protections to limit the number of hours women could work and the physicality of their labor. Pressured by this reformist movement, in the first decades of the twentieth century a growing number of states implemented Mothers' Pension programs to assist mothers who lacked the support of a man's income. This kind of legislation reinforced women's roles as mothers and wives—the arbiters of social reproduction—and was often favored by craft unions who feared women's growing workforce participation.[37]

Thus in the late nineteenth and early twentieth centuries, this private reformist impulse contributed to the incremental expansion of protective legislation, which took particular interest in families and households. These concerns were shaped not only by capitalism's instability, but also by hardening ideas of national purity. For example, by the turn of the century, the majority of states implemented a compulsory education system that served contradictory social purposes. If these public institutions subsidized care and promised new opportunities to the children of immigrants and working classes, they also served to inculcate, "Americanize," and propagate certain ideologies and cultural behaviors that were essential to forging a workforce and a nation. Progressives' education movement thus complemented an obsession with racial purity and nationalism. The results of these reformist initiatives were particularly extreme for Native American children, many of whom were literally forced by the federal government to leave their communities for industrial schools, where they learned the skills of manual or domestic labor.[38]

Despite this expansion in state regulations and policing, Progressive reform was geographically uneven and generally patchwork. This was largely because reforms were located in the individual state governments rather than the federal government, whose growth was constrained by constitutional barriers and the architecture of federalism.[39] Execution, then, typically fell to local municipalities, and even the most robust welfare programs were significantly underfunded.[40] Thus while the states became a more powerful force in the material lives of working people, these reforms paled in comparison to what would come next.

THE HISTORIC COMPROMISE

The catastrophe that was the Great Depression irreversibly transformed social reproduction in the United States. Having grown so dependent on the wage, the sudden economic collapse proved disastrous for most working-class households. In the wake of the crash, unemployment climbed to 25 percent, and nearly thirteen million Americans searched for work. With wages collapsing, and millions out of work, American workers struggled to survive. Food was simply too expensive for impoverished households, and many American cities experienced food shortages—too poor to harvest their crops, farmers let them rot in the fields. Thousands of families could not afford rents. Evicted from homes, they built shantytowns, known as Hoovervilles, around American cities. Many used cardboard, tin, and salvaged materials to jerry-build shelters; other families dug holes into the earth; while in some cases proletarians moved into empty conduits and water mains. Infant mortality soared; one-quarter of school children were malnourished; diseases, like tuberculosis, spread unchecked; suicide rates increased across the country, and the great disparities in living conditions throughout the country were fully revealed.[41]

This crisis had enormous consequences for the composition of households. Hoping to pool more incomes in order to weather the crisis, many households grew substantially larger during the 1930s. In other cases, the Depression tore households apart.[42] Couples divorced, families collapsed, and many Americans, both men and women, took to the road. It is estimated that during the early 1930s over half a million transient men wandered across the country, either on foot or by train, searching for jobs.[43] In this context, some experimented with alternative ways of organizing social life. Hobos, for example, created "hobo jungles" to share food, fuel, water, fire, and information, and to care for and protect one another. Occasionally, homeless proletarians formed large-scale autonomous communities, sometimes within major cities.[44]

With the Great Depression, capitalism faced a crisis of unprecedented proportions. Far more serious than the fall in the rate of profit, capitalist accumulation had effectively halted the continued reproduction of the working class, and with it, labor power, its very condition of possibility. What is more, workers began to fight back. Unemployed workers organized mass marches in nearly every major American city.[45] In the spring of 1932, thousands of hungry veterans marched on Washington,

D.C., occupying parts of the capital. In 1934, a general strike paralyzed the city of San Francisco for four days. In 1936, autoworkers in Flint, Michigan organized a sit-in strike against General Motors. Widespread struggles soon translated to the rapid growth of formal organizations. The United Auto Workers, for instance, saw its membership soar from 30,000 to 500,000 members in under a year. Even the Communist Party (CPUSA) boasted 100,000 members by the late 1930s, drawing its greatest numbers from the unemployed rather than wage-earners.[46]

In light of this crisis, the distinctions between production and social reproduction, waged and unwaged workers, were once again blurred. Struggles unfolded not only on the factory floor, but on the terrain of social reproduction.[47] Women organized bread, meat, and milk strikes against high prices.[48] In 1931, several hundred famished women and men raided a grocery market in Minneapolis, pilfering bread, fruit, meat, and canned foods. Although the media refused to publicize the riots for fear of contagion, these actions still spread to such a degree that by 1932 "organized looting of food was a nation-wide phenomenon," as Irving Bernstein has written.[49] These food riots were soon joined by "rent strikes." Bands of workers, often led by Communists, turned the gas back on, blocked marshals from evicting families, and in some cases battled the police to reinstall evicted families.[50]

But social reproduction was not simply a terrain of struggle; it rapidly emerged as a site of class recomposition.[51] Through struggles over social reproduction—over food, housing, and relief—different sectors of the American working class began to articulate themselves into a broader class unity. In cities like Chicago and Harlem, rent actions united black and white workers; in Detroit, the labor movement connected with the unemployed movement; in the South, Communists tied struggles over unemployment to anti-racism; across the country, women fought alongside men, workers overcame occupational divisions to demand greater relief, and women struggled to link domestic concerns with the sphere of production.[52] Although this process was uneven and fraught with contradictions, social reproduction nevertheless became a primary site of class formation during one of the most militant moments in American history. It was in neighborhoods, apartment buildings, parks, schools, and streets that the working class made itself into a political subject.[53]

Crucial to this political class recomposition was the recognition that the crisis stemmed not from any individual failing, but rather from the system itself. Instead of treating poverty as a sign of personal failure, workers banded together to demand that the system that caused the crisis should be held accountable. This took many forms, but the most central was the demand for greater relief.[54] Workers raided local relief offices demanding monetary aid, free health care, meals, and work. As a report from the American Public Welfare Association later described:

> Relief offices were approached by large committees, numbering ten, fifteen, twenty, and sometimes more persons, which demanded immediate audience, without previous appointment and regardless of staff members' schedules. . . Frequently these large committees were buttressed by neighborhood crowds which gathered outside the relief office and waited while committees within presented "demands."[55]

In places like Harlem, if relief officers refused, workers would camp in the offices or even begin breaking desks and chairs, provoking pitched battles with the police.[56]

When these local and state institutions were overwhelmed, many workers demanded that the federal government shoulder the responsibility. In this way the 1930s, marked a significant transformation in working-class attitudes toward the state. Many workers began to believe that the federal government had a responsibility to provide relief that had until then fallen under the purview of philanthropists, welfare capitalists, or local governments. In greater numbers, workers demanded that the US government had a duty to cover the costs of their social reproduction.[57]

Indeed, even militant workers who wanted to overthrow capitalism began to voice such demands. Although the CPUSA was one of the first to organize the unemployed, calling for unemployment insurance and emergency relief in 1930, the party initially insisted that workers should "have no illusions that the government will grant these measures of partial relief."[58] Yet the experiences of everyday organizing soon led activists to rethink their dismissal of struggles for immediate needs. As Steven Nelson, a Communist leader in Chicago, put it,

> We spent the first few weeks agitating against capitalism.... But even if people listened to our arguments, we couldn't offer them much hope for the immediate future. How were they going to pay the rent, buy food, and survive in the meantime?[59]

In fall 1930 the Communist International itself criticized the CPUSA for not going far enough in its fight for federal relief, prompting the party to reorient its strategy.[60] By 1935, when the Comintern formally adopted the Popular Front strategy, the CPUSA agreed to collaborate with the Democratic Party, table calls for maximalist revolution, and channel the anger of the working classes to demand that the state subsidize social reproduction.

The working class's changing attitude toward the state prompted the state to change its attitude toward the working class. In response to these pressures, the federal government, under the administration of President Franklin D. Roosevelt, began to experiment with new approaches to managing capitalism.[61] What began as inchoate, disconnected projects soon developed into a coherent governing logic over the course of the 1930s. Under the "New Deal," the central state intervened directly in the economy, regulated capitalist firms, devised new monetary policies, and managed class struggle by making major concessions to workers.[62] With this new approach, workers were no longer treated as an impediment to profit, but necessary partners in the pursuit of continued growth.[63] As Silvia Federici and Mario Montano put it, the working class's "needs can no longer be violently repressed; they must be satisfied, to ensure continued economic development."[64] Thus, wages were allowed to rise, labor unions were protected, and millions of unemployed workers were hired by the state.

A central aspect of this new state strategy was to help cover the costs of social reproduction, a pattern which took many different forms.[65] Perhaps the most dramatic program was the Federal Emergency Relief Act (FERA), which, in addition to work relief and payments in kind, transferred funds directly to workers. In a significant break with the recent past, relief was not limited to widows, children, or the disabled, but open to all those who were unemployed. In fact, by winter 1934, 20 million people, nearly one-sixth of the total population, received such payments.[66] While many have argued that workers resisted the dole out of shame, evidence suggests that many workers not only welcomed direct federal aid, but felt they deserved it. As one social worker observed in 1934, "There is a noticeable tendency to regard obtaining relief as another way of earning a living."[67] In this way, some men and women came to see direct state payments as a crucial component of total household income. As an emergency measure, FERA soon expired, but the state did formalize cash benefits in 1935 when President Roosevelt signed the Social Security Act, a pathbreaking piece of legislation that shifted the responsibility for relief from local and state bodies to the federal government. Establishing the outlines of the modern "welfare state," the Social Security Act established provisions for unemployment compensation, old age insurance, and workers' compensation. It also established public assistance for the poor, including direct aid to dependent children (ADC, later AFDC).

In addition to providing various forms of social insurance, the federal government also began to issue payments in kind. For instance, in 1933, the Federal Surplus Relief Corporation (FSRC) began distributing food and fuel, beginning with pork, to impoverished households. In December 1933, the FSRC delivered three million tons of coal to unemployed workers in the Northwest.[68] By the fall of 1934, the FSRC had supplied households in thirty states with nearly 700 million pounds of foodstuffs, such as apples, beans, and beef.[69] But the central state not only provided workers with raw materials for social reproduction; in some cases it offered to take over socially reproductive activities altogether. For example, the Emergency Nursery Schools, which were originally designed to provide work for unemployed teachers, custodians, cooks, and nurses, ended up offering childcare for many impoverished working-class households in the United States.[70]

Perhaps the best-known programs of the New Deal involved massive public works projects, which built up new infrastructures and improved the quality of life for millions of impoverished Americans, ultimately reshaping the conditions of reproductive processes. Under the Public Works Administration, for instance, the federal government invested in thousands of new bridges, roads, waterworks, hospitals, and schools. This type of investment had an especially dramatic impact outside of urban centers, where economic development was uneven. For example, the Rural Electrification Act used federal money to electrify huge swathes of the country, especially poor rural areas, helping to bring the proportion of US farms with electricity from 20 percent in 1934 to ninety percent by 1950.[71] With access to electricity, agricultural production improved, and many more homes could benefit from new labor-saving products such as electric stoves and refrigerators. In addition to developing public infrastructures and utilities, the central state also came to assume an important role in the affective work of entertainment and social care, creating new parks, stadiums, museums, and other recreational facilities. For instance, under the Works Progress Administration (WPA), the federal government built over 750 swimming pools and renovated hundreds more between 1933 and 1938.[72] Thus in addition to providing millions of jobs, these various federal projects changed the contours of social life for millions of people, reorganizing the routines of care, work, transportation, and consumption.

These social programs came with a steep price. Although they saved many working people from poverty, the New Deal's programs also reorganized the composition of the working class, reinforced internal divisions, and foreclosed experiments in self-reproduction. In fact, the New Deal revolved around social hierarchies among workers in crucial ways. For example, the Roosevelt administration regarded the influx of women into the waged workforce as a potential threat, and thus used New Deal programs to re-establish gendered divisions of labor: women whose husbands worked for the government were fired from the civil service, married women were denied jobs, the so-called "family wage" was formalized, and the notion of "women's work" confirmed.[73] Through these kinds of policies, the New Deal reinforced the heterosexual, two-parent household as the primary site of social reproduction. Indeed, it was the family, based on women's domestic labor, Mariarosa Dalla Costa argues, that became the social institution holding together this historic compromise: "In the overall task of defending the purchasing power of wages, reabsorbing and reproducing individuals not immediately active, successfully producing new labor power and reproducing the active labor power, and therefore defending the capacity of consumption in general, the family functioned at the center of Roosevelt's New Deal."[74]

In addition to shoring up the nuclear family, the New Deal institutionalized racism into its most lauded social programs. This discrimination was built in by design: under pressure from southern Democrats, the Social Security Act denied insurances to domestic and agricultural workers, industries in which African Americans predominated. As a result, vast numbers of black workers were denied the benefits of the New Deal compromise. Thus the very same policies that helped defray the costs of social reproduction also worked to reinforce inequality and to maintain a divided, fragmented working class shot through with racial and gendered oppressions.[75] That the Roosevelt administration aligned black workers and southern segregationists within the same political party suggests just how limited and contradictory the New Deal's programs could be.[76]

Finally, social welfare programs reinforced American workers' dependence on the wage. At a time when some workers were calling for the right to life, the state doubled down on the ideology of work. After providing emergency relief, the US government eschewed direct income transfers for fear of the expectations they might cultivate. Instead, the state reinforced the sanctity of work, solidifying the idea that in capitalist society, one had to work to survive. Thus by October 1934, President Roosevelt publicly announced that direct payments should be terminated, and pursued the new policy of employing millions of workers in government programs. Through programs like the WPA, workers' reproduction was covered indirectly through the wage, and the social relations of capitalism were stabilized. In some respects, these relations were even deepened: on plantations throughout the South, the New Deal incentivized landowners to reduce production and mechanize, marking another enclosure movement that forced sharecroppers and tenants to search for bona fide wage work elsewhere.[77]

In this sense, what we are calling the "historic compromise" was not simply a detente between capital, labor, and the state, but resulted in an exchange—the state began to subsidize many of the costs of social reproduction while working-class households became largely dependent on capitalist relations.

EXPANDING THE COMPROMISE

Although many New Deal programs were scaled back, transformed, or dismantled in the late 1930s, the compromise took hold. Indeed, in some ways, the Second World War deepened the federal government's presence in the daily routines of reproduction, as the need for women's labor participation compelled federal officials to expand child care.[78] After the war, President Harry Truman's "Fair Deal," though limited in many respects, continued the New Deal legacy, laying the groundwork for new government programs.[79] But the crowning moment of the compromise came in the 1960s with President Lyndon Johnson's "Great Society."

In important ways, the Great Society went further than the New Deal by aiming to incorporate many of the groups who were initially excluded from the historic compromise—particularly African Americans, Latinx, and women. Responding to the pressure of escalating social movements, federal officeholders showed a new, albeit limited willingness to use social welfare to combat racism, sexism, and other forms of discrimination.[80] Mass social protest not only succeeded in including more people, but also worked to significantly expand the terms of the compromise.[81] The civil rights movement, certain currents of the women's movement, and the welfare rights movement fought for dignity, better coverage, independence, and a greater voice in the process, overturning many of the punitive, degrading, discriminatory, and authoritarian aspects of social welfare.[82]

It was in this context that the Great Society enriched the compromise by creating a new array of social programs to subsidize social reproduction and improve the quality of life. Among the most significant expansions in federal assistance involved payments in kind to poor households. For example, federal spending on food stamps, initially designed as a stopgap measure during the Depression, increased from 36 million in 1965 to 1.9 billion in 1972. By the 1970s, Congress had made food stamps available to working-class families above the poverty line, and added budgets for school lunches and nutritional supplements. In addition to subsidizing working Americans' food consumption, the Johnson administration unveiled the Department for Housing and Urban Development in 1965, embarking on a ten-year federal project to build 600,000 low-income homes. And in July 1965, Johnson created Medicare, and Medicaid, which provided much-needed health care services to low-income Americans. The effects were enormous and immediate—to take a single metric, between 1965 and 1972 infant mortality in the United States declined by 33 percent.[83]

As the welfare state expanded and reformed, political activists disagreed sharply over long-term strategic goals. Some groups wished to widen, democratize, and ultimately improve social relief from the government, even if the capitalist foundations of federal welfare remained intact. Others hoped to use these various federal programs to build power and deploy the welfare state against other forms of oppression, for example domestic abuse.[84] Still others argued that the compromise, however beneficial to workers in the short run, functioned to manage or recuperate class struggle, unite competing capitalists, and keep profits flowing smoothly, ultimately strengthening the capitalist mode of production. The underlying capitalist logic of the welfare state was no secret; Lyndon B. Johnson, for instance, praised the food-stamp program precisely because it "raised the diets of low-income families substantially while strengthening markets for the farmer and immeasurably improving the volume of retail food sales."[85] Thus, for many radicals, the task was not to improve the welfare state or use it to build power but to overthrow it altogether.

Yet even the most revolutionary activists of the 1960s and 1970s incorporated the welfare state's precepts into their movements, even as they tried to subvert them. For example, some radical feminists framed the struggle to destroy the wage system in the language of social welfare, calling for the state to pay wages for housework.[86] This contradictory orientation to federal welfare reflected the ambiguous impact of what President Johnson once called "responsible capitalism."

These ambiguities were especially pronounced within the Black Power movement. It is well known that Bobby Seale and Huey Newton, founding members of the Black Panther Party, developed their party's program at the North Oakland Neighborhood Anti-Poverty Center, where they used federal resources to educate, organize, and reflect on putting theory into practice. The party even used the government's lists of welfare recipients to perform inquiries into "the desires of the community," as Newton put it.[87] It is not coincidental that the Black Panthers' "survival programs"—such as free breakfast, after-school programs, health clinics, and GED classes—closely resembled the Great Society's antipoverty initiatives.[88] In many ways, the Panthers exemplified radical activists' complex and sometimes contradictory relationship to the welfare state. At the same time the party program insisted that the "federal government is responsible and obligated to give every man employment or a guaranteed income," its members called for the overthrow of the capitalist state.[89]

While revolutionaries were correct to point to the capitalist foundations of the welfare state, the expansion of social welfare programs had undeniable benefits for working-class men and women. Workers led healthier lives; enjoyed greater access to housing, education, and food; and could count on the state to compensate for lost income from old age, illness, disabilities, or unemployment.[90] For many households in the United States, particularly those in poverty, federal assistance became central to everyday survival. Thus in 1982, Frances Fox Piven and Richard A. Cloward could write that "nearly half the income of the bottom fifth of the population is derived from social welfare benefits. The poorest people in the country are now as much dependent on the government for their subsistence as they are on the labor market."[91]

If many households grew to rely on federal aid, still more grew dependent on rising wages and mass consumption. Indeed, social struggles against discriminatory barriers allowed more and more white women and people of color to enter waged work across sectors. For those in the expanding "middle" class, higher wages and stronger unions created greater disposable incomes and life revolved increasingly around consumption. With this income, as well as access to credit, loans, and expanding infrastructures, the consumption of homes, cars, televisions, and household appliances reached new heights among working people.

For many social and political elites, these patterns confirmed a liberal consensus that the welfare state was good for capitalism and that healthy worker-consumers were a crucial ingredient for ever-growing profits. As President Johnson reflected in 1964,

> Why shouldn't we try to obtain peace at home between business, the men who employ our people, the capitalists who make the investments, the workers who produce the goods, the government who has a 52 percent take in everything that they make?[92]

It is worth noting that this consensus did not end with Johnson but continued well into the 1970s. Between 1965 and 1976, social welfare spending increased at an average rate of 4.6 percent. In 1974, it accounted for 16 percent of the total gross national product.[93] Thus, while the political fault lines of a conservative backlash were already in formation, the federal subsidization of social reproduction nevertheless reached its high point under Republican administrations. Let us not forget that it was Richard Nixon who proposed a guaranteed income. For a time, then, the welfare state encouraged unity between different fractions of the ruling bloc, even if the basis of this unity was fragile, contradictory, and fleeting.

THE SUBSUMPTION OF SOCIAL REPRODUCTION UNDER CAPITALISM

High wages, public subsidies, and mass consumption, the pillars of the historic compromise, did not only augment socially reproductive activities, they also heralded their qualitative transformation. The 1960s and 1970s witnessed a technological quantum leap in work processes, as capitalist firms transformed entire forms of reproductive activity into labor-saving commodities like dishwashers, washing machines, and vacuum cleaners. To be sure, social reproduction was always changing, and even the technologies of the late twentieth century were not necessarily brand new. The commercial "automatic" washing machine, for example, first became available in 1913. But it was not until the 1960s that washing machines became more accessible to US households. This was indeed, a slow process—as late as 1983, only 25 percent of households owned a microwave. Nevertheless, the transformation was dramatic. Today, many of these commodities, like refrigerators, can be found in even the poorest of households.[94]

As anyone who washes dishes, does the laundry, or prepares food knows, owning a dishwasher, washing machine, or microwave did not magically reduce the work to zero. Indeed, in some cases, time spent working at home remained relatively constant—and the time saved was often offset by new kinds of domestic work. Nor did these technologies make housework any more pleasant or fulfilling. But these commodities nevertheless changed daily work routines, especially when it came to the laborious tasks of laundering or preparing and preserving meals.[95]

These technological innovations, along with advances in the women's movement and structural changes in the US economy, ultimately contributed to a transformation in the landscape of waged domestic work. The percentage of households that employed servants declined, while increasing numbers of women entered the expanding service economy, finding jobs in health care, education, and the food industry, among many others.[96] These patterns in turn reproduced racial divisions within service work. As Evelyn Nakano Glenn has written, women of color were disproportionately

> employed to do the heavy, dirty, "back-room" chores of cooking and serving food in restaurants and cafeterias, cleaning rooms in hotels and office buildings, and caring for the elderly and ill in hospitals and nursing homes, including cleaning rooms, making beds, changing bed pans, and preparing food, while white women tended to fill the professional, administrative, and supervisory occupations in the very same settings.[97]

The overarching consequence of these changes was that socially reproductive activities, many of which had long retained relative autonomy, became deeply, though differentially, integrated into capitalist relations by the 1970s. Indeed, although much of the work of social reproduction has remained unwaged and confined to the home—and may well stay that way—the vast majority of this unwaged work was nevertheless mediated by waged incomes and purchased commodities. From the increasingly ubiquitous condition of relying on wages to obtain life's necessities to the conversion of unpaid reproductive activity into paid productive work to the wholesale transformation of socially reproductive work into commodities, reproductive labor was thoroughly reorganized by capitalism, even if unwaged work endured.

Thus we might say that the history of capitalism can be understood as a complex process of subsuming forms of social reproduction under capitalist relations: as with forms of production, capitalism first laid hold of preexisting reproductive processes without fundamentally altering them, then subsumed them altogether, unevenly modifying their very materiality.[98] These different forms of subsumption did not follow one another as stages in history but overlapped in contradictory ways. Waged social reproduction has not fully supplanted unwaged reproductive activities, just as capitalism cannot transform all of those activities into commodities. Instead, in the same way that relative surplus value has not "replaced" absolute surplus value, so too have different forms of social reproduction's subsumption developed one another in reciprocal ways. By the late 1970s, the combined result of these manifold forms of subsumption was the thoroughgoing assimilation of socially reproductive activities into capitalist relations.

THE CRISIS OF SOCIAL REPRODUCTION

Although the "historic compromise" served capitalist interests quite well, challenges to expanded accumulation began to emerge as early as the 1960s. By the mid-1970s, growing international competition, declining US hegemony, financial instability, difficulty accessing cheap raw materials such as oil, a gnawing recession, and a strong, organized working class all contributed to a falling rate of profit. For a number of reasons, instead of attempting to reinforce the compromise established in the 1930s, a segment of the ruling bloc decided to violate its accord with the working class.

American capitalists, backed by the federal government, began to push for a new strategy of capitalist accumulation. Its basis was an outright, continuous assault on the working class, which capitalists once again regarded as an obstacle to profitability. This story, when told from the perspective of the point of production, is well known. Capitalists, working with the state, attacked unions, transplanted factories to the

South or to foreign countries, fired workers, drove real wages down, reduced benefits, began replacing workers with robots, and allowed unemployment to rise.

Yet the assault on the working class was waged just as much, if not more so, on the terrain of social reproduction.[99] Indeed, this battle played a decisive role in the new, state-driven strategy for managing the crisis, later called "neoliberalism," that allowed the ruling classes to disarticulate and discipline the working-class, reunite themselves into a coherent ruling bloc, and restore profitability.[100] This was a two-pronged attack, involving the simultaneous expansion and retrenchment of the state. The state launched a violent offensive to irreversibly disrupt the political bases of working-class social reproduction: the War on Drugs, for example, was deliberately designed to destroy black communities, the real base of black power. The rhetoric of "law and order," which became a permanent feature of American politics, justified tougher laws, longer prison sentences, and expanded police forces across the country. The exponential growth of the US prison population, disproportionately black and Latinx, must be understood within this overall assault on social reproduction.[101]

At the same time, the state began to unilaterally devolve the costs of social reproduction back onto the working class. Although social insurance, such as Social Security remained largely, albeit tenuously, intact, the state dismantled the vast array of public assistance programs, slashing funds, tightening eligibility requirements, rewriting legislation, using tax cuts for the wealthy to reduce resources, and privatizing social services. Branded as "handouts," programs such as food stamps and school lunches were retrenched—by 1998, for example, food-stamp rolls had declined by 33 percent. Other programs, such as Aid to Families with Dependent Children (AFDC), were completely restructured. In 1988, for example, the Family Support Act transformed AFDC, in the words of Mimi Abramovitz, "from a program that allowed single mothers to stay home with their children into a mandatory work program."[102] In 1996, Clinton transitioned AFDC into Temporary Assistance for Needy Families, which set a lifetime limit of five years on welfare, excluded college from its list of training activities, barred legal immigrants from important sources of support, and forced thousands of single mothers to find low-waged work, overwhelmingly in the service industry. In this way, the attack on social reproduction created a reserve army of highly vulnerable and exploitable labor just as the country transitioned to a predominantly service economy—once more demonstrating the close connection between transformations in social reproduction and production.[103]

It is also no coincidence that the assault on social welfare spoke a racist and sexist language.[104] Black mothers were demonized as dishonest, irresponsible, and promiscuous; blacks and Latinx people were vilified as criminals or indolent abusers.[105] The hope was to convince other workers, such as poor or unemployed white males, to blame the "black welfare queen" or "reverse racism" for their own conditions, rather than the capitalists. In this way, the battle over social reproduction played an unsurpassed role in turning the heterogenous sectors of the working class against one another.

The consequences of this attack on workers' social reproduction cannot be exaggerated. As we saw, over the course of the twentieth century, most Americans found themselves deeply integrated into capitalist relations, which meant above all that working-class households grew dependent on the wage for social reproduction, at the expense of other sources of income such as direct subsistence, petty commodity production, and barter. With the "historic compromise," the federal government further institutionalized this shift by subsidizing the costs of social reproduction through social welfare programs, public institutions, and financial regulations. Indeed, by the 1990s, nearly 50 percent of all US households were dependent on some kind of government assistance to cover the costs of social reproduction.[106] Thus, by the last decade of the twentieth century, many working-class households had become heavily dependent on two major sources of income: state support and wages. In this context, the federal government's decision to diminish, retrench, or dismantle a range of social services in the 1980s and early 1990s not only proved devastating on its own terms but forced many American workers to rely heavily on low-wage, "unskilled" work.

It is not incidental that, just when workers found themselves more dependent on the wage than ever before, real wages fell to some of their lowest levels. Indeed, for most workers, real wages in the early 1990s were lower than they had been in the 1970s, even if productivity continued to rise. To make matters worse, workers had great difficulty finding other sources of support to supplement such low wages. After all, a century of capitalist development had effectively eradicated other forms of support. Gone were the nineteenth-century custom of turning to municipal relief houses and the possibility of subsisting on common lands and resources.

The kind of direct subsistence so many Americans had once relied on for their social reproduction was no longer a viable option. Alternative knowledges, practices, and forms of life had disappeared. Many workers found themselves without reserves.

An improved economy in the mid- to late 1990s temporarily masked the gravity of the situation, but the 2008 crash shattered all illusions. More than 8 million jobs vanished, unemployment climbed to 10 percent, and millions of workers lost their homes, assets, and savings. In just two years the poverty rate rose 15 percent. Despite disagreements within the ruling bloc about how best to manage the crisis, the decades-long process of demonizing taxes, unions, and state aid legitimized a regime of austerity. Without consistent federal investment, the country's public infrastructures—like roads, bridges, and rails—were left to rot. Public education continued its terminal decline. Rents became too expensive. Water supplies were contaminated. Millions of Americans found themselves behind bars, their social reproduction now subsidized, but in exchange for virtual enslavement. Following others, we are calling this the "crisis of social reproduction."[107]

In response, a wave of social struggles has exploded in the United States, many—unsurprisingly—on the terrain of social reproduction. American workers are fighting to keep their water from being turned off and struggling over their rents, their cost of living, and the state of transportation and education. They fight to keep their neighborhoods safe from racist police. They fight for access to welfare, health care, and child care. They are organizing against climate change. Some of these struggles are beginning to link up with those in workplaces, once more raising important questions about how social reproduction can act as a site of class recomposition and unity.[108]

The crisis of social reproduction constitutes the horizon of the new cycle of struggle unfolding today. Recognizing this is crucial to adequately comprehending our own conjuncture. A full analysis is beyond the confines of this essay, but we hope that in illuminating the origins of the present crisis of social reproduction we have made a useful contribution to that necessarily collective project. To that end, we would like to close by briefly indicating a few areas of further research.

The first relates to recent transformations in patterns of accumulation, and specifically to financialization in the era of neoliberalism. Enabled by consecutive waves of deregulation from the 1970s through the present, financial capital's increasing detachment from productive processes and reorientation toward speculation has proven well suited to capitalizing on the sources of social reproduction.[109] The recent growth of credit, bank fees, and debt-financed consumption among US households indicates how the finance sector has profited as real wages decline and the government withdraws from its midcentury bargains. Mortgage-refinancing packages, the repeal of federal usury laws, and the proliferation of mortgage-backed securities are other examples of how finance capitalists have capitalized on, and in turn deepened, the crisis of social reproduction. Especially illuminating is the recent trajectory of pension funds, one of the beacons of welfare capitalism and now one of the primary institutional investors in the private-equity industry, contributing 43 percent of the capital invested in the last decade.[110] In light of these patterns, we must further ask how exactly the recent dismantling of government functions and the corresponding attack on workers' power have allowed finance capitalists to speculate on social reproduction. What are the material relationships between the crisis of social reproduction and the growing financial sector in the United States? To what extent has finance capital depended on restructuring postwar relations of social reproduction—from household consumption to home ownership to public schools and utilities?

In addition to examining patterns of accumulation and the changing relationship between social reproduction and production, we must also consider how the crisis has affected the dominant classes. The crisis of social reproduction is also a crisis of hegemony. It has aggravated tensions within the ruling bloc, with different fractions proposing rival solutions to crisis management. Despite broad consensus about preserving capitalism, these solutions are distinct and will have different consequences for working people in the United States and beyond. Further research into the composition of the ruling bloc is desperately needed today. How has the crisis created or revealed intra-elite fault lines? How have different fractions of the ruling bloc responded to the crisis, and what are the rival solutions they propose? What are the overlapping points between ruling-class strategies of crisis management and the new wave of struggles unfolding on the terrain of social reproduction? How has the dismantling of the central state's functions affected the balance of power between and within the state system and ruling classes? What role has the US federalist system played in this shifting balance of power, and in capitalists' abilities to control processes of social reproduction at subnational levels?

Another important research agenda relates to the heterogeneity of working classes, both within the United States and around the world. The crisis of social reproduction is not a uniform condition; it affects different sectors of the US working class in different ways and is implicated in uneven processes of accumulation and dispossession on a global scale. Within the United States, a recomposed working class has responded to this crisis in part by articulating discontent into different political forms—autonomous initiatives aiming to rebuild communal life; the formation of a new social-democratic current calling for the revitalization of the welfare state; the return of right-wing populism. We must ask precisely how the crisis has transformed the working class as a whole, how workers have responded, and why they have supported these specific political forms. Based on this investigation, we might consider what possibilities exist for a deeper articulation of social forces.

The meanings of this crisis outside of the United States are beyond the scope of this essay, but are no less significant. In the last forty years, millions of people around the world have seen inherited forms of social reproduction annihilated, a process accompanied by the emergence of massive slums and the creation of migrant populations. In many cases, these dispossessed men and women travel into the United States or other countries and, with few legal protections, take up low-paying jobs in the field of social reproduction—domestic labor, child care, food preparation, sex work, and so on. Thus we must ask: How has the crisis of social reproduction in the United States affected and been shaped by other parts of the world? What are the specific connections between transnational processes of dispossession, the crisis of social reproduction, and the patterns of capital accumulation that have developed since the 1970s?[111] What are the roles of US military interventionism, financialization, and the structural adjustment policies of bodies like the International Monetary Fund in the transformation of social relations abroad? How has the restructuring of the US state contributed to these processes? What does social reproduction or class struggle in slums or informal economies look like?[112] And most importantly, if this crisis is indeed global, what are the possibilities for international resistance or solidarity?

The perspective of social reproduction is therefore essential not only to understanding the historical origins of the present conjuncture but to answering the burning strategic questions of our time.

4

How Not to Skip Class: Social Reproduction of Labor and the Global Working Class

Tithi Bhattacharya

> Labour-power is a commodity which its possessor, the wage-worker, sells to the capitalist. Why does he sell it? It is in order to live.
>
> —Karl Marx, *Wage-Labor and Capital*

Since its very formation, but particularly since the late twentieth century, the global working class has faced a tremendous challenge—how to overcome all its divisions to appear in shipshape, full combative form to overthrow capitalism.[1] After global working-class struggles failed to surmount this challenge, the working class itself became the object of a broad range of theoretical and practical condemnations. Most often, these condemnations take the form of declarations or predictions about the demise of the working class or arguments that the working class is no longer a valid agent of change. Other candidates—women, racial/ethnic minorities, new social movements, an amorphous but insurgent "people," or community, to name a few—are all thrown up as possible alternatives to this presumed moribund or reformist or masculinist and economistic category, the working class.

What many of these condemnations have in common is a shared misunderstanding of exactly what the working class really is. Instead of the complex understanding of class historically proposed by Marxist theory, which discloses a vision of insurgent working-class power capable of transcending sectional categories, today's critics rely on a narrow vision of a "working class" in which a worker is simply a person who has a specific kind of *job*.

In this essay, I will refute this conception of class by reactivating fundamental Marxist insights about class formation that have been obscured by four decades of neoliberalism and the many defeats of the global working class. The key to developing a sufficiently dynamic understanding of the working class, I will argue, is the framework of social reproduction. In thinking about the working class, it is essential to recognize that workers have an existence beyond the workplace. The theoretical challenge therefore lies in understanding the relationship between this existence and that of their productive lives under the direct domination of the capitalist. The relationship between these spheres will in turn help us consider strategic directions for class struggle.

But before we get there, we need to start from the very beginning, that is, from Karl Marx's critique of political economy, since the roots of today's limited conception of the working class stem in large part from an equally limited understanding of the economy itself.

THE ECONOMY

The allegations that Marxism is reductive or economistic only make sense if one reads the economy as neutral market forces determining the fate of humans by chance, or in the sense of a trade-union bureaucrat whose understanding of the worker is restricted to the wage earner. Let us here first deal with why Marx often criticizes this restrictive view of the "economic." His contribution to social theory was not simply to point to the historical-materialist basis of social life, but to propose that, in order to get to this materialist basis, the historical materialist must first understand that reality is not as it *appears*.[2]

The "economy," as it appears to us, is the sphere where we do an honest day's work and get paid for it. Some wages might be low, others high. But the principle that structures this "economy" is that the capitalist and the worker are equal beings who engage in an equal transaction: the worker's labor for a wage from the boss.

According to Marx, however, this sphere is "in fact a very Eden of the innate rights of man. There alone rule Freedom, Equality, Property and Bentham." In this one stroke Marx shakes our faith in the fundamental props of modern society: our juridical rights. Marx is *not* suggesting that the juridical rights we bear as equal subjects are nonexistent or fictive, but that such rights are anchored in market relations. The transactions between workers and capitalists take the form—insofar as they are considered purely from the standpoint of market exchange—of exchange between legal equals. Marx is not arguing there are no juridical rights, but that they mask the reality of exploitation.

If what we commonly understand as the "economy" is then merely surface, what is this secret that capital has managed to hide from us? That its animating force is human labor. As soon as we, following Marx, restore labor as the source of value under capitalism and as the expression of the very social life of humanity, we restore to the "economic" process its messy, sensuous, gendered, raced, and unruly component: living human beings capable of following orders—as well as of flouting them.

THE ECONOMIC AS A SOCIAL RELATION

To concentrate on the surface "economy" (of the market) as if this was the sole reality is to obscure two related processes:

1. the separation between the "political" and "economic" that is unique to capitalism; and
2. the actual process of domination and expropriation that happens beyond the sphere of "equal" exchange.

The first process ensures that acts of appropriation by the capitalist appear completely cloaked in economic garb, inseparable from the process of production itself. As Ellen Meiksins Wood explains:

> Where earlier [precapitalist] producers might perceive themselves as struggling to keep what was rightfully theirs, the structure of capitalism encourages workers to perceive themselves as struggling to get a share of what belongs to capital, a "fair wage," in exchange for their labor.[3]

Since this process makes invisible the act of exploitation, the worker is caught in this sphere of juridical "equality," negotiating rather than questioning the wage form.

However, it is the second invisible process that forms the pivot of social life. When we leave the Benthamite sphere of juridical equality and head to what Marx calls the "hidden abode of production":

> He, who before was the money-owner, now strides in front as capitalist; the possessor of labor power follows as his laborer. The one with an

> air of importance, smirking, intent on business; the other, timid and holding back, like one who is bringing his own hide to market and has nothing to expect but—a hiding.[4]

Marx emphasizes here the opposite of "economism," or "free trade vulgaris" as he calls it. He is inviting us to see the "economic" as a social relation: one that involves domination and coercion, even if juridical forms and political institutions seek to obscure that.

Let us pause here to rehearse the three fundamental claims made about the economy so far. One, that the economy as we see it is, according to Marx, a surface appearance; two, that the appearance, which is steeped in a rhetoric of equality and freedom, conceals a "hidden abode" where domination and coercion reign, and those relations form the pivot of capitalism; hence, three, that the economic is also a social relation, in that the power that is necessary to run this hidden abode—to submit the worker to modes of domination—is also by necessity a political power.

The purpose of this coercion and domination, and the crux of the capitalist economy considered as a social relation, is to get the worker to produce more than the value of their labor power. "The value of labour-power," Marx tells us, "is the value of the means of subsistence necessary for the maintenance of its owner" (i.e., the worker).[5] The additional value that she produces during the working day is appropriated by capital as surplus value. The wage form is nothing but the value necessary to reproduce the worker's labor power.

In order to explain how this theft occurs every day, Marx introduces us to the concepts of necessary and surplus labor time. Necessary labor time is that portion of the workday in which the direct producer, our worker, makes value equivalent to what is needed for her own reproduction, surplus labor time is the remainder of the workday, where she makes additional value for capital.

The ensemble of conceptual categories that Marx proposes here form what is more generally known as the labor theory of value. In this ensemble, two core categories that we should particularly attend to are (a) labor power itself—its composition, deployment, reproduction, and ultimate replacement—and (b) the space of work, i.e., the question of labor at the point of production.

LABOR POWER: THE "UNIQUE COMMODITY" AND ITS SOCIAL REPRODUCTION

Marx introduces the concept of labor power with great deliberation. Labor power, in Marx's sense, is our capacity to labor. "We mean by labour-power or labour-capacity," Marx explains, "the aggregate of those mental and physical capabilities existing in the physical form, the living personality, of a human being, capabilities which he sets in motion whenever he produces a use-value of any kind."[6] Obviously, the *capacity* to labor is a transhistoric quality that humans possess irrespective of the social formation of which they are a part. What is specific to capitalism, however, is that only under this system of production does commodity production become generalized throughout society and commodified labor, available for sale in the marketplace, become the dominant mode of exploitation.[7] Thus, under capitalism, what is generalized in commodity form is a human *capacity*. In several passages Marx refers to this with the savagery that such a mutilation of self deserves: "The possessor of labour-power, instead of being able to sell commodities in which his labour has been objectified, must rather be compelled to offer for sale as a commodity that very labour-power which exists only in his living body."[8]

Further, we can only speak of labor power when the worker *uses* that capacity, or it "becomes a reality only by being expressed; it is activated only through labour."[9] So it must follow that as labor power is expended in the process of production of other commodities, thereby "a definite quantity of human muscle, nerve, brain, etc.," the rough composite of labor power, "is expended, and these things have to be replaced."[10]

How can labor power be restored? Marx is ambiguous on this point:

> If the owner of labour-power works today, tomorrow he must again be able to repeat the same process in the same conditions as regards health and strength. His means of subsistence must therefore be sufficient to maintain him in his normal state as a working individual. His natural needs, such as food, clothing, fuel and housing vary according to the climatic and other physical peculiarities of his country. On the other hand, the number and extent of his so-called necessary requirements, as also the manner in which they are satisfied, are themselves the product of history, and depend therefore to a great extent on the level of civilization attained by a country; in particular they depend on the

> conditions in which and consequently on the habits and expectations with which, the class of free workers has been formed.[11]

Here we falter and sense that the content of Marx's critique is inadequate to his form. There are several questions the above passage provokes and then leaves unanswered.

Social reproduction Marxists and feminists, such as Lise Vogel, have drawn attention to the "production" of human beings—in this case, the worker—which takes place away from the site of production of commodities. Social reproduction theorists rightly want to develop further what Marx leaves unexamined. That is, what are the implications of labor power being produced outside the circuit of commodity production, yet being essential to it? The most historically enduring site for the reproduction of labor power is of course the kin-based unit we call the family. It plays a key role in biological reproduction—as the generational replacement of the working class—and in reproducing the worker through food, shelter, and psychical care to become ready for the next day of work. Both those functions are disproportionately borne by women under capitalism and are the sources of women's oppression under that system.[12]

But the above passage needs development in other respects as well. Labor power, for instance, as Vogel has pointed out, is not simply replenished at home, nor is it always reproduced generationally. The family may form the site of individual renewal of labor power, but that alone does not explain "the conditions under which, and . . . the habits and degree of comfort in which" the working class of any particular society has been produced. What other social relationships and institutions are comprised by the circuit of social reproduction? Public education and health care systems, leisure facilities in the community, and pensions and benefits for the elderly all compose those historically determined "habits." Similarly, generational replacement through childbirth in the kin-based family unit, although dominant, is not the only way a labor force may be replaced. Slavery and immigration are two of the most common ways in which capital has replaced labor within national boundaries.

Relatedly, let us suppose that a certain basket of goods (x) is necessary to "reproduce" a particular worker. This "basket of goods" containing food, shelter, education, health care, and so on is then consumed by this mythical (or, some would say, universal) worker to reproduce herself. But does the size and content of the basket goods not vary depending on the race, nationality, and gender of the worker? Marx seemed to think so. Consider his discussion of the Irish worker and her or his "needs" as compared to other workers. If workers lowered their consumption (in order to save), Marx argues, then they would

> inevitably degrade . . . [themselves] to the level of the Irish, to that level of wage laborers where the merest animal minimum of needs and means of subsistence appears as the sole object and purpose of their exchange with capital.[13]

We will have occasion to discuss the question of differential needs producing different kinds of labor powers later; for now, let us simply note that the question of reproduction of labor power is by no means a simple one. As we can see, there is already intimation of a complex totality when considering Marx's "hidden abode of production" and its structuring impulse on the surface "economy." Marx's original outline, enriched now through the framework of social reproduction of labor power, thoroughly complicates, in fundamental ways, the narrow bourgeois definition of the "economy" and/or "production" with which we began.

Beyond the two-dimensional image of individual direct producer locked in wage labor, we begin to see emerge myriad capillaries of social relations extending between workplace, home, schools, hospitals—a wider social whole, sustained and coproduced by human labor in contradictory yet constitutive ways. If we direct our attention to those deep veins of embodying social relations in any actual society today, how can we fail to find the chaotic, multiethnic, multigendered, differently abled subject that is the global working class?

THE TWAIN OF PRODUCTION AND REPRODUCTION

It is important in this regard to clarify that what we designated above as two separate spaces—(a) spaces of production of value (point of production) and (b) spaces for reproduction of labor power—may be separate in a strictly spatial sense, but they are actually united in the theoretical and operational senses.[14] They are particular historical forms of appearance in which capitalism posits itself. Indeed, sometimes the two processes may be ongoing within the same space. Consider the case of public schools. They function both as work places or points of production and also as spaces where labor power (of the future worker) is socially reproduced. As in the case of pensions, so in the case of public health or education, the state outlays some funds for the social reproduction of labor power. It is only within the home that the process of social reproduction remains unwaged.

The question of separate spheres and why they are historical forms of appearance is an important one and worth spending some time on. A common misunderstanding about "social reproduction theory" is that it is about two separate spaces and two separate processes of production, the economic and the social—often understood as the workplace and home. In this understanding, the worker produces surplus value at work and hence is part of the *production* of the total wealth of society. At the end of the workday, because the worker is "free" under capitalism, capital must relinquish control over the process of regeneration of the worker and hence of the *reproduction* of the workforce.

Marx, however, has a very specific understanding and proposal for the concept of social reproduction. First, this is a theoretical concept he deploys to draw attention to the reproduction of society as a whole, not only with the regeneration of labor power of the worker or reproduction of the workforce. This understanding of the theater of capitalism as a totality is important because, at this point of the argument in *Capital* Volume 1, Marx has already established that—unlike bourgeois economics, which sees the commodity as the central character of this narrative (supply and demand determine the market)—in his view labor is capitalism's chief protagonist. Thus what happens to labor—specifically, how labor creates value and consequently surplus value—shapes the entirety of the capitalist process of production. "In the concept of value," Marx says in the *Grundrisse*, capital's "secret is betrayed."[15]

Social reproduction of the *capitalist system*—and it is to explain the reproduction of the system that Marx uses the term—is therefore not about a separation between a noneconomic sphere and the economic, but about how the economic impulse of capitalist production conditions the so-called noneconomic. The "noneconomic" includes, among other things, what sort of state, juridical institutions, and property forms a society has—while these in turn are conditioned, but not always determined, by the economy. Marx understands each particular stage in the valorization of capital as a moment of a totality that leads him to state clearly in *Capital*: "When viewed, therefore, as a connected whole, and in the constant flux of its incessant renewal, every social process of production is at the same time a process of reproduction."[16]

This approach is best outlined in Michael Lebowitz's *Beyond Capital*. Lebowitz's work is a masterful *integrative* analysis of the political economy of labor power, in which he shows that understanding the social reproduction of wage labor is not an outer or incidental phenomena that ought to be "added" to the understanding of capitalism as a whole, but actually reveals important inner tendencies of the system. Lebowitz calls the moment of the production of labor power "a second moment" of production as a whole. This moment is "distinct from the process of production of capital" but the circuit of capital "*necessarily* implies a second circuit, the circuit of wage-labor."[17]

As Marx sums it up, rightly, and with a bit of flourish:

> The capitalist process of production, therefore, seen as a total connected process, i.e. a process of reproduction, produces not only commodities, not only surplus-value, but it also produces and reproduces the capital relation itself; on the one hand the capitalist, on the other the wage-labourer.[18]

Here, by *social reproduction* Marx means the reproduction of the entirety of society, which brings us back to the unique commodity, labor power, that needs to be replenished and ultimately replaced without any breaks or stoppages to the continuous circuit of production and reproduction of the whole.

There is a lot at stake, both theoretical as well as strategic, in understanding this process of the production of commodities and the reproduction of labor power as unified. Namely, we need to abandon not just the framework of discrete spheres of production and reproduction, but also—because reproduction is linked within capitalism to production—we need to revise the commonsense perception that capital relinquishes all control over the worker when she leaves the workplace.

Theoretically if we concede that production of commodities and the social reproduction of labor power belong to separate processes, then we have no explanation for why the worker is subordinate before the moment of production even takes place. Why does labor appear, in Marx's words, "timid and holding back, like one who is bringing his own hide to market"?[19] It is because Marx has a unitary view of the process that he can show us that the moment of production of the simple commodity is not necessarily a singular entry point for the enslavement of labor. Therefore, "in reality," Marx tells us,

> the worker belongs to capital before he has sold himself to the capitalist. His economic bondage is both at once mediated through, and concealed by, the periodic renewal of the act by which he sells himself, his change of masters, and the oscillations in the market-price of his labour.[20]

But this link between production and reproduction, and the extension of the class relationship into the latter, means that (as we will see in the next section) the very acts where the working class strives to attend to its own needs can be the ground for class struggle.

EXTENDED REPRODUCTION: THE KEY TO CLASS STRUGGLE

What binds the worker to capital?

Under capitalism, since the means of production (to produce use values) are held by the capitalists, the worker only has access to the means of subsistence through the capitalist production process—selling her labor power to the capitalist in return for wages with which to purchase and access the means of her life, or subsistence.

This schema of capital-labor relationship is heavily predicated upon two things: (a) that the worker is forced to enter this relationship because she has needs as a human being to reproduce her life, but cannot do so on her own because she has been separated from the means of production by capital; and (b) she enters the wage relation for her subsistence needs, which is to say that the needs of "life" (subsistence) have a deep integral connection to the realm of "work" (exploitation).

So far we are more or less in undisputed territory of Marxist theory.

The exact delineations of the relationships between the value of labor power, the needs of the worker, and how those in turn affect surplus value are, however, neither undisputed nor adequately theorized in *Capital*; it is on this that we will spend the remainder of this section.

Let us revisit the moment in *Capital* where even the individual consumption of the worker is also part of the circuit of capital because the reproduction of the worker is, as Marx calls it, "a factor of the production and reproduction of capital." A central premise that Marx offers us about labor power is that the value of labor power is set by the "value of the necessaries required to produce, develop, maintain, and perpetuate the laboring power."[21] But there is something else to this formulation. For the sake of making a logical argument (as opposed to a historical one), Marx treats the *standard of necessities* as constant: "In a given country at a given period, the average amount of the means of subsistence necessary for the worker is a known *datum*."[22]

In *Capital*, the *value* of labor power on the basis of the standard of necessity (U) is taken as constant and the changes in *price* of labor power are attributed to the introduction of machinery and/or the rise and fall of the supply and demand of workers in the labor market. As Lebowitz has pointed out, taking this methodological assumption as fact would put Marx at his closest to classical economists: endorsing the formulation that supply shifts in the labor market and the introduction of machinery adjust the price of labor to its value, *just as it does for all other commodities*.

But there is a reason why Marx deems the worker's labor power is deemed a *unique* commodity, unlike, say, sugar or cotton. In the case of labor, a reverse process can and may take place: the *value* of the worker's labor power may adjust to *price*, rather than the other way around. She may adjust (lower or raise) her needs to what she receives in wages.

According to Lebowitz, Marx *does not have a generalized concept of constant real wages* (means of subsistence, U) but only adopts it as a "methodologically sound *assumption*."[23] In contrast to bourgeois political economists, Marx always "*rejected* the tendency . . . to treat workers' needs as naturally determined and unchanging." It was patently mistaken, Marx thought, to conceptualize subsistence level "as an unchangeable magnitude—which in [bourgeois economists'] view is determined entirely by nature and not by the stage of historical development, which is itself a magnitude subject to fluctuations."[24] Nothing could be "more alien to Marx," emphasizes Lebowitz, than "the belief in a fixed set of necessities."[25]

Let us consider a scenario where the standard of necessity (U) is fixed as Marx dictates, but there is an increase in productivity (q). In such a case, the value of the set of wage goods (our original basket of goods, x) would fall, thereby reducing the value of labor power. In this scenario, Marx says that labor power "would be unchanged in price" but "would have risen above its value." This means that, with more money wages at their disposal, workers can go on to buy more goods or services that satisfy their needs. But, according to Lebowitz, this never happens. Instead, money wages tend to adjust to real wages, and capitalists are thus able to benefit from the reduced value of labor power. Lebowitz proceeds to explain why capitalists, rather than workers, benefit from this scenario.

Briefly put, he points out that the standard of necessity (U) is not invariable but is actually "enforced by class struggle." Thus, with a rise in productivity (q) and a "decline in the value of wage goods providing slack in the workers' budget, capitalists . . . [are] emboldened to attempt to drive down money wages to capture the gain for themselves in the form of surplus value."[26] But once we see that the standard of necessity is variable and can be determined by class struggle, then it becomes clear that the working class can fight on this front as well. Indeed, this is one of the consequences of understanding the expanded sense in which the economic is actually a set of social relations traversed by a struggle for class power.

Once we acknowledge class struggle as a component of the relations of production it becomes clear, as Lebowitz shows, that there are two different "moments of production." They are composed of

> two different goals, two different perspectives on the value of labor power: while for capital, the value of labor power is a means of satisfying its goal of surplus value...for the wage-laborer, it is the means of satisfying the goal of self development.[27]

Reproduction, in short, is therefore a site of class conflict. However, this conflict is inflected with certain contradictory tendencies. For instance, as the orchestrator of the production process, the capitalist class strives to limit the needs and consumption of the working class. However, to ensure the constant realization of surplus value, capital must also create new needs in the working class as consumers, and then "satisfy" those new needs with new commodities. The growth of workers' needs under capitalism is thus an inherent condition of capitalist production and its expansion.

A further complication in this class struggle over the terms of reproduction is that the growth of needs for workers is neither secular or absolute. The position of the working class under capitalism is a relative one; that is, it exists in a relationship with the capitalist class. Hence any changes in the needs and in the level of satisfaction of workers are also relative to changes in the same for the capitalists. Marx uses the memorable example of how the perception of the size of a house (its largeness or smallness) was relative to the size of the surrounding houses.[28] Thus one generation of a working class may earn, in absolute terms, more than the previous generation; however, their satisfaction will never be absolute, as that generation of capitalists will always have more. Since the growth of workers' needs, then, is part of the process of capital's valorization and their satisfaction cannot take place within the framework of the system, *workers' struggle to satisfy their own needs* is also an inherent and integral part of the system.

If we include the struggle for higher wages (to satisfy ever-increasing needs) in the argument in *Capital*, is it an exogenous, hence eclectic, "addition" to Marxism? Lebowitz shows this not to be so.

What *Capital* lays out for us is the path of reproduction for capital. Marx represents capital's movement as a circuit:

$$M - C\,(M_p, L_p) - P - C' - M'$$

Money (M) is exchanged for commodities (C): that is, a combination of means of production (M_p) and labor power (L_p). The two elements combine through capitalist production (P) to produce new commodities and surplus value (C') to then be exchanged for a greater amount of money (M'). Such a circuit is both continuous and complete upon itself, ruling out any exogenous elements.

But what about the circuit of reproduction of wage labor?

The "uniqueness" of labor power lies in the fact that, although it is not produced and reproduced by capital, it is vital to capital's own circuit of production. In *Capital* Marx does not theorize this second circuit, but simply notes that "the maintenance and reproduction of the working class remains a necessary condition for the reproduction of capital" and that "the capitalist may safely leave this to the worker's drive for self-preservation and propagation."[29] This is where Lebowitz argues there ought to be acknowledged a *missing* circuit of production and reproduction, that of labor power. Marx perhaps would have addressed this in later volumes of *Capital*, but it remains incomplete as the "Missing Book on Wage Labor."

Once we theoretically integrate the *two* circuits: that of production and reproduction of capital and that of the same for labor power, commodities themselves reveal their dual functions.

Commodities produced under capitalist production are both means of production (bought by capital for money), and articles of consumption (bought by workers with their wages). A second circuit of production then must be posited, distinct from that of capital, though in relation with it. This circuit is as follows:

$$M - A_c - P - L_p - M$$

Money (M), in the worker's hands, is exchanged for articles of consumption (A_c) which are then consumed in a similar process of production (P). But now what is produced in this "production process" is a unique commodity—the worker's labor power (L_p). Once produced (or reproduced), it is then sold to the capitalist in exchange for wages (M).

The production of labor power then takes place outside the immediate circuit of capital but remains essential for it. Within *capital's circuit*, labor power is a means of production for capital's reproduction, or valorization. But within *wage labor's circuit*, the worker consumes commodities as use values (food, clothing, housing, education) in order to reproduce herself. The second circuit is a process of *production of self for the worker or a process of self-transformation*.

The second circuit of production encloses a purposeful activity, under the workers' own self-direction. The goal of this process is not the valorization of capital, but the self-development of the worker. The historically embedded needs of the worker, which themselves change and grow with capitalist growth, provide the motive for this labor process. The means of production for this circuit are the manifold useful values that the working class needs in order to develop. These are more than just means to simple biological reproduction; they are "social needs":

> Participation in the higher, even cultural satisfactions, the agitation for his own interests, newspaper subscriptions, attending lectures, educating his children, developing his taste etc., his only share of civilization which distinguishes him from the slave, [which] is economically only possible by widening the sphere of his pleasures at the times when business is good.[30]

Whether the working class can access such social goods, and to what extent, depends not only on the existence of such goods and services in society but on the tussle between capital and labor over surplus value (which reproduces capital) and the basket of goods (which reproduces the worker). The worker consumes use values to regenerate fresh labor power, but the reproduction of labor power also presupposes, as Lebowitz perceptively shows, an *ideal* goal for the worker:

> The second aspect of the worker considered as a labor process is that the activity involved in this process is "purposeful activity." In other words, there is a preconceived goal, a goal that exists ideally, before the process itself . . . [and this goal] is the worker's conception of self—as determined within society. . . . That preconceived goal of production is what Marx described as "the worker's own need of development."[31]

However, the materials necessary to produce the worker in the image of her own needs and goals—food, housing, "time for education, for intellectual development," or the "free play of his [or her] own physical and mental powers"—cannot be realized within the capitalist production process, for the process as a whole exists for the valorization of capital and not the social development of labor. Thus the worker, due to the very nature of the process, is always-already reproduced as *lacking* in what she needs, and hence built into the fabric of wage labor as a form is the struggle for higher wages: class struggle. Here, finally, we arrive at the strategic implications of social reproduction theory, or why an integrative sense of capitalism is necessary in our actual battles against capital.

SOCIAL REPRODUCTION FRAMEWORK AS STRATEGY

The "actual degree" of profit, Marx tells us,

> is only settled by the continuous struggle between capital and labor, the capitalist constantly tending to reduce wages to their physical minimum, and to extend the working day to its physical maximum, while the working man constantly presses in the opposite direction.

This struggle "resolves itself into a question of the respective powers of the combatants."[32]

Note that as he lays out here the inner logic of the system, Marx does not talk of individual capitalists and the workplaces they command, but capital as a whole. Indeed, Marx is clear that although the system appears to us as an ensemble of "many capitals," it is "capital in general" that is the protagonist; the many capitals are ultimately shaped by the inherent determinants of "capital in general."

If we apply what I call this *method* of social reproduction of labor theory to the question of workplace struggle, we can now have a few givens:

1. That the individual capitals, in competition with each other, will try to increase surplus value from the worker.
2. That the worker will pull in the opposite direction to increase the time (quantity) and wages, benefits (quality of life) she can have for her own social development. This most frequently will take the form of struggle for a shorter work week or higher wages and better work conditions in the workplace.

What is the ideal situation for the worker? That she pulls all the way in the opposite direction and annihilates surplus value altogether—that is, she only works the hours necessary to reproduce her own subsistence, and the rest of the time is her own to do as she pleases. This is an impossible solution, in that capital will then cease to be capital. The struggle for higher wages, benefits, and so on in a workplace, against a boss, or even in a series of workplaces and against specific bosses, then is only part of the pivotal struggle of capital *in general* versus wage labor *in general*. The worker can even "leave" an individual boss, but she cannot opt out of the system as a whole (while the system as it stands exists):

> The worker leaves the capitalist, to whom he has sold himself, as often as he chooses, and the capitalist discharges him as often as he sees fit, as soon as he no longer gets any use, or not the required use, out of him.
>
> But the worker, whose only source of income is the sale of his labor-power, cannot leave the whole class of buyers, i.e., the capitalist class, unless he gives up his own existence. He does not belong to this or that capitalist, but to the capitalist class; and it is for him to find his man—i.e., to find a buyer in this capitalist class.[33]

Most trade unions, even the most militant ones, are typically equipped to fight against the individual boss or a collective of bosses, which in Marx's terms takes the form of "many capitals." Trade unions leave the task of confronting "capital in general" alone. There is a very good reason why this is so.

As Lebowitz shows, capital's power "as owner of the products of labor is . . . both absolute and mystified"—this ultimately undergirds its ability to buy labor power and submit workers to its will in the production process. If the worker is to transcend the partial struggle for better work conditions and direct all social labor to producing only use values for social and individual development, then it is this underlying power of capital as a whole that must be confronted. But capital's power in this arena is qualitatively different from that in workplace struggles:

> There is no direct area of confrontation between specific capitalists and specific wage laborers in this sphere comparable to that which emerges spontaneously in the labor market and the workplace. . . . [Instead] the power of capital as owner of the products of labor appears as the dependence of wage labor upon capital-as-a-whole.[34]

Consider the two ways surplus value is increased: by the absolute extension of the workday, and by cutting wages or reducing the cost of living, thereby reducing the necessary labor time. While Marx is clear that absolute and relative surplus are related concepts, it is quite clear that some aspects of this process of realization (the boss's efforts to reduce wages, for instance) are more easily confronted in the workplace than others.

Let us take a historical example of how the system as a whole will sometimes increase relative surplus value by reducing the cost of living of the working class as a whole. During the eighteenth century, a section of the working class in Britain was put on a diet of potatoes, a cheaper food option than wheat, such that the cost of feeding workers was forced down, thereby cheapening the cost of labor as a whole. One of the best and undoubtedly one of the most lyrical historians of working class life, E.P. Thompson, called this a "regular dietary class war" waged for over fifty years on the English working class. What concrete forms did this class war take? While the cheapening of labor increased surplus value at the point of production and hence benefited the bosses in the workplace, it was not just in the workplace or at the hands of the bosses that the cheapening of labor took place. Thompson gives us a moving account of how "landowners, farmers, parsons, manufacturers, and the Government itself sought to drive laborers from a wheaten to a potato diet."[35] The ruling class, as a class, then forced the increase of potato acreage over wheat, prompting the historian Redcliffe Salaman to rightly claim that "the use of the potato . . . did, in fact, enable the workers to survive on the lowest possible wage."[36] Similarly, Sandra Halperin has shown how, in the late nineteenth century, British overseas investment and control over colonies, with its railways, harbor and shipbuilding for Baltic and North American grain, "produced a backflow of cheaply produced . . . raw materials and foodstuffs that did not compete with domestic English agriculture and drove domestic working class wages down."[37]

Trade unions, even the best ones, by nature struggle against specific and particular capitals, but the above examples show the need to confront capital in its totality. Lebowitz accurately concludes that "in the absence of such a total opposition, the trade unions fight the effects within the labor market and the workplace but not the causes of the effects."[38]

To his comrades in the First International, Marx pointed out precisely this caveat in trade-union struggles. The trade unions, he argued, were "too exclusively bent upon the local and immediate struggles with capital" and had "not yet fully understood their power of acting against the system of wages slavery itself." The proof of their narrowness? That "they had kept too much aloof from general social and political movements." Marx's advice was to overcome this narrowness and go beyond the purely economic struggle for wages:

> They must now learn to act deliberately as organizing centers of the working class in the broad interest of its complete emancipation. They must aid every social and political movement tending in that direction. Considering themselves and acting as the champions and representatives of the whole working class, they cannot fail to enlist the non-society men into their ranks. They must look carefully after the interests of the worst paid trades, such as the agricultural laborers, rendered powerless [the French text reads: "incapable of organized resistance"] by exceptional circumstances. They must convince the world at large [the French and German texts read: "convince the broad masses of workers"] that their efforts, far from being narrow and selfish, aim at the emancipation of the downtrodden millions.[39]

If we take our lead from Marx himself, then it is utterly unclear why *only* the economic struggle for wages and benefits at the workplace must be designated as class struggle. Every social and political movement "tending" in the direction of gains for the working class as a whole, or of challenging the power of capital as a whole, must be considered an aspect of class struggle. Significantly, one of the greatest tragedies of the destruction of working-class power and the dissolution of proletarian living communities in the last forty years has been the loss in practice of this insight about the social totality of production of value and reproduction of labor power.

At any given moment of history, a working class may or may not be able to fight for higher wages at the point of production. Labor unions may not exist or may be weak and corrupt. However, as items in the basket of goods change (fall or rise in quality and quantity of social goods), the members of the class are acutely aware of such changes to their lives; those battles may emerge away from the point of production but nevertheless reflect the needs and imperatives of the class. In other words, where a struggle for a higher wage is not possible, different kinds of struggles around the circuit of social reproduction may also erupt. Is it then any wonder that in the era of neoliberalism, when labor unions agitating at the point of production (for wages) are weak or nonexistent in large parts of the globe, we have rising social movements around issues of living conditions, from the struggles for water in Cochabamba and Ireland, against land eviction in India, and for fair housing in the United Kingdom and elsewhere? This pattern is perhaps best summarized by the antiausterity protesters in Portugal: *Que se lixe a troika! Queremos as nossas vidas!* (Fuck the troika! We want our lives!)

THE WORKING CLASS: SOLIDARITY AND "DIFFERENCE"

We should then reconsider our conceptual vision of the working class. I am not suggesting here a concrete accounting of who constitutes the global working class, although that would be an important exercise. Instead, leading from our previous discussion about the need to reimagine a fuller figuration for "economy" and "production," I am proposing here three things: (a) a theoretical restatement of the working class as a revolutionary subject; (b) a broader understanding of the working class than those employed as waged laborers at any given moment; and (c) a reconsideration of class struggle to signify more than the struggle over wages and working conditions.

The premise for this reconsideration is a particular understanding of historical materialism. Marx reminds us that

> the specific economic form, in which unpaid *surplus labor* is pumped out of direct producers, determines the relationship of rulers and ruled, as it grows directly out of production itself and, in turn, reacts upon it as a determining element.[40]

Under capitalism, wage labor is the generalized form through which the rulers expropriate the direct producers. In the abstract, capital is indifferent to the race, gender, or abilities of the direct producer, as long as her or his labor power can set the process of accumulation into motion. But the relations of production, as we saw in the earlier section, are actually a concatenation of existing social relations, shaped by past history, present institutions, and state forms. The social relations outside of wage labor are not accidental to it but take specific historical form in response to it. For instance, the gendered nature of reproduction of labor power has conditioning impulses for the extraction of surplus value. Similarly, a heterosexist form of the family unit is sustained by capital's needs for the generational replacement of the labor force.

The question of "difference" within the working class is significant in this respect. As mentioned before, Marx gestures toward differently "produced" sections of the working class in his discussion of the Irish worker, where the English worker is "produced" with access to a better basket of goods—his or her needs adjusted to this higher level—while the Irish worker remains at a brutal level of existence with only "the most animal minimum of needs." Obviously Marx did not believe that the value of the labor power of the Irish worker was a constant that remained below that of her English counterpart due to ethnicity. Instead it was a result of class struggle, or lack thereof, and it was English workers who needed to understand the commonality of their class interest with the Irish against capital as a whole.

Incorporating class struggle as a crucial element that determines the extent and quality of social reproduction of the worker then enables us to truly understand the significance of a Marxist notion of "difference" within the class. Acknowledging that at any given historical moment the working class might be differently produced (with varying wages and differential access to means of social reproduction) is more than simply stating an empirical truth. By showing how concrete social relations and histories of struggle contribute to the "reproduction" of labor power, this framework points to the filaments of class solidarity that must be forged, sometime within and sometimes without the workplace, in order to increase the "share of civilization" for *all* workers.

Writing in the Britain of the early eighties, when the working class was being physically brutalized by Thatcherism and theoretically assaulted by a range of liberal theories, Raymond Williams understood very well the dangers of a false dichotomy between "class struggles" and "new social movements":

> All significant social movements of the last thirty years have started outside the organized class interests and institutions. The Peace movement, the ecology movement, the women's movement, human rights agencies, campaigns against poverty and homelessness . . . all have this character, that they sprang from needs and perceptions which the interest-based organizations had no room or time for, or which they simply failed to notice.[41]

Today, we can add to the list the recent anti-police-brutality struggles in the United States.

While these struggles may arise outside the workplace or be understood as struggles for extra-class interests, however, Williams points to the absurdity of such a characterization:

> What is then quite absurd is to dismiss or underplay these movements as "middle class issues." It is a consequence of the social order itself that these issues are qualified and refracted in these ways. It is similarly absurd to push the issues away as not relevant to the central interests of the working class. In all real senses they belong to these central interests. It is workers who are most exposed to dangerous industrial processes and environmental damage. It is working class women who have most need of new women's rights.[42]

If, for whatever historical reasons, organizations that are supposed to champion "class struggle," such as trade unions, fail to be insurgent, it does not mean then that "class struggle" goes away, or that these struggles are "beyond class." Indeed as Williams astutely observes, "there is not one of these issues which, followed through, fails to lead us into the central systems of the industrial-capitalist mode of production and . . . into its system of classes."[43]

Understanding the complex but unified way the production of commodities and reproduction of labor power takes place helps us understand how the concrete allocation of the total labor of society is socially organized in gendered and racialized ways through lessons capital has learned from previous historical epochs and through its struggle against the working class. The process of accumulation thus cannot be indifferent to social categories of race, sexuality, or gender but seeks to organize and shape those categories, which in turn act upon the determinate form of surplus labor extraction. The wage-labor relation suffuses the spaces of nonwaged everyday life.

"A DEVELOPMENT OF THE FORCES OF THE WORKING CLASS SUSPENDS CAPITAL ITSELF"

If the social reproduction of labor power is accorded the theoretical centrality that I propose it should, how useful is that to my second proposal—rethinking the working class?

Social reproduction theory illuminates the social relations and pathways involved in reproducing labor power thereby broadening our vision of how we ought to approach the notion of the working class.

The framework demonstrates why we ought not to rest easy with the limiting understanding of class as simply those who are currently employed in the capital versus waged labor dynamic. To do so would restrict both our vision of class power and our identification of potential agents of class solidarity.

The "waged worker" may be the correct definition for those who currently work for a wage, but such a vision is, again, one of "the trade-union secretary." The working class, for the revolutionary Marxist, must be perceived as everyone in the producing class who has in their lifetime participated in the totality of reproduction of society—irrespective of whether that labor has been paid for by capital or remained unpaid. Such an integrative vision of class gathers together the temporary Latinx hotel worker from Los Angeles, the flextime working mother from Indiana who needs to stay home due to high child-care costs, the African American full-time schoolteacher from Chicago, and the white, male, unemployed erstwhile United Automobile Workers (UAW) worker from Detroit. But they come together not in competition with each other, a view of the working class still in terms of the market, but in solidarity. Strategic organizing on the basis of such a vision can reintroduce the idea that an injury to the schoolteacher in Chicago is actually an injury to all the others. When we restore a sense of the social totality to class, we immediately begin to reframe the arena for class struggle.

What has been the form of the one-sided class struggle from the global ruling class in the past four decades of neoliberalism? It is crucial to understand that it has been a twin attack by capital on global labor to try and restructure *production* in workplaces and the social processes of *reproduction* of labor power in homes, communities, and the niches of everyday life.

In the workplace, the assault has primarily taken the form of breaking the back of union power. The neoliberal edifice, as I have argued elsewhere,[44] was built on the back of a series of defeats for the global working class, the most spectacular examples being those of the air-traffic controllers in the United States (1981), the mill workers in India (1982) and the miners in the United Kingdom (1984–85).

If the ruling-class attack in the workplace or on productive labor took the form of violent antiunionism, it certainly did not end there. Outside the workplace, the attack on reproductive labor was equally vicious. For specific countries, this second line of attack may be said to have been even greater. In the case of the United States, several scholars, including David McNally, Anwar Shaikh, and Kim Moody, have shown how an absolute decline in working-class living and working standards built the capitalist expansion of the 1980s. Key areas of social reproduction were attacked through increased privatization of social services and the retrenchment of important federal programs such as Aid to Dependent Children, Temporary Aid to Needy Families, unemployment insurance, and Social Security. In the Global South this took the form of the International Monetary Fund and the World Bank forcibly raising the price of imports—the bulk of which for these countries were food grain, fuel, and medicines.

This was open class war strategically waged on the entire working class, not just its waged members; it became so effective precisely because it extended beyond the confines of the workplace. By systematically privatizing previously socialized resources and reducing the quality of services, capital has aimed to make the work of daily regeneration more vulnerable and precarious while simultaneously unloading the entire responsibility and discourse of reproduction onto individual families. These processes of degrading the work of social reproduction have worked most effectively in social contexts where capital could bank on, create anew, or reenergize practices and discourses of oppression. From racist clarion calls against "welfare queens" to new ways of sexualizing bodies that diminished sexual choices to rising Islamophobia, neoliberalism has found increasingly creative ways to injure the working class. It has destroyed class confidence, eroded previously embedded cultures of solidarity, and—most importantly in certain communities—succeeded in erasing a key sense of continuity and class memory.

SPACES OF INSURGENCY: CONFRONTING CAPITAL BEYOND THE FACTORY FLOOR

One of the leaders of a recent factory occupation in India explained to a shocked business reporter: "The negotiating power of workers is the most in the factory, but no one listens to you when you reach Jantar Mantar" (the traditional protest square in the Indian capital of Delhi).[45]

The experiential discernment of this rebel worker is often the political-economic common sense of revolutionary Marxism about capital-labor relations. The "dominant" reading of Marx locates the possibilities for a critical political engagement of the working class with capital chiefly at the point of production, where the power of workers to affect profits is the most.

This essay, so far, has been a counterintuitive reading of the theoretic import of the category of "production"; we must now consider the strategic import of the workplace as a pivotal organizing space. Recent scholarship on the Global South, for instance the "coolie lines" in India or the "dormitory labor regime" in China, brings to striking analytical prominence not only the places where the working class works, but the spaces where workers sleep, play, go to school— in other words, live full, sensual lives beyond the workplace. What role do such spaces play in organizing against capital? More importantly, do point-of-production struggles have no strategic relevance anymore?

The contours of class struggle (or what is traditionally understood as such) are very clear in the workplace. The worker feels capital's dominance experientially on an everyday basis and understands its ultimate power over her life, her time, her life chances—indeed, over her ability to exist and map any future. Workplace struggles thus have two irreplaceable advantages: one, they have clear goals and targets; two, workers are concentrated at those points in capital's own circuit of reproduction and have the collective power to shut down certain parts of the operation. This is precisely why Marx called trade unions "centers of organization of the working class."[46] This is also why capital's first attack is always upon organized sections of the class: in order to break this power.

But let us rethink the theoretical import of extra-workplace struggles, such as those for cleaner air, for better schools, against water privatization, against climate change, or for fairer housing policies. These reflect, I submit, those social needs of the working class that are essential for its social reproduction. They also are an effort by the class to demand its "share of civilization." In this, they are also class struggles.

Neoliberalism's devastation of working-class neighborhoods in the Global North has left behind boarded buildings, pawnshops, and empty stoops. In the Global South it has created vast slums as the breeding ground for violence and want.[47] The demand by these communities to extend their "sphere of pleasure" is thus a vital class demand. Marx and Engels, writing in 1850, advanced the idea that workers must "make each community the central point and nucleus of workers' associations in which the attitude and interests of the proletariat will be discussed independently of bourgeois interests."[48]

It is our turn now to restore to our organs and practices of protest this integrative understanding of capitalist totality. If the socialist project remains the dismantling of wage labor, we will fail in that project unless we understand that the relationship between wage labor and capital is sustained in all sorts of unwaged ways and in all kind of social spaces—not just at work.

When the UAW went to organize a union at the Volkswagen plant in the US South, its bureaucratic leaders maintained a religious separation between their union work at the plant and the workers' lived experience in the community. The union leaders signed a contract with the bosses that they would never talk to workers in their homes. But these were communities that had never experienced union power, had never sung labor songs or held picnics at union halls. Unions played little role in the social texture of their lives. In such a community, devastated and atomized as it was by capital, the union movement could only be rebuilt if doing so made sense in the total aspect of their lives and not just in a sectoral way at work alone.

Contrast this tactic to the one the Chicago teachers used to rebuild their union. They did what the UAW did not: they connected the struggles in the workplace with the needs of a wider community. For years, every time they were about to lose a school to the privatizers, they brought their union banner to one grieving neighborhood after another and protested school closures. In the deeply racialized poverty of Chicago, the struggle of a union trying to save a working-class child's right to learn made a difference. So when this very union went on strike, it had already established a history of working and struggling in extra-workplace spaces, which is why the wider working class of Chicago saw the strike as their own struggle, for the future of their children. And when striking teachers in red shirts swelled the streets of the city, working-class people gave them their solidarity and support.

We want working-class insurgents to flood city streets like they did in Chicago during the Chicago Teachers Union strike. To prepare our theory and our praxis to be ready for such times, the first stop should be a revived understanding of class, rescued from decades of economic reductionism and business unionism. The constitutive roles played by race, gender or ethnicities on the working class need to be re-recognized while we reanimate the struggle with visions of class power broader than contract negotiations.

Only such a struggle will have the power to rupture capital's "hidden abode" and return the control of our sensuous, tactile, creative capacity to labor, to where it truly belongs—to ourselves.

5

Intersections and Dialectics: Critical Reconstructions in Social Reproduction Theory

David McNally

> In reproduction life is *concrete* and is vitality. . . . Each of the individual moments is essentially the totality of all; their difference . . . is posited in reproduction as concrete totality of the whole.
>
> —G.W.F. Hegel, *Science of Logic*

> The leaders of the women's rights movement did not suspect that the enslavement of Black people in the South, the economic exploitation of Northern workers and the social oppression of women might be systematically related.
>
> —Angela Davis, *Women, Race and Class*

We are at an inflection point in the development of materialist theories of multiple social oppressions. The most influential approach in the area—intersectionality theory—has been struggling to overcome the atomism that appears to be foundational to its conceptual outlook, as I show below. At the same time, social reproduction theory, which grew out of historical materialist analyses of gender relations, is being renovated in part as a response to critical challenges from intersectionality and antiracism. In what follows, I suggest that a dialectically revitalized social reproduction theory—one that rises to the critical challenges posed by intersectional analysis—offers the most promising perspective for those interested in an historical materialist theory of multiple oppressions within capitalist society.

Moving in this direction will require a fundamental protocol of dialectical theory: *immanent* criticism. It is all too typical for critical analyses to engage in wholesale rejection of alternative approaches, which may be all well and good where purely vulgar ideological formations are in question. But it will not do when we are trying to move beyond the limits of theory animated by a spirit of genuine inquiry. Here, dialectical criticism insists that a more comprehensive standpoint can be gained only by absorbing the strengths of a theoretical perspective in the course of overcoming its internal weaknesses. Rather than dogmatically dismissing a contending theory, dialectical criticism instead enters into its system of thinking, engages it on its own terms, and integrates its most critical insights. Truth, Hegel urges, is not a thing; it "is not a minted coin that can be given and pocketed ready-made." Rather, truth resides in the *process* of critical thinking, which can only move through partial and one-sided understandings toward richer and more comprehensive ones. The theoretical approach that prevailed at a particular point in time cannot then be glibly dismissed as "false." Even where it is transcended by a more robust theory, an earlier perspective full of false starts is still part of the history of truth, as a process of discovery, exploration, and theoretical formulation. "This truth thus includes the negative, what would be called the false, if it could be regarded as something from which one might abstract. The evanescent itself must, on the contrary, be regarded as essential, not as something fixed, cut off from the True."[1]

Hegel also describes this mode of criticism as a form of *determinate negation*. In contrast to abstract negation, which merely rejects one position in favor of another, determinate negation shows how the contradictions within a system of thought push toward their own overcoming. It thus engages these contradictions in a dual process of appropriating and overcoming. It is in this spirit that I engage intersectionality theory. Convinced that intersectional analyses bear deep theoretical flaws, I also recognize the critical insights they have generated. Yet, as many intersectional theorists themselves acknowledge, their perspective flounders in the face of some fundamental internal problems. So, while engaging this approach and its contradictions, I seek to show how they might be dialectically overcome—and their critical insights retained and repositioned—in a dialectically reconstructed social reproduction theory.

IMPASSES OF INTERSECTIONALITY THEORY

Intersectionality emerged through efforts to comprehend the multiple oppressions that constitute the social experience of many people, particularly women of color. Yet, from its beginnings, intersectionality struggled with the spatial metaphor that defines it. An intersection, after all, is a space in which discrete roads or axes cross paths. Indeed, at the 2001 World Conference Against Racism, one of the key founders of intersectional analysis, Kimberlé Crenshaw, illustrated her theorization with a visual image of a person standing at a junction of multiple roads as vehicles careened toward her from many angles.[2] Notwithstanding a growing dissatisfaction with this sort of imagery, intersectionality theorists have repeatedly resorted to describing multiple oppressions with spatialized terms such as *lines*, *locations*, *axes*, and *vectors*. Christine Bose, for instance, has deployed the image of "intersecting axes" of oppression, while Helma Lutz has enumerated "fourteen lines of difference," a view amended in Charlotte Bunch's suggestion that social differences run along "sixteen vectors."[3]

Dissatisfaction with the idea that all of these "axes" or "vectors" of power are independently constituted has propelled a number of analysts to amend the notion of intersecting relations with a vision of *interlocking* ones. Patricia Hill Collins, for instance, has proposed that we think in terms of interlocking systems of oppression that comprise a "matrix of domination," one which constitutes a "single, historically created system."[4] Sherene Razack pushes this approach slightly farther, urging that interlocking systems "need one another," implying perhaps that they are co-constituted.[5] More recently, Rita Kaur Dhamoon has suggested that the term *interactions* is preferable to *intersections*.[6] All of these theoretical moves rightly seek to overcome the conceptual image that has haunted intersectionality theory: that of reified, preconstituted identities or locations that come into some kind of external contact with each other. But at the same time, these modifications continue to be plagued by the ontological atomism inherent in the founding formulations of intersectionality theory: the idea that there are *independently constituted* relations of oppression that, in some circumstances, crisscross each other.

An especially clear expression of the atomism underlying intersectional accounts is offered by Floya Anthias, who overtly resists the idea that relations of power and oppression are co-constituting. A key problem with the idea of "mutual constitution," urges Anthias, is that it "disrupts the saliency of the categories in and of themselves."[7] The idea here seems to be that if we recognize, say, that relations of race and class are internally constitutive parts of gender, then the saliency of gender as a category is imperiled. This is ontological atomism to its core; it insists that one entity or relation cannot be understood as constituted in and through another without losing the very identity of the thing itself. Things—be they entities, processes, or relations—can thus only be understood as utterly discrete atomic bits whose identities exclude the co-constituting effects of others. Nira Yuval-Davis makes this position even more theoretically explicit in claiming that, while each social difference is "intermeshed in other social divisions," nevertheless "the ontological basis of each of these divisions is autonomous."[8] If this is so, then intermeshing can only really be a kind of external contact among ontologically discrete relations, as if every power relation were capable of careening off of every other without its internal constitution being affected. The result is a sort of social Newtonianism, a mechanics of colliding bits of social reality.

By *social Newtonianism*, I refer in the first instance to Isaac Newton's theoretical model of the universe as composed of discrete atomic bits. Each of these bits has a principle of self-movement ("inertial motion") inscribed within it. Of course, Newton knew that other forces, such as gravity, acted upon these atoms. Indeed, he knew that every body exercises a gravitational pull on every other. Nevertheless, he argued that gravity operated *externally*, affecting each and every bit of matter from the outside (and thus modifying their internally generated motion). But if every bit was affected by gravity, how was it that gravity was not essential to their very nature? How was it, in other words, that gravity was not acknowledged as something constitutive of every bit, i.e., as something that inherently makes these atomic parts what they are? Part of the answer here is that such a position inherently challenges the atomism to which Newton was committed. After all, if what things are is significantly determined by forces that appear to be "outside" of them, then the world would appear to be a complex and dynamic organic system in which the boundaries between parts are always porous. Newton was very much aware of the degree to which the world is one of unending flux and transformation. What allowed him to insist upon the stability and identity of its parts was his conception of absolute space and time.

Rather than his dynamic model of the universe leading him toward a philosophy of internal relations—in which every part is in constant motion and interaction and thus internally affected and *intrinsically constituted* by its interrelations with other parts—Newton held that this world-in-flux was ultimately stabilized by the absoluteness of time and space. Each object and each atomic part, he insisted, occupies a unique location in unchanging space and time. To clarify this concept, Newton urged that absolute space and time were mathematical in nature. Just as a pure geometric figure, like a circle or a triangle, can be constructed in an abstract space outside of any sensible form (for example, in our minds), so absolute time was independent of our sensations, and absolute space of any actual material substances. Thus, in his *Principia*, Newton claimed of "absolute, true and mathematical time" that it is "in and of itself and of its own nature, without reference to anything external." And in the same idiom he depicted an absolute space that "without reference to anything external, always remains homogeneous and immovable."[9] With this conception of homogeneous and unmoving space and time, Newton placed his dynamic world in constant motion upon fixed and unchanging foundations. This static metaphysics, with its conception of absolutely fixed space and time, thus rescued Newton's atomism, that is, his notion that the universe consists of discrete, independent atomic parts that are internally driven until modified by external collisions and interactions with other parts and forces. As much as our world appears to be one of endless flux and interaction among parts—which would seem to threaten an atomistic conception in which the bits of the world are utterly discrete and independent of each other—things are in fact stabilized, according to Newton, by the fixed, if invisible, coordinates of absolute space and time. The famous billiard-ball model of the universe, in which parts behave like colliding and careening balls that have been set in motion on a billiard table by an unseen mover, rests on just this static vision. A dynamic world in motion was thus held in check by an immutable (mathematically regulated) order.

Classical liberalism, particularly in the realm of political economy, adapted this mechanical philosophy to social life. For theorists like Adam Smith, the social universe is composed of self-moving atomic parts (self-seeking individuals) whose colliding movements are regulated by morality, law and, crucially, the market. In the hectic pell-mell of collisions among self-interested individuals, a stable social order thus emerges, one that can be analyzed in much the same way Newton deciphered the order amid the flux of the physical world. Smith's "invisible hand" of the market, which generates harmony out of the chaotic, self-interested behavior of individuals, is a deliberate analogue to the unseen forces that harmonize Newton's physical world.[10] Indeed, Newton's universe of abstract mathematical space-time is thoroughly consonant with the world of the capitalist market. "To the physical abstraction of space corresponds the economic abstraction of the market, which renders different types of labour and wealth commensurable through the monetary relation," writes Daniel Bensaïd. "To homogeneous, empty physical time corresponds the linear time of circulation and accumulation."[11] Newtonian space is thus a corollary of the abstracting social space of commodified social life governed by capitalist markets.

In suggesting that intersectionality theory is haunted by social Newtonianism, I am referring precisely to the idea that different axes and vectors of difference can be mapped in social space as ontologically separate and autonomous "bits" that enter into external relations with other "bits." Just like every atom must be measurable and every commodity must have its measure in price, so a theory of distinct axes or vectors requires each relation to be enclosable, measurable, mappable. Ironically, major currents in modern science—from systems theory to chaos and complexity theory—have moved far beyond such an approach. As one commentator observes, "In modern science, dynamic interaction appears to be the central problem in all fields of reality."[12] With dynamic interaction—as opposed to external collisions among things—comes, at least implicitly, the notion that things are *internally* related, i.e., that one thing (part or relation) is intrinsically constituted by the relations it has with others. In this respect, contemporary scientific thought can often be found moving away from mechanics and toward dialectics.[13] Let us return to our examination of intersectionality theory in this light.

While intersectional theorists tend to work with locations and vectors rather than the atomic individuals of liberal theory, they confront a similar methodological problem. They too are challenged when it comes to deriving some kind of social order or system from these parts. Why, after all, do we have reason to hold that independently constituted axes of oppression will come into contact? If they do, why should an ordered pattern emerge, rather than random chaos? And why should such contact not internally affect the axes or vectors in question? Perhaps because intersectionality originates in legal theory—with its foundational doctrine of discrete and autonomous legal subjects who possess property and rights—it regularly finds itself trapped within an atomism that its most sophisticated proponents seek to escape (as in Hill Collins's efforts to theorize a singular "matrix of domination"). Atomic individuals, of course, can only collide, or avoid colliding, in social space. When the former happens, we witness violations of the personal space of rights and property. Little surprise, then, that intersectionality theory, notwithstanding admirable efforts to the contrary, regularly reverts to spatialized conceptions of the social whole. Indeed, Anthias ends up advocating a merger of intersectionality with stratification theory and its vulgar depiction of social relations of power in terms of geological strata.[14] The result is the adding of one rigidly spatial metaphor—strata—to those of axes, vectors, and locations.

Even where intersectional theorists try to move toward a conception of "interactions" between different relations of domination, they remain trapped in what Hegel describes as *chemism*, an outlook which acknowledges "reciprocal adjustment and combination" among elements but remains "infected . . . with externality," that is, with the idea that discrete, preconstituted ingredients can only affect each other from the outside, not in a truly formative manner.[15] Dialectical organicism, however, sees a diverse and complex social whole as constitutive of every part, and each part as reciprocally constitutive of every other. This enables it to overcome the aporias of intersectional atomism. In this way, dialectics can transcend what Himani Bannerji describes as "the habit of fragmentive or stratified thinking so prevalent among us, which ends up by erasing *the social* from the conception of ontology."[16]

ONTOLOGY AND DIALECTICS

In his *Science of Logic*, Hegel sets out a tripartite typology of models of interaction in the natural and human sciences. He identifies the three models in question as *mechanism*, *chemism*, and *teleology*. These models summarize the state of scientific thinking in his age and, I would suggest, continue to shed significant light on debates in the social sciences, including those concerning intersectionality and social reproduction theory.

Mechanism, which Hegel clearly associates with Newtonianism, involves "a mechanical style of thinking" in which discrete objects come into external relations with one another. To the degree to which mechanism conceives of a plurality of things, it considers them as an "aggregation"—recall here the lists of fourteen and then sixteen axes or vectors of difference that we have seen—in which the "unity" of all the parts is "an external indifferent one." Rather than the parts being unified as internally related aspects of a whole, the whole is instead considered to be a mere sum of indifferent parts. In this outlook, "the objects are self-subsistent in regard to one another" and exist in the form of "mutual externality."[17]

Chemism, according to Hegel, has the merit of acknowledging interactions among differentiated elements. But because it too begins with the presumptions of atomism, with its vision of independently constituted bits of the world whose most basic properties are unaffected by other parts, it can only imagine interaction on the lines of "reciprocal adjustment and combination" of parts with each other. So, chemism may recognize the combination of two parts hydrogen with one part oxygen that produces water, but it does not theorize the qualitative transformations that this combination entails—the emergence of forms of life that are not reducible to these two chemical elements. As a result, the interactions of which chemism speaks are "still infected . . . with externality."[18] One can observe precisely this approach in intersectional accounts that speak in terms of "interactions between inequality-creating social structures."[19] These structures are taken to be discrete and relatively fixed "things" that preexist their interaction. A similar problem persists within accounts of interconnectivities and interlocking relations among multiple systems of oppression.[20] New combinations may be created by interactions and interconnectivities, but the structures themselves are viewed as constituted prior to their contact with one another.

In dialectical opposition to mechanism and chemism—by which, following Hegel, I mean a negation that overcomes theoretical contradictions and blockages while retaining a theory's most scientific insights—Hegel turns to teleology. Here, given the dominance of analytical and positivist modes of thought, a few clarifications are in order.

Positivism and postmodern theory converge today in their hostility to teleology. Positivism wants "the facts and just the facts," its hyper-empiricism displaying an allergy to any larger causes or purposes that might superintend the immediately observable "facts." Events, such as wars or economic crises, are *merely* events; any larger theorization in terms, say, of the dynamics of capitalism and imperialism is considered illicit, as these transcend the particularity of the phenomenon taken as a discrete, atomic happening. In a different idiom, postmodern theory too has rejected teleology as a search for grand narratives, for stories that illegitimately seek an overarching directionality to discrete phenomena and events.[21] As critics have pointed out, both antiteleological positions are caught up in a performative contradiction. After all, a claim for no larger purposes or directionalities in nature and society is itself a grand narrative, a universal claim that cannot be disclosed from single events in and of themselves.

Hegel's fundamental argument in this regard is that life itself has a teleological dynamic, i.e. life is purposeful. As Hegel explains, all life obeys a tendency to preserve and reproduce itself. We cannot comprehend our world and ourselves outside of an understanding of such life purposes. So, to use a familiar example, if I build a table, its *material cause* is wood. Its *formal cause* is the form of a table: that is, it must be formed with legs of roughly equal length in order to balance it, and so on. Its *efficient cause* is the activity—sawing wood, joining pieces, hammering nails, sanding the tabletop, and so on that I perform as a table maker. But the final cause (*telos*)—the purpose that informs its making—is the reproduction of the lives of those in my household.[22] It is around the table that we will gather to eat, drink, celebrate, and regenerate our communal bonds. It is around the table that we will socially and materially reproduce ourselves as interconnected living persons. For Hegel, the concept of teleology is both as simple and as profound as that.

The standpoint of teleology can only be an organic one. A part of a living system is not a discrete, self-sufficient atomic bit. The lungs do not exist simply to process oxygen unto themselves; they exist in relation to the heart, the circulatory system, and so on. It is the total organism that is alive—not the hands, eyes, or liver on their own. All of these organs have one overriding imperative—the reproduction of the total process of life—to which they are not equal on their own. Their functions make teleological sense only as an ensemble, only in their interconnections as parts whose purpose pertains to the whole, the living organism in its totality. The same applies to a product of human labor, such as a table. When I build a table for use in my household, table legs, joints, and wooden top are produced as elements of an organic whole, not as discrete ends in themselves. Similarly, when I build concepts with which to understand something, they are informed by the broader purpose of making sense of the world as part of living in it—and this applies as well to the vulgar empiricist, for whom the denial of general knowledge is part of her account of life. Living systems—from the body to the objects in a household to systems of knowledge—are all informed by purposes. Hegel holds that the same is true for social collectivities, from the family to the state.[23]

Among the most materialistic elements in Hegel's dialectic is his insistence that what pertains to life also pertains to thought. If life is animated by the purposefulness of a dynamic organic system, then thought, as an aspect of life, must obey the same imperative. Thought must be equal to the complex, manifold richness of life. It must seek out "the real organic Concept or the whole."[24] Just as life is a journey that describes a dynamic, contradictory path, the same is true of thought. As a good and true life is one that increases in the richness of its relations, knowledge, and experience, the same is true of thought. True thinking endeavors not to produce fixed thought-objects, but to trace a *process* of ever richer comprehension. "Truth is not a minted coin that can be given and pocketed ready-made." Instead, truth is the process of ever richer, more detailed, more concrete comprehension of ourselves and our world. All quests for knowledge begin with specific bits of information (or "contents" of thought), says Hegel. The scientific method of philosophy, he argues, "is the necessary expansion of that content into an organic whole. Through this movement the path by which the concept of knowledge is reached becomes likewise a necessary and complete process of becoming."[25]

This is why Hegel, in a move that is radically at odds with formal logic, introduces the concept of life into his *Science of Logic*.[26] For if the task of thought—and what could be a higher goal?—is to comprehend life, then this requires a conceptual system adequate to life's complex, dynamic, multidimensional unfolding. However, this necessitates not formal-logical categories, but dialectical ones; not the fixed and static concepts of analytical philosophy, with its minted coins, but concepts that are internally dynamic and self-transforming, concepts that capture the very *becoming* of things in their many-sidedness. Dialectical concepts, Hegel insists, "become fluid" as one passes into another and attains a greater richness. This requires that the differences that constitute a phenomenon, its "differentiated moments," must lose their "fixity," as thought grapples with their fundamental dynamism and relationality—which is, of course, the dynamism and relationality of the elements of life itself.[27] Dialectical thinking thus drives beyond the "method of labelling . . . and pigeon-holing everything" in which "the living essence of the matter has been stripped away or boxed up." It resists the abstracting tendencies of analytical thinking, which endeavors to decompose phenomena into ever smaller bits that can be boxed up and labeled. By contrast, dialectics traces "the *coming to be of the object*," the dynamic and changing interrelations among the elements of life that comprise a concrete (and hence internally differentiated) totality.[28]

For Marx, this mode of dialectical thinking was second nature, something upon which he rarely reflected, so much did he take it for granted. Yet, after Marx's death, Engels recognized how foreign it would be for many readers of Marx's work. As a result, Engels advised that readers of *Capital* should not look for

> fixed, cut-to-measure, once and for all applicable definitions in Marx's works. It is self-evident that where things and their interrelations are conceived, not as fixed, but as changing, their mental images, the ideas, are likewise subject to change and transformation, and they are not encapsulated in rigid definitions, but are developed in their historical or logical process of formation.[29]

This rejection of formal-logical methods of definition corresponds to a dialectical view of life as dynamic becoming. Concepts cannot be fixed and rigid because life is nothing of the sort. It follows that the multi-dimensionality of social life cannot be grasped by presupposing its parts to be "ontologically autonomous." On the contrary, as much as there are analytically identifiable components of living wholes—hands and eyes, or concrete individuals—they can only be fully understood relationally. For dialectical organicism, objects are in fact *relations*;[30] these relations are in flux, undergoing temporal transformations that reconfigure them as elements of a living system.

It is instructive that, in her critique of intersectionality theory, Himani Bannerji too insists on the priority of life, or lived experience. "Non-white and white people living in Canada or the West know," she writes,

> that this social experience is not, as lived, a matter of intersectionality. Their sense of being in the world, textured through myriad social relations and cultural forms, is lived or felt or perceived as being all together and all at once.[31]

From this perspective, Bannerji advocates an understanding of the concrete social whole in "its multiple mediations of social relations and forms."[32] "We need to venture," she writes, "into a more complex reading of the social, where every aspect can be shown to reflect others, where every little piece of it contains the macrocosm in the microcosm."[33] The distinct parts of a social whole are thus *internally* related; they mediate each other and in so doing constitute each other. And things (or relations) that are intermediated and co-constituting are not ontologically separate, even if they have properties that differentiate them and constitute a relative distinctiveness.

To be sure, there are properties specific to the different parts of a whole. The eye has particular functional properties quite different from those of the hand. Racism has specific characteristics that allow us to distinguish it in the first instance from sexism. But these distinctions do not provide exhaustive definitions. They afford a starting point from which thought unfolds the internal relations of parts to other parts and to the organic system as a whole. Racism, in other words, can be understood as a *partial totality* with unique features that must ultimately be grasped in relation to the other partial totalities that comprise the social whole in its process of becoming. Each partial totality, each partial system within the whole, has unique characteristics (and a certain "relative autonomy" or, better put, relational autonomy). The "heart-lung system," for instance constitutes such a partial totality within the human organism as a whole. But no part (or partial totality) is ontologically autonomous per se. Each part is both (partially) autonomous and dependent, (partially) separate and ontologically interconnected. Consequently, none can be grasped adequately as a self-sufficient unit outside of its membership in a living whole. Of course, the organic whole is constituted in and through its parts—it is these that give it determinateness and concreteness—but it is not reducible to its parts. It is something greater and more systematic than a mere additive sum. There are, insists Hegel, relations of reciprocity, rather than mechanism, between parts and between parts and the whole. Indeed, this is what it means to be a living organism rather than a lifeless mechanism.

It is at this point in his analysis of life that Hegel introduces his concept of reproduction. A living organism, after all, must reproduce itself; without reproduction—be it daily, seasonal, or generational—life ceases. Moreover, it is the organism as a whole that must reproduce itself, for it is the total organism that lives, biological or social. Individual organs live only through the reproduction of the entire organism. It follows that parts and whole are bound together in a single life-process:

> in reproduction life is *concrete* and is vitality. . . . Each of the individual moments is essentially the totality of all; their difference constitutes the ideal form determinateness, which is posited in reproduction as the concrete totality of the whole.[34]

A concrete totality attains concreteness ("determinateness") through the differences that comprise it. At the same time, each of these different parts carries the whole within it; as elements of life, their reproduction is impossible outside of the living whole. It is with just this conception in mind that Marx famously writes, "The concrete is concrete because it is the concentration of many determinations, hence unity of the diverse."[35] Totalities or universals are not abstractions from the concrete diversity and multiplicity of things for Hegel and Marx. On the contrary, totalities are constituted in and through the diversity and dynamism of real life processes. This is what distinguishes the abstract universals of formal logic from "the concrete totality of the whole" that animates dialectical thinking. The dialectical concept of totality thus involves comprehending a process of *totalization* that unifies (without suppressing) the partial totalities constitutive of it. The social totality is thus grasped as existing "in and through those manifold mediations through which the specific complexes—i.e. 'partial totalities'—are linked to each other in a constantly shifting and changing, dynamic overall complex."[36]

This sort of conception, I submit, is what an intersectional theorist like Patricia Hill Collins aspires to when she writes that interlocking systems of oppression ought to be understood as "part of a single, historically created system." Hill Collins rightly points here toward a unitary ("single"), historically developing system. In so doing, her critical insight points beyond the spatial metaphor that constrains intersectional theory. Dialecticized, Hill Collins's move opens the way toward an organic conception of society as a dynamic system of internally connected (and thus co-constituting) social relations. The conundrum for intersectionality theory has been that the cartography of locations, vectors, and axes and the atomistic conceptual framing built upon it are unamenable to this sort of dialectical theorization.

Hill Collins's insightful reminder that social systems are "historically created" also gestures toward an aspect of Hegel's conception of teleology that is utterly crucial to his theory—and utterly foreign to empiricist and positivist forms of thought. I refer here to his concept of *retrodetermination*, a concept that is unthinkable by means of mechanism or chemism. After all, nondialectical thought is dominated by a concept of causation that pivots on temporal succession: first arrives a cause, then its effects. But Hegel's conception of life pushes beyond that. In life, after all, the full meaning of what I did in the past will only come to fruition in the present or the future. If I plant seeds in a garden, what I have done remains to be seen. Perhaps my failure to tend these seeds, or a lack of rainfall will bring my efforts to naught. Perhaps war will drive me from my land. On the other hand, a whole series of *subsequent* actions may allow me to bring these seeds to fruition. Only after the fact might I be able to say that my planting was an act of creating food crops. Similarly, the meaning of my past social relationships and activities is open-ended and amendable. A painful childhood relation may be transformed into something quite different in adulthood. The meaning of my past would thus have been retroactively reworked. To take a political example, the meaning of activities by socialists today are indeterminate. If a socialist future were one day to arrive, this would give new meaning to the small and often thankless tasks we performed in the past. Understood in these terms, we may say that in life endings determine beginnings—or indeed that they *are* the beginnings. Hegel writes, "It can therefore be said of teleological activity that in it the end is the beginning, the consequent the ground, the effect the cause, that it is a becoming of what has become."[37]

This is one reason why abstract debates of the "is racism necessary to capitalism?" sort are so decidedly flawed. One cannot know such things in advance, on the basis of principles abstracted from concrete historical life. What we can say is that the actual historical process by which capitalism emerged in our world integrally involved social relations of race and racial domination. From the standpoint of "the effect"—racialized capitalism—we can say definitively that racism is a necessary feature of the historical capitalism in which we live. The effect has thus become a cause—and it is systematically reproduced in and through the reproduction of the capitalist mode of production. In the "single, historically created system" (Hill Collins) in which we live, all of these relations of social power—from gender, racial, and sexual domination to capitalist exploitation—form a complex social whole, one in which "each of the individual moments is essentially the totality of the whole." This, it seems to me, is precisely what Bannerji intends when she urges that "'race' cannot be disarticulated form 'class' any more than milk can be separated from coffee once they are mixed, or the body divorced from consciousness in a living person."[38] These relations do not need to be brought into intersection because each is already inside the other, co-constituting one another to their very core. Rather than standing at intersections, we stand in the river of life, where multiple creeks and streams have converged into a complex, pulsating system.

REVISITING SOCIAL REPRODUCTION THEORY WITH ANGELA DAVIS'S *WOMEN, RACE AND CLASS*

As we have seen, Hegel's teleological model of life culminates in the concept of reproduction. There can be little doubt that this Hegelian insight lies at the basis of Marx's concept of the (expanded) reproduction of capital. As an organic system, the capitalist mode of production must be capable of reproducing itself in time and space. One of the purposes of *Capital* is to show the essential laws through which it does so, and the antagonisms, conflicts, and contradictions they generate.

Starting in the late 1960s, Marxist-feminist scholars began deploying a distinctive approach to how working-class households reproduce the essential commodity upon which capitalism revolves—labor power. Rather than focusing exclusively on capital's reproduction, they interrogated that of the working class, taking up the gendered dynamics through which the daily and generational reproduction of labor power occurred. In so doing, they underscored the daily and generational reproduction of living laborers, which is an essential precondition for the ongoing reproduction of capital. While some advocates of this approach—dubbed social reproduction theory or social reproduction feminism—lapsed into a fundamental dualism which posited distinct modes of production and reproduction (known as "dual systems theory"), the most sophisticated contributions to the field sought out a unitary conceptualization in which these were theorized as two moments of a complexly unified social process.[39] Yet, notwithstanding the powerful insights generated by social reproduction approaches, most commentators failed to integrate processes of racialization into their analysis. The great accomplishment of intersectionality theory was to expand the framework of discussion—initially to race, gender, and class, and more recently to other relations of oppression, such as those of sexuality and ability.

Yet, like dual systems approaches, intersectional theorists tended toward the *additive method* we have described in the first section of this paper. Where the dualists added together relations of class and gender, intersectionalists added a third element—race—to the mix, in efforts to arrive at a more complex picture of the social whole. Subsequent interventions have expanded the number of additional factors, to the point at which we now have discussions about the "sixteen vectors" of difference that define social being. Rarely, however, have attempts been made to think all of these relations as co-constituting parts of the differentiated unity that comprises a concrete social totality. And as a postmodern cultural climate took hold—where plurality was celebrated and universality condemned—the emphasis on ontologically autonomous regions (locations, axes, vectors, etc.) of social life predominated, generating the intellectual fragmentation and stratification of the social bemoaned by Bannerji. More recently, however, in tandem with a broader renewal of historical materialism, imaginative theorists have undertaken to renovate social reproduction theory by accenting its emphasis on social labor in its widest sense as *human practical activity*. Highlighting embodied labor activities in concrete social-spatial relations, they have shown how the ensemble of practices which reproduce social life are simultaneously organized via multiple relations of domination and power, centrally including race. Lately, work in this vein has been developed in social reproduction theorizations of the global reproduction of labor power, including its cross-border organization.[40]

This renewed emphasis on the differentiated unity of practical activities through which human beings produce and reproduce themselves, their social relations, and their relations with the natural environment offers a compelling basis for dialectical theorization of the sort we have advocated above. As Ferguson argues, "such a theory encourages us to understand those layered and contradictory experiences as part of a much broader, dynamic, and materialist set of social relations—relations created, contested, and reproduced by our labor inside and outside the household."[41] In so doing, such a theoretical approach returns us to the complex unity of the multifaceted but internally connected processes by which life is reproduced in determinate social forms.

Here I want to venture a further claim. I want to insist that, largely because of its historical materialist orientation and its overriding emphasis on the interplay of the production of value and the reproduction of human beings, Angela Davis's seminal work, *Women, Race and Class* (1981), ought to be considered a social reproduction text in just the ways I have been outlining. In proposing this, I do not mean to deny the status Davis's text has in intersectionality literature. But I do mean to redeem its historical materialist core and its power as a classic in antiracist and feminist Marxism, one that shares the spirit of the most compelling work in social reproduction theory.

Davis's text, after all, repeatedly grounds the *labors* of Black women—as both wage-earners and members of households—in organizing their lives. Davis regularly underlines the much higher proportion of Black women employed as wage workers compared to white women, and she highlights their struggles over conditions of employment. Crucially, she points out that for huge numbers of Black women, wage labor *was* household labor—for *other* households, that is, for wealthy white families—with overwhelming numbers of Black women employed as domestics.[42] Davis further demonstrates the complex unity of both racism and sexism toward Black women workers, particularly with respect to sexual assault on the job—showing the utterly interwoven character of sexism, racism, and class exploitation in the experience of Black working-class women. At the same time, she accents how involvement in labor in both the slave and post-slavery periods bestowed a distinctive independence upon Black women within African American households.[43] What holds the various elements of this analysis together is the text's insistence that the gendered and racialized relations of capitalist production and reproduction give an overriding unity to all these dimensions of social experience. Indeed, in an implicitly Hegelian-Marxist gesture, Davis urges that in the American situation, "the enslavement of Black people in the South, the economic exploitation of Northern workers and the social oppression of women" should be seen as "systematically related."[44]

Now, to be *systematically* related involves considerably more than mere intersection. Intersections can be relatively random and haphazard; systems cannot. In a system, all the parts are ordered and integrated in ways that are determined by the other components. For this reason, a system is always more than the sum of its parts. There is an inseparability here in which the whole determines the parts, even as it is reciprocally determined by its subunits in turn. Davis's formulation strongly suggests that black slavery, women's oppression, and the economic exploitation of wage labor comprised "a single, historically created system" (Hill Collins) in the United States, a complexly unified capitalist social formation. Seen in these terms, *Women, Race and Class* emerges as an explicitly historical materialist text that seeks to anatomize the social reproduction of a racist, male-dominated capitalist mode of production in the United States. Indeed, there seems no other way to fully appreciate the text's claim that, for Black and working-class women, an end to gender oppression can only mean the socialization of housework, whose precondition is "an end to the profit-motive's reign over the economy."[45] In other words, gender oppression is inextricably entwined (as is its overcoming) with the capitalist structure of the economy—so much so that, to overturn one, the other must be transformed. This, of course, is another way of saying that, however much they are differentiated relations, they constitute an integral system.

For Davis, in other words, we are dealing with a capitalist mode of production and reproduction that entails historically specific relations of gender and racial oppression. Rather than enumerating discrete axes and vectors, she shows the systematic interrelations in and through which racial and gender domination are utterly interwoven with capitalist exploitation—so much so that they cannot legitimately be considered separable, even if they remain analytically distinct at a certain rough-and-ready level of abstraction. As a result, changes in one subset of relations presuppose changes in all the others and in the system as a whole.

There was a time, during the ascendance of neoliberalism and the flowering of the postmodern moment, when talk of system transformation was treated as hopelessly modernist. But that sociopolitical moment has waned in the face of an enduring global economic slump, a grinding age of austerity, and the resurgence of movements against capitalist social inequality. Our new conjuncture has given rise to an intellectual renaissance of historical materialism in the context of new anticapitalist struggles. After all, the fundamentally capitalist character of our world system is on dramatic display; the most inspiring radical social movements are posing the problem of system transformation rather than partial amelioration.[46] In this political-intellectual climate, it is not surprising that Marxist-inspired social reproduction theory has similarly resurged as a response to crucial aporias in intersectionality approaches, while also drawing upon critical insights about multiple forms of oppression that the latter has advanced. As I have tried to show here, to be equal to the tasks of the moment, a dialectically reconstructed social reproduction theory is vital if we are to understand the "unity of the diverse" that is the shape of our world—and if we are to change it.

6

Children, Childhood and Capitalism: A Social Reproduction Perspective

Susan Ferguson

INTRODUCTION

Children, we now know, have entered the marketplace. Few if any serious critics still hold that "childhood" is a time and space apart, untouched and unsullied by capitalist economics. It is precisely this problematic—the child in and of a global capitalist nexus—that animates a great deal of research and public discussion today. And insofar as Global North childhoods are at issue, it is the corporate-consumerist nexus—and children's participation as its victims or savvy interpreters—that usually comes under the most intense scrutiny.[1]

While a focus on children's encounters with a rampantly globalizing market captures an important range of experiences, it is a limited view of capitalist childhoods. Capitalism is not only, or even fundamentally, a system of exchange relations. The market in consumer goods and services owes its very existence to the ongoing availability of another market: a market of potentially exploitable labor power.[2] However deeply they are or are not implicated as capitalist *consumers*, the vast majority of children, even in the Global North, cannot escape their fate as capital's present and future *laborers*. If the goal is to understand "capitalist childhoods," analysis needs to also account for children's experiences and navigation of capitalist *productive* relations, for, despite appearances, these are at least as much a part of their everyday lives as is commodity culture.

What exactly are capitalist productive relations? And how are children implicated in them? Conventional Marxist analyses define productive relations narrowly, as constituted by workplace (i.e., direct labor/capital) relations. The child subjects of capitalist productive relations are accordingly *workers*, child laborers. A social reproduction feminism perspective, on the other hand, directs our attention to a broader definition—one that includes those relations that generate and sustain workers for capital. While children's direct encounters with capitalist value production are a crucial part of the story, they are not the full story. As present and future laborers, children also participate directly in the processes and institutions of social reproduction. To begin, they are the objects of the (feminized, gendered, and racialized) reproductive labor of others. But they are also agents of their own self-transformation into capitalist subjects—subjects, that is, who are able and willing to both sell their labor power for a wage, *and* who over time take increasing responsibility for their own social reproduction (and possibly that of other people, too). Whatever else it may be, childhood under capitalism is incontrovertibly the space and time in which such a transformation is set in motion.

To claim this as a purpose or objective of childhood is not to *reduce* explanation of childhood to its systemic functions. I am not suggesting, in other words, that we explain childhood and children as shaped in any straightforwardly functional or simplistic way as a response to capital's demand for productive and reproductive labor power. Rather, as I elaborate below, there exists a deeply contradictory relationship between the social reproduction of children and childhoods, on the one hand, and the continued thriving and expansion of capital, on the other. I do, however, want to insist that capitalist productive relations determine the terrain upon which children and childhoods are produced and reproduced.[3] As such, the systemic requirements of capital's reproduction establish certain limits of possibility. Although children and childhoods vary historically, geographically, and socially between and within capitalist societies, the fundamental demands of capital for a renewable supply of labor power exert strong pressures for certain (privatized) forms, (disciplining) practices, and (alienated) states of being to emerge. At the same time, they generate forces that obstruct the likelihood that other (communal, open-ended, integrated) childhoods will develop.[4]

Be that as it may, my primary emphasis in this chapter is not on limits and functions. It is on the ways in which children and childhoods can and do represent a challenge and/or alternative to capitalist social reproduction, and thus also to capitalist value production. A social reproduction feminist perspective is especially well equipped to highlight the *contradictions* ingrained in the systemic reproduction of capitalism because it begins from an expansive definition of labor. It reminds us that although value-productive forms of labor dominate, capitalism does not—indeed cannot—exist without other forms of labor. And it insists that those labors, and the social reproductive processes and institutions they sustain, are geared to navigating the systemic contradiction between meeting human need and producing labor power for capital.[5]

To inquire about children's involvement in this navigation does, however, stretch this analytic framework. It pushes social reproduction feminism to account for two facts that are rarely, if ever, queried:

(i) That children do not begin life under the direct control of capital, but instead their bodies and minds must learn their way into those capitalist subjectivities;[6] and
(ii) That children participate in their own socio-specific transformations into capitalist subjects.

A social reproduction feminist approach, I propose, opens up pathways to address these facts by grappling with the specificities of children's "labor"—by which I mean the practical human activity (which, as I explain below, involves both work and play) children engage in to transform their own worlds and selves. It makes it possible to ask how this "labor" figures in the management of capitalism's social reproductive contradictions. My reading of this—developed in the remaining pages of this paper—is that capitalist children and childhoods are engaged in a constant negotiation between a playful, transformative relationship to the world and the more instrumental, disembodied state of alienation required to become laborers for capital. This negotiation occurs throughout the entirety of children's everyday lives, be they at home, at work, at school, or at the mall. Thus, any discussion of capitalist childhoods and subject formation needs to consider not just children's interactions with the consumer market and/or their experiences as workers. It also needs to grapple with how their bodies and minds experience—how they bend with *and against*—capital's relentless drive for access to exploitable labor power.

In highlighting this bending with and against capital, I advance a conception of children's practical activity that avoids reifying the child subject as victim or agent and instead attends to the praxic quality of their agency or interactions with the world.

WORK

Certainly children directly reproduce capitalism as workers. As Marx describes in detail in chapter 15 of the first volume of *Capital*, industrial capitalism sucked children in from a young age and profited massively off their labors. One hundred and fifty years later, the regular workforce in the Global North is decidedly more adult, but children's exit from it has been neither swift nor complete. For all the nineteenth-century alarms raised about the very young toiling in factories and mines or hawking goods and running errands on city streets, children remained a fixture in labor markets well into the next century. To offer just two North American snapshots of many possible: in 1911, twenty-five years after Ontario's legislature outlawed the hiring of boys under twelve and girls under fourteen to work in factories and roughly two decades after other legislation restricted children's work in retail and street trades, a full third of the average family income in the industrial city of Hamilton could be tracked to children's wages.[7] That same year in the United States, where similar regulations existed, a survey of Polish immigrant families found that children contributed up to 46 percent of household income.[8] While reliance on children's wages in North America declined for most families as the century proceeded, child labor did not disappear completely. It remains an everyday fact of life today for a minority—especially, but not simply, for children of migrant workers.[9] There's little sign that it will disappear completely, as some Canadian provinces and US states have eased restrictions in recent years, allowing younger children to work longer hours in a handful of the least regulated, most dangerous industries, such as farming and construction.[10]

However, while capitalism has not dispensed with child labor in the Global North, it has sidelined it. The vast majority of children today are no longer part of the regular workforce. Instead, they take on jobs after school and during summers. As such—and in contrast to the nineteenth century, when the profitability of everything from coal mining to lace- and basket-making depended upon industrialists' ability to exploit children's labor[11]—young people are now widely understood to be marginal, if relevant at all, to capitalist patterns of accumulation. Accordingly, their contribution to a family's survival has diminished. Rather than turning over most or all of their wages to household heads as they did in the past, today's working children tend to keep their earnings to spend or save as they see fit.[12] These patterns help to cement a conception of children's work as dispensable or trivial, while also confirming the notion that the capitalist child is more consumer than producer. Indeed, it is not just that the unproductive child is the norm, the very definition of children and childhood situates them *in opposition to* work. A child's "job" in the Global North (and increasingly in modernizing middle classes in the Global South) is not to work, but to play—and to attend school.

The radical distinction of work and play that this common adage implies pervades thinking about childhoods, shaping the very way we investigate them. For example, work on "consumer-capitalist" childhoods tends to assume a nonlaboring child and rarely crosses paths with research into child labor. When it does, it is usually to emphasize the divergent experiences of children in the Global North from those in the Global South, pointing out the rich irony that "labor-free," consumption-driven childhoods are in fact dependent upon the exploitation of majority-world children's labor.[13] Although astute, this observation hinges on a distinction that in fact begins to falter on closer examination of children's participation in the broader social reproduction of capitalism—the distinction between work and play. I turn to that discussion after first teasing apart the question of participation as it is generally understood in relation to theorizing the nature of children's subjectivity.

BEING AND BECOMING A CAPITALIST SUBJECT

Both child cultural studies and labor studies explore children's participation in a public arena that is seen as potentially damaging and contrary to children's interests. This raises some tricky, possibly unanswerable questions: To what extent do or can children exercise agency in these situations? Should we conceive of them as willing and able participants, or are they victims of their circumstances? It was precisely these sorts of questions—and the theorization of children's subjectivities they invited—that launched childhood studies as a scholarly field.

In the 1970s, a handful of scholars and children's rights advocates challenged traditional conceptions of children as passive and infinitely malleable and began emphasizing their essential resilience and creativity instead. Children, they argued, should not be conceived only as objects of social institutions, whose worth and welfare is judged by how well they are shaping up to be productive adults of the future. Rather than "works" or "persons-in-progress," children are active subjects, with rights, responsibilities, and powers of their own; they are competent to challenge or reject the ideas and practices they inherit as subordinate members of an adult-organized world. So, for instance, while marketers try to pull them ever more deeply toward consumerism and other market-based values, children become increasingly market-savvy, able to decode and resist commercial messages. The key for social theory and policy is to recognize this and create environments in which children's voices and meaningful contributions can be acknowledged, understood, and attended to.

This new paradigm of children's subjectivity took hold swiftly, providing a productive framework for empirical work and bolstering a children's rights participation agenda. The 1989 Convention on the Rights of the Child, for example, includes rights to participation alongside protection and provision, while the United Nations General Assembly pledged in 1992 to change the world *with*, rather than *for*, children.[14] Yet it also spawned a tendency to overestimate the potential of children's voices and agency while underplaying their relative social powerlessness. By the 1990s, one critic notes, it had become "an ethical imperative" as well as an orthodox methodological approach to treat the child as a competent social actor, akin to the liberal autonomous subject.[15] The earlier model of the vulnerable, passive child had been swept away only to be supplanted by another, equally static and reified model of subjectivity.[16]

Rejecting both these models, a more nuanced theorization of children's subjectivities has emerged from the field of children's geography. Rather than simply assessing the impact children make on the world—*what they achieve* as social actors—these geographers focus as well on *how children relate* to their environments. In a series of empirically rich and theoretically penetrating studies, they highlight the embodied and transformative nature of that relationship. Children, they show, come to know the spaces they occupy through manipulating them physically and imaginatively and in ways that are charged with affect. This is an essentially playful mode of being, and it is not only observable in young children "at play." It is also characteristic of older children surviving life on the streets of Yogyakarta, organizing community service projects in Chula Vista, herding cattle in Howa, or traveling to and from school in Manhattan.[17] Whatever else it reveals, in inquiring into the *quality* of children's interactions with the world (what do those interactions look—and feel—like?), this alternative understanding of subjectivity, among other things, troubles the hard and fast distinction between work and play. In so doing, it takes us to the heart of Marxist philosophy and to the social reproduction feminist development of those Marxist premises.

WORK AND PLAY

Close observations of children's interactions with their worlds are nothing new. Indeed, bourgeois society has long been entranced by the child, and by the child's body in particular, as the history of portraiture, film, and photography attest.[18] By the end of the nineteenth century, "child-watchers"—spurred on by Charles Darwin's article recounting his own children's sensual, imaginative, and pleasurable gestures and interactions—had turned that fascination into the building blocks of a science, namely developmental psychology.[19] Early work in that field closely documented children's tendency to embrace the world in ways that are especially sensuous and imaginative, with psychologists such as Jean Piaget and Lev Vygotsky defining the childish mode of existence as "playful." While these scientists studied primarily European, bourgeois babies and young children more than a hundred years ago, this basic premise of their work has since been affirmed across cultures and through time. Other psychologists, anthropologists, historians, and geographers tend to agree that, notwithstanding considerable cultural variation in the forms and purposes of play, there is strong evidence that virtually all children play.[20]

Leaving aside for the moment the obvious question about fetishism that the ongoing fascination with children raises, I want to suggest that all this close observation yields some important clues about what, for Marx, is the premise of all human history: the conscious, practical activity that transforms the world—that which is generally called *work* or *labor*.[21] The above accounts (and the theorization of childish subjectivities they inspire) highlight the "praxic" nature of a child's interaction with the world. Like workers, players transform their environments, but they do so in ways that are simultaneously imaginative and sensual, and often pleasurable and/or aimed at creating something better. Such, proposes Thomas Henricks, is the very essence of play:

> Play is the laboratory of the possible. To play fully and imaginatively is to step sideways into another reality, between the cracks of ordinary life. Although that ordinary world, so full of cumbersome routines and responsibilities is still visible to us, its images, strangely, are robbed of

> their powers. Selectively, players take the objects and ideas of routine life and hold them aloft. Like willful children, they unscrew reality or rub it on their bodies or toss it across the room. Things are dismantled and built anew.[22]

The creative and delightful transformation of the world Henricks describes can also be found in Vygotsky's famous case study of a child who takes a stick and, positioning it between his legs, turns it into a horse before proceeding to have a lot of fun "riding" around the room. So too is it evident in observations of older children who, for example, take hold of established public spaces and "reconfigure" their boundaries to suit their own needs, to create a meandering pathway home from school or a place to hang out with friends.[23] There is open-endedness and fluidity to this "childish" way of being in the world that is both familiar and strange to many adults. As Curti and Moreno write, "In emerging action, function, effect, assembling, doing—becoming—children move and change in and through their own affective strivings, endeavoring and imaginings, actively becoming with—while simultaneously transforming the identity, constitution and form of—objects, places, bodies and spaces."[24] *Creation* in these instances is a thoroughly two-sided affair: tactile and intellectual. Whatever else play might be, it is this two-sidedness that allows children to transform their worlds in ways that allow new meanings and possibilities to flourish.

Consider too how the distinction here between work and play is blurred. Worlds are built in work-like ways (with intention and focus), yet the interactions are brimming with feeling (both physical and emotional) and imagination. Such a mode of being approximates the sort of unalienated self-objectification that Marxists identify with self-actualization and freedom.[25] It engages all the senses and brings imagination and concrete interactions with the environment together to produce a material and social world that satisfies human desires and needs. This, in other words, is the conscious practical human activity Marx identifies in the *Economic and Philosophical Manuscripts of 1844* as the very generator of society.[26] In a world in which people have unimpeded access to resources and freedom to explore their potentialities, the "work" of reproducing ourselves and our worlds can be both sensuous and imaginative. That is, it can be "playful." It can also be decidedly pleasurable. "Play" is synonymous with "fun" in the sense that any activity ceases to be play when the fun—or perhaps more accurately, the good feeling—goes out of it.[27] But capital, Marx (and experience) tells us, cannot tolerate this pleasurable shifting along a work/play continuum. Capital needs instrumentalized workers who are alienated not just from the products of their labor but also from each other, and from their own sensibilities and sensualities. It needs workers who are willing and able to subsume their more expansive life needs and potentialities to a de-eroticized, narrowly functional relationship with the world and others.[28]

Children—the future laborers on whom capitalism depends—thus pose a problem for capitalism: they are not as prepared, as adults are, to abandon the play end of the work/play continuum and all that comes with it. This is not to suggest that children are fundamentally noncapitalist. Nor am I suggesting that play represents a purely unalienated state of being, one that is not inflected with and circumscribed by capitalist realities. Let me take a short detour here to properly explain the premises and categories I'm relying on to make my argument.

Capitalism is, and must be, a totalizing system in the sense that the dispossession and privatization of property it presumes constitute conditions affecting all practical, conscious human activity, playful and work-like. Yet it imposes (in the sense that it establishes a strong logic behind) a radical separation of work and play. Workers and future workers are encouraged to play only at times and in spaces that are not reserved for work (e.g., value-productive *and* much social reproductive labor). Indeed, the history of class struggle can be seen as a history of contestations over the work/play or work/leisure divide. Childhood—insofar as it is a time and space set apart from the *direct* domination of labor by capital—is a byproduct of those struggles.[29] Because children are, especially in the Global North, afforded considerable distance from the direct labor/capital relation, they can explore and exercise capacities and affects that are otherwise not just discouraged or redirected but in fact repressed.

That is, the separation of work from play in capitalism does not reflect some natural or pre-ordained polar opposition between these two forms of activity. Rather, it results from an ongoing attempt to *repress* the sensuous, imaginative—concrete—engagement with the world that typifies play, and to channel activity to instrumentalized, alienated work or labor. That attempt takes multiple forms (all mediated by socio-specific gendered, racialized, heterosexist, ableist, settler-colonial logics). These include, for example, disciplinary policies and practices in workplaces (everything from scheduled breaks and productivity quotas to distributing mobile phones to executives so they are on call 24/7 or distributing birth-control pills to women factory workers in an effort to limit leaves for pregnancy and maternity) and in schools (such as rules against running in the halls and detentions for uncompleted homework), as well as the scientific and social norms informing parenting, education, health care (such as parental and professional strictures governing standards of cleanliness, developmental growth, and sexualities), and so much more. All such measures help shape a labor force that is willing and able to forego physical, intellectual, and emotional self-fulfillment. They instead aim at restricting the range of human interaction with the world to that which is required to produce value for capital and, in the case of social reproductive work, to produce labor power suitable for exploitation. This repression—which comes about in the first instance because the worker is alienated from both her means of production and the product she produces—also comprises the worker's alienation from her (creative, sensuous) *self.*

Children are not born outside of this history. Childhood does not shield them from it. Rather, childhood, children, and their practical human activity are its products, just as children are also contributors to its ongoing-ness. However, while their play is subject to the (temporal and spatial) conditions that make abstract labor the necessary and dominant form of labor, it is not directly subject to the process of abstraction that produces capitalist value. Global North capitalist childhoods are about as far removed from that process as one can imagine within a capitalist society, steeped in a deeply rooted ideology affirming the essentially sacred nature of childhood, a status which (supposedly) protects children from the "profanity" of the market. It is precisely the degree of this spatial and temporal distance from the direct labor/capital relation (and thus from the rule of abstract time) that allows the foregrounding of other (sensuous, creative) dimensions of human activity to flourish.[30]

Although capitalist relations require the repression and alienation of the self, processes of concrete labor—those performed under the direct purview of the boss and those performed as unpaid domestic work—hold at least the potential for greater self-fulfillment (that is, for the exercise of imaginative, sensuous pleasures). Usually that potential is (and can only be) expressed in partial ways. Consider, for instance, the autoworker who takes pride in solving a breakdown in the assembly line, or the custodial staff who linger during break to finish a game of cards. In different ways, these workers shape their concrete labors according to their personal motivations, realizing something of their fuller selves in the course of their labor time for capital. They mitigate their own alienation insofar as they resist the temporal and spatial limits prescribed by the law of value. The custodians claim back their time and good humor, while the autoworker's pride is a claim on the finished product. Indeed, Ursula Huws proposes that the model subject of neoliberal capitalism, the "creative" or "knowledge" worker, is especially likely to experience their job, at least some of the time, "as unalienated," as constituting

> a source of genuine satisfaction, creating a motive to work that cannot be subsumed into the simple economic motive of earning a living. The worker [cares] about the work's content (or intellectual property), which, even after it has been sold, may still be experienced as in some sense "owned."[31]

As for the concrete labor of raising children and maintaining one's self or household members, it too can be inflected with the same sort of personal attachments and pleasures. Helping a toddler learn to eat from a spoon is part and parcel of reproducing labor power, to be sure. It is shaped by capitalist temporalities (meals are scheduled and often rushed to accommodate the workday, for instance) and spaces (the child generally eats in private homes or daycares). But it can also be an overwhelmingly playful activity whose pleasure derives in part from the caregiver's and baby's efforts. Similarly, teachers who work with older children, introducing more abstract concepts in math or science perhaps, often feel a pride in and "ownership" over the child's *aha!* moments. The social reproductive labor of caretaking and teaching *is* subject to capitalist conditions of dispossession, and it is in a subordinate relation to processes of value production. But the "reproduction process" of creating a human being is inflected not just by capital's demand for future labor power; it is also, crucially, shaped by the personal needs and desires of the caretaker and teacher as well as the psycho-physiological needs and desires of the child. As such, it can be both more playful and less fully alienated.

The capitalist law of value then ensures that abstract labor dominates production, but it cannot ever fully subsume concrete labor. This dual nature of labor—the origin of abstract labor in concrete labor, and their lived simultaneity—is, David McNally reminds us, the crux of capitalism's internal contradiction and the reason it is prone to crisis. Labor is and must be attached to a living body, a body whose reproduction adheres to concrete times and spaces that the logic of capitalist reproduction necessitates but works nonetheless to extinguish. "Capital's drive to fully subsume labour, to instrumentalise it, to strip it of all embodiment and subjectivity, runs up against its dependence on concrete, living labour—sentient, embodied, thinking, self-conscious labour."[32] In other words, that body, and hence the concrete practical human activity it performs, exceed abstraction even as they are dominated by it. As John Holloway puts it: concrete labor exists—simultaneously—*in, against, and beyond* capitalist processes of abstraction.[33] Furthermore, insofar as bodies at play or engaged in concrete labor are absorbed in and retain some control over their conscious, practical human activity, they not only provide the basis for an immanent critique of capitalism but also signal an alternative to the mode of being upon which the reproduction of capitalism depends.

That is to say, then, that play is a form of concrete (social reproductive) labor that is, in many senses, freer (I'll come back to this term in a minute) than the form of waged and abstracted concrete labor (i.e., work) that directly produces value. It is also freer than the form of much unwaged concrete labor that goes into socially reproducing workers (i.e., household labor). This greater freedom has everything to do with the relative distance separating spaces and times of play from, on the one hand, workplaces where the dictates of value production straightforwardly privilege abstract labor over concrete labor, and on the other hand, from the sites and times of much social reproductive labor. The latter, although not directly dominated by the law of value—not directly disciplined by the logic of abstract labor-time valuation and appropriation processes—are nonetheless deeply inflected with this capitalist time-discipline.[34]

This relative distance allows for a less instrumentalized, more expansive form of conscious practical human activity. Freed from the direct discipline of the market and carving time and space away from those activities required to sustain the labor market, players engage the sensual and creative potentialities of conscious, practical human activity more, and more intensely, than do (productive and social reproductive) "workers." But their play is still social reproductive activity insofar as it is integral to the creation of present and future labor power.[35] It is simply the case that, being at some distance from the times and spaces of market compulsion, their activity is shaped more by the needs and desires of the (re)producers themselves, than by the dictates of capital. It is this, Marx tells us in the *Grundrisse*, which is essential to freedom. A "liberating activity," he writes, occurs as "the external aims become stripped of the semblance of merely external natural urgencies, and become posited as aims which the individual himself posits—hence as self-realization, objectification of the subject, hence real freedom, whose action is, precisely, labour"[36] (or, I might suggest, whose action is play/work). Much more can and needs to be said about the distinctions I'm proposing; in particular, we need to take a closer look at how concrete and abstract temporalities figure in play and other social reproductive activities. But the key point for the purposes of this paper is that play represents an alternative to—and because it is an alternative, also a potential resistance and challenge to—the instrumentalization and disciplining of concrete labor that is enforced by the law of value. Children's playful or praxic tendencies thus constantly butt up against the socio-political forces of capitalist subject formation. Children's negotiation of this dynamic also helps shape the sites of social reproduction of which they are both subjects and objects.

CONTESTED SITES OF SOCIAL REPRODUCTION: SCHOOLS AND THE WORK/PLAY CONTINUUM

A social reproduction feminist approach can challenge the reification of child subjectivities one finds in conventional notions of child agency while also pointing to how capitalist childhood, and thus children's subject formation, is central to the reproduction of labor power. It does so by theorizing labor power as an aspect of living, capitalist personhood. That is, it refuses to forget that a person's capacity to labor for capital does not exist separately from their potentialities and needs dictated by the reproduction of life as a whole. Life is lived and reproduced in and through multidimensional, concrete individuals. Thus—and this is crucial to developing a robust understanding of capitalist childhood *as well as* understanding capitalism—capital's demand for laboring subjects exists in tension with other dimensions of forming and reproducing life in general (dimensions which could be considered productive of the "good life"). This tension abides throughout the vast majority of people's lives. It is particularly evident, however, in childhood, because children are less subject to and less adapted to capital's direct demands. Indeed, in the Global North, childhood has been constructed such that children are at least partially sheltered from those demands.[37]

To take up the question of subject formation is to examine the individual in a way that acknowledges that processes of subject formation are not just sociological and political. They are also physiological and psychological. Thus while the state, for example, is a powerful force in our subject formation in that it restricts or outlaws certain ways of being in the world (sleeping on park benches, skipping school, disturbing the "peace"), so too are physiological and psychological impulses (pursuing pleasure, releasing aggression, loving and caring for others) that promote alternative ways of being or subjectivities. Children, who begin life under the sway of a powerful primary narcissism, only gradually attend to and learn to negotiate the wider world. As a result, the physiological and psychological processes of subject formation are especially relevant and influential in their lives. With this negotiation in mind, the final section of this paper takes a (highly schematic) look at one key site of social reproduction, schooling. I suggest that the perspective outlined above can enrich our understanding of the contested nature of schooling as a site of social reproduction.

With settlement of the "new world" came schooling, both private and (locally funded) public schooling. But it was only in the nineteenth century that a sizeable proportion of children (up to 50 percent in some US states from mostly white and better-off families) enrolled in public schools. Despite plenty of evidence that many working-class families preferred to send their children to schools rather than factories, the decision rested largely upon how much they needed the child's wages or their unpaid work as caregivers and farmhands. So while, for instance, by 1850 in Ontario, children of artisans were as likely to attend school as children of professionals and of other affluent families, their enrollment was not stable. It dropped considerably in subsequent years when a more mechanized economy threatened family livelihoods, creating new "unskilled" jobs for which children were considered well suited.[38] Economic compulsion also trumped legal compulsion, as mandatory-schooling laws passed in Canada and the United States in the 1870s had little effect on enrollment numbers. Only after the recession of the 1890s, during a new phase of capital combination and centralization and a surge in immigration lasting until the eve of World War I, do we begin to see a gradual and uneven decline in industry's demand for child labor. This—along with extended mandatory schooling legislation and reinforced truancy regulation—still only haltingly expanded enrollments. Schooling only became the norm for most children in the 1920s, a period of relatively sustained prosperity among "low-skilled" and "unskilled" working-class families permitted them to forgo the contributions of child labor wages.[39]

However much there is a mutually reinforcing relationship between schooling and child labor, clearly the former does not, *in any direct sense*, originate or develop as a function of capital's need for supplies of future labor power. Employers, in fact, generally opposed funding schools through taxation and compulsory-attendance legislation. The political will to establish schools—and then to compel children to attend—instead originated primarily with religious communities and civic-minded political reformers and was supported (albeit with considerable ambivalence) by many working-class families. While the motivations among and within these different groups varied, two dominant discourses prevailed throughout the century: those of child protection and child discipline.[40]

As my analysis will suggest, child-protection rhetoric and reform reflect a wider public sentiment that there is something very special about children. A growing romantic fascination with the child and childhood was consolidated among the bourgeoisie in the nineteenth century, arguably because the burgeoning numbers of middle-class children freed from the necessity of labor were given the space and time to display the "childish" ways of being in the world discussed above. It is the foreign yet strangely familiar quality of the child's interactions with the world that fuels this fascination, as the study of play morphed into social policies that promote and protect playful childhoods: kindergartens (partially inspired by Friedrich Fröbel's child studies in the 1830s and his German Play Institute) cropped up in European, North American, and British school districts, for example, while reformers convinced city councils to build (ill-used) urban playgrounds to protect children from the growing dangers of the streets. There was clearly something about children's participation in their newly emerging spaces of childhood that was both curious and inspiring to those who had the time and resources to ponder it—something about their playful way of being in the world that moved these adults to organize to preserve, develop, and protect it.

Yet that same fascination with the child was—as any fetish is—intensely anxiety-provoking. The work/play continuum children exhibit may well be celebrated but, for those middle-class scientists, reformers, and politicians and for the members of the working class who supported public schooling, it was something that must also be contained. "The child who resists, who preserves something against, the demands of cultural life . . . can thrust the spectator back towards the mute, but still agitating, states of being and mind in infancy and early childhood," suggests Vicky Lebeau in her work on the cinematic child. "Bordering on an otherness within, a space and time we have all known without knowing it, this is a child that must be left behind . . . [but with whom] we must too, continually negotiate."[41] Children's "excess" of sensuality and imagination (their "leaky bodies," to use Margrit Shildrick's evocative term) poses a threat to the given order of social reproduction—as was evident in the inflated reformer and popular discourse about street "urchins" and "lay-abouts."[42] Supervised playgrounds, summer camps, youth organizations, and schooling are all "solutions" to this supposed "problem." Meanwhile, those presumed to be the most sensual and "dirty" children (depending on the context, this could include girls, and black, Indigenous, working-class, and poor children, who therefore stoke the greatest fears) invite more severe forms of social control such as reform schools, prison, and other forms of discipline that deny them the opportunity to play and pursue pleasure. But for the most part, efforts to preserve, develop, and protect "childhood" are at the same time efforts to organize and control children's more playful ways of being in the world. "Protection," that is, is always at the same time "regulation." Individual employers and capitalists as a class may not be directly pushing for these policies, but plenty of people— from middle-class professionals to skilled and "unskilled" workers who have already adapted to and largely internalized capitalist subjectivities—know in their bones (if not always in their hearts too) how necessary it is to repress the sensual, creative qualities of living. They know that the reproduction of life depends upon the ability to earn a wage, which in turn depends upon learning one's way into capitalist subjectivities.

Schools (like all social reproductive institutions) were established to deal with the tension between children's pursuit of pleasure and the anxieties that pursuit elicited. They did so, in the first instance, largely through corporal punishment of "misbehaving" children and the policing of truants.[43] Today, with compulsory schooling more normalized, a softer discipline (backed up by legal force, of course) is generally adequate. This much has been well documented in many excellent analyses of schooling. But most such analyses assume rather than query that need for discipline. They don't usually ask, in other words, why children in particular require it, why it takes the forms that it does, or what it might indicate about schooling's relationship to capitalism that children in fact keep asserting alternative modes of being in the face of such punishment. Perhaps this is not surprising, given the hegemony of the ideology of child development that asserts that the transition from a willful, playful child into a rational, restrained individual is natural and inevitable. Yet when one questions the naturalness of this "progression," children's agency in provoking the disciplinary nature of schooling becomes more evident—as does the fuller purpose of such practices.

Schooling is fundamentally about disciplining children. But it is about more than that. Because they are not directly under the thumb of capitalist control, schools (and other institutions of social reproduction) can and do regularly make time and space to attend to the psychological and physiological impulses. They encourage children to tell stories, draw pictures, sing, play sports, and work together to solve problems, activities that are oriented to pleasure, affect, physicality, and sociality. As such, they stoke and preserve the sensual and imaginative life of the child in a way that the work world rarely if ever does. They actively cultivate, that is, alternative ways of being or subjectivities (while also working to repress these in other ways). To the extent that turn-of-the-century working-class parents and middle-class reformers perceived schooling as an alternative to child labor—notwithstanding other motives for educating their children—schools continued to be imagined as places in which the play/work continuum could be protected and even encouraged to some extent. The kindergarten movement secured this for very young children, and reformers like Maria Montessori, John Dewey, and others who introduced child-centered learning in the 1930s opened up possibilities for that continuum to be encouraged and safeguarded in older children, too. Ongoing adjustments in the official curriculum in most Global North countries can be understood as a struggle over the degree to which children can or should be encouraged to use these spaces of social reproduction to explore noninstrumentalized ways of being. We see in the early twentieth century, for example, that public education systems generally shifted from teaching Latin, grammar, and basic mathematics to incorporate lessons in music, visual arts, and sports. The current-day emphasis in many schools on "inquiry-based" learning also addresses and provides scope for children's more curious, creative, and playful relationship to the world.

This is not to say that such initiatives are not also simultaneously attempts to channel these open-ended childish energies into "productive" ends—they are—or that all children enjoy or benefit from them. Further, these initiatives never completely supplant or even overshadow the more work-like curriculum based on rote learning and standardized testing. Because capitalist social relations establish the terrain on which social reproduction occurs, there are real limits to the degree to which individual children and the institutions of social reproduction can allow expansive human needs and potentialities to flourish. But the point is that *both dynamics can be found within schools and other such institutions—precisely because the social reproduction of labor cannot be separated from the social reproduction of life and because children and childhoods are generally afforded a greater distance from the temporal and spatial compulsions of capitalist value creation (even as they are an essential condition to its reproduction).* Children themselves are thus constantly negotiating between their more sensual, imaginative subjectivities and the denial or repression of these. In the process they provide a window onto an alternative way of being that many adults recognize as valuable and something to be preserved, even fought for. Seen in this light, children are not powerless victims of a disciplinary educational regime. Rather, they are social negotiators whose playful ways shape the school systems that are essential to today's reproduction of labor power. That role, however, is deeply contradictory because, as children remind us by their alternative mode of being, labor power is not a thing. It is a capacity of concrete, potentially playful individuals whose needs and desires come into conflict with the capitalist impulse to separate play and work.

CONCLUSION

Institutional responses to that conflict—orphanages, schooling, the private family, prisons—tend by and large to discipline and disempower children. At the same time, because the social reproduction of labor does not take place under the direct control of capital and because children provide a window onto an alternative way of being, one that adults remember and are in fact also always repressing in order to maintain their own capitalist subjectivities—those institutions are also shaped by a noncapitalist impulse that prioritizes making space and time for meeting those expansive needs and inspiring those expansive potentialities. In other words, schools and families in particular are not simply reproducers of labor power. They are also reproducers of life. As such, they become sites of struggle over the types of determinations that will hold sway in the process of subject formation. Moreover, children themselves help shape their own social reproduction as they constantly negotiate between their more expansive, playful subjectivities and the denial or repression of these, as they too struggle to reproduce themselves as capitalist subjects. This negotiation is never resolved under capitalism. It cannot be resolved. But recognizing it is essential to understanding the nature of capitalist children and childhood and seeing capitalist children as producers—not just as consumers—of their world. Doing so not only valorizes children's (nonreified) agency but also highlights the possibilities for greater freedom in struggles to change our world.

7

Mostly Work, Little Play: Social Reproduction, Migration, and Paid Domestic Work in Montreal

Carmen Teeple Hopkins

INTRODUCTION

Feminist political economy has given us many perspectives from which to analyze social reproduction. Margaret Reid's *Economics of Household Production* (1934) was one of the first studies to critique the exclusion of unpaid domestic labor from statistical data collection.[1] Unpaid domestic labor has continued to be a crucial site of feminist inquiry to uncover the oppression of women in capitalist patriarchal societies. Yet Marxist feminists have been long divided on how to analyze the position of women in capitalism, notably on whether unpaid domestic labor is value-producing in the capitalist production process. Autonomist Marxist feminists Mariarosa Dalla Costa, Selma James and Silvia Federici argue that unpaid domestic labor has an exchange value while Margaret Benston, Lise Vogel, Paul Smith and others disagree, holding that unpaid domestic labor only has a use value.[2] While I side with the latter tradition, the autonomist Marxist feminists provide an important base from which to understand the necessity of unpaid domestic labor to the reproduction of labor power. Indeed, these autonomists were among the first people to raise the issue of unpaid domestic labor so we owe a debt of gratitude to the contributions of these activist-writers.

Currently understood in three principal ways, social reproduction refers to the biological reproduction of people (e.g., breastfeeding, commercial surrogacy, pregnancy), the reproduction of the labor force (e.g., unpaid cooking, caring and cleaning tasks) and individuals and institutions that perform paid caring labor (e.g., personal home care assistants, maids, paid domestic workers).[3] This definition has made important inroads to consider the ways in which race and citizenship status impact paid social reproduction. Indeed, working-class women of color and migrant workers perform many types of paid cooking, cleaning and caring tasks.[4] Often missing, however, from the recognized social reproduction canon are the analyses of Black feminists who have discussed both the unpaid labor of enslaved African American women during US slavery and the lack of attention to the paid domestic labor that many African American women performed in the post-slavery period, which continues today.[5]

In this chapter, I trace the conceptual lineages of unpaid and paid domestic labor in social reproduction theory (including Black feminism) to examine migrant work in contemporary neoliberalism in Canada. I argue that faith-based communities operate as an important site of social reproduction for migrant live-in caregivers whose homes (sites of reproduction) are also places of work (sites of production). Specifically, there is a spatial and temporal distancing of the spheres of production and reproduction for migrant caregivers to meet their own social reproductive needs. The empirical side of this chapter is based on the vignettes of two paid domestic workers in Montreal, Quebec. I interviewed four paid domestic workers as part of a study of 28 interviews with precarious women workers across industries and neighborhoods and anti-precarity activists in Montreal between 2013 and 2015.[6] Of the four paid domestic workers that I interviewed, two of them were from the Philippines and arrived in Canada through the Live-In Caregiver Program (LCP).[7]

This chapter unfolds as follows. First, I review the domestic labor debate as an entry point to then examine paid domestic work in the second section. Indeed, both unpaid domestic labor and paid domestic work share a characteristic: neither produces exchange value. My analysis of paid domestic work leads into a discussion of both the overlap and separation of the spheres of production and reproduction in this industry. I then introduce the Canadian context of paid domestic work and gendered migration through the LCP. In the final section, I build on both Silvia Federici and Barbara Ellen Smith and Jamie Winders to show how the church and church-based communities are integral to understanding many forms of socially reproductive support that the two paid domestic workers receive.[8] I conclude by using Cindi Katz's notion of countertopography[9] as a way for future research to compare the role of faith-based communities for racialized migrants in Montreal.

UNPAID DOMESTIC LABOR

In 1960s Italy, autonomist Marxists tended to focus on the role of working-class struggle against capitalists that was taking place in both factories and in communities, rather than emphasizing the importance of Communist Party politics.[10] The emphasis on worker autonomy and working-class struggle in what became known as the "social factory" instead of the factory workplace became front and center. The term *social factory* was coined by Mario Tronti in 1963, a leading Italian Marxist at the time.[11] Tronti established that productive work in factories, in Marx's terms, was insufficient to analyze the totality of social life. Accumulation was not only about production in the workplace as it was traditionally understood, but also about those who reproduced workers, i.e., labor power. The factory, then, was social, because the working class was "society as a whole" and the "working class had to be redefined to include nonfactory workers."[12]

Clearly, Tronti's work provided the occasion for Italian autonomist Marxist feminists to elaborate on reproduction.[13] In so doing, Mariarosa Dalla Costa and others had a significant theoretical and political impact within and outside Italy. Theoretically, they extended Tronti's work to develop a conception of unpaid work outside of the formal factory, demonstrating how the reproduction of labor power in the home underpinned capitalism.[14] Dalla Costa and James in particular argued for unpaid labor in the home to be valued and paid as labor. While Marx focused on the wage relation as central to capitalism, these feminists argued that women's work was the unpaid caring labor necessary to reproduce the wage labor force.[15]

Dalla Costa and James use Tronti's term, *social factory*, to situate it within the processes of capitalist production and reproduction from a specifically feminist standpoint:

> The community therefore is not an area of freedom and leisure auxiliary to the factory, where by chance there happen to be women who are degraded as the personal servants of men. The community is the other half of capitalist organization, the other area of hidden capitalist exploitation, the other, hidden, source of surplus labor. It becomes increasingly regimented like a factory, what we call a social factory, where the costs and nature of transport, housing, medical care, education, police are all points of struggle. And this social

> factory has as its pivot the woman in the home producing labor power as a commodity, *and her struggle not to.*[16]

To talk conventionally about work as factory production tells only half the story of life under capitalism. The other half consists of the reproductive sphere, and this sphere is not one of leisure. It is one of unwaged, labor-intensive housework that can also operate like work in the factory understood in the classical Marxist sense: cooking, cleaning, and caring for one's partner, children, and one's self.

Federici also refers to and expands upon *social factory* by focusing on social relations at home. The social factory "was centered above all in the kitchen, the bedroom, the home—insofar as these were the centers for the production of labor power—and from there it moved on to the factory, passing through the school, the office, the lab."[17] The feminist conception of the social factory thus exposed women's unpaid domestic labor and feminists formulated this idea concretely through the Wages for Housework campaign that began in 1972.[18] This campaign attributed an exchange value to unpaid domestic labor, thus embedding it within the capitalist production process.

A number of Marxist feminists disagreed with the autonomist Marxist feminist position that domestic labor produced exchange value.[19] This latter group of theorists argued that the line between work and leisure was porous. In Global South countries, for instance, it was difficult to distinguish between unpaid household labor and peasant labor carried out on farms for subsistence purposes. Did the gathering of water for household consumption count as subsistence or household work? It could be categorized as both. Moreover, neither form of labor produced commodities.[20] In many ways this argument generalized the inability to distinguish neatly between temporal and spatial categories of productive and unproductive work.

The malleability of unpaid domestic labor meant that a new set of relations—external to definitions of exchange value—were needed to understand unpaid domestic labor.

> If we want to recognize the contribution of caring and self-fulfilling activities to the well-being of society, we need a different type of analysis which resists the tendency to polarize. Not everything needs to be seen as either work or nonwork. Rather than reinforcing this dichotomy, by insisting that if women's contributions to society are

> to be recognized they have to fit into a category designed around the ways in which men enter into a capitalist economy, we need to transcend it.[21]

The task, then, is to go beyond the terms of production and reproduction in order to value and theorize unpaid caring labor.

An additional argument was the distinction between productive labor and socially necessary labor.[22] To be sure, unpaid domestic labor is socially necessary. Despite the primacy of this labor to capitalist relations of production, one did not need to define it as productive in the sense that it generated surplus value. The "reproduction of labor power," Paul Smith writes, "takes place outside the capitalist mode of production."[23] Put simply, unpaid domestic labor is not affected by changes in the market price of labor power when wages increase or decrease.[24] So while unpaid domestic labor is socially necessary for capitalist production because the labor force needs to receive care, meals, and emotional support, it cannot produce profit, nor is it affected by profit losses in the market.

While the domestic-labor debate is often considered the theoretical and political backbone of what is now known as social reproduction theory, black feminism has made important interventions that demonstrate how unpaid labor performed by African American women date to US slavery. Carmen Teeple Hopkins states:

> During U.S. slavery, there was a gendered division of enslaved labor where Black women performed field work with Black men but also domestic work that Black men would not do. Black women's labor as field workers, i.e. harvesting crops in fields, and as domestic workers, was devalued by Black men because it was seen as feminine … During this time period enslaved labor was unwaged for both women and men, yet women's labor often differed from that of men and was not considered as important. Black women's enslaved labor was thus central to both production and socially productive processes. Furthermore, since Black women worked outside the home in unpaid labor during slavery, the traditional public/private sphere division has not applied to U.S. Black women.[25]

US slavery changes the focal point of unpaid work to highlight the exploitation of enslaved African American women both in the homes and in the fields of white slave owners.

I have discussed three distinct traditions that analyze unpaid domestic labor. First, autonomist Marxist feminists hold that unpaid domestic labor generates exchange value and that the realm of reproduction is temporally and spatially separate from the sphere of production. Second, Marxist feminists define unpaid domestic labor only along the terms of use value. Finally, black feminists show that unpaid labor began during the transatlantic slave trade. They deconstruct the neat divisions of home/work time and private/public space: enslaved women could be asked to perform tasks at any time, and some women worked within the homes of slave owners while others worked in agricultural fields.

PAID DOMESTIC WORK: RACE AND MIGRATION

Social reproduction theorists have gone beyond the domestic labor debate to theorize a racial division of labor in paid reproductive work.[26] For example, surveys conducted on 97 women in Grand Rapids, Michigan, found that African American women were more likely to perform low-waged work (e.g. as nurse aides and childcare aides), whereas Anglo-American women often held higher-waged, skilled, and valued employment in positions such as nurses, mid-wives, and occupational health therapist assistants.[27] At a general level, reproductive labor is devalued; for racialized women, however, it is even further devalued.

When employers of contemporary paid domestic workers are families or households (versus agencies or companies), the employment relation is often grounded in the master-servant relations of historical slavery.[28] Although paid social reproduction is generally degraded, there are specific characteristics in paid domestic work for employers who are individuals or households that distinguish it from maid agencies, nurses, personal home care attendants, teachers, and janitors. Paid domestic workers tend to be socio-spatially isolated because they do not have colleagues, they are also not unionized and are often excluded from labor laws.[29]

Although migration is not new, the global movement of people arguably began at a large scale during the transatlantic slave trade; since the neoliberal time period of the 1970s, migration programs have interrelated employment and citizenship status.[30] Particularly since the 2001 war on terror, there is an increased disciplining of migrant workers who tend to be racialized in global north countries.[31] Migrants are tied to an employer and are removed from the respective country of employment if they lose their job. Many European welfare states exclude migrant workers from the social benefits of full citizenship,[32] a phenomenon that lowers labor standards for everyone.[33] Put simply, legalized forms of discrimination that entrench precarious work with precarious citizenship are fundamental features of neoliberal capitalism.

Neoliberal migration is gendered and has come to be known as the feminization of labor migration.[34] Women increasingly migrate globally for employment in paid domestic work, sex work, and caring work. As the demographic shift in Europe and North America means that more middle-class women are employed in the formal labor market and people are living longer, there is a need for workers to perform the cooking, cleaning, and caregiving tasks that middle-class women no longer wish to perform in the home.[35]

The economic contributions of migrant women workers to their countries of origin cannot be overestimated. At the scale of transnational social reproduction, women migrants often send remittances to their home countries as a way to compensate for the decline in state social provisioning following World Bank and International Monetary Fund reforms.[36] In fact, transnational social reproduction is key to understanding precarity in Global South countries, which have different histories than Global North countries due to colonialism and structural adjustment.[37] A case in point comes by way of the Philippines, a country that received its first structural adjustment program in 1980 and then two more from 1983 to 1985 and 1990 to 1992.[38] In 1977 remittances represented 1.7 percent of the country's gross domestic product (GDP); by 2015, remittances represented 10.3 percent of its GDP.[39]

Transnational gendered migration is also inflected with the social dimensions of race and citizenship. The racialized dimensions, however, differ based on context. In Canada, as in many Global North countries, there is often a racialized class difference, as migrant domestic workers tend to be women of color who hail from Global South countries while their employers are white middle-class families.[40] In contrast, in paid domestic work in Malaysia or Singapore, employers tend to be Malay and Muslim while domestic workers are Indonesian and Muslim, the latter "requiring complicated negotiations, using a finer mesh, of sameness as much as difference."[41] While the racialization of paid domestic work is pronounced in certain contexts and less so in others, a common thread is the precarious citizenship that these women experience often interlocks their place of employment with their place of home.

This interlocking of home and work has made paid domestic work a prime example of the overlapping spaces of production and reproduction. Migrant women may work as either live-in or live-out caregivers,[42] though the blurring of these two spheres is particularly visible when paid migrant domestic workers live in the homes of their employers, as they cannot leave the physical place of work at the end of the day.[43]

Federici specifies that this intersection of home and work is not necessarily straightforward. To be sure, paid reproductive labor in the United States and Europe is one sphere is which the distinction between production and reproduction is "blurred."[44] Federici counters this point by arguing, however, that women continue to do unpaid domestic labor in addition to paid reproductive labor; the spheres of production and reproduction thus remain analytically and politically distinct.[45] Although Federici would agree that the spatial overlap of home and work occurs for both live-in and live-out migrant workers, she argues that there is a temporal distinction between the work tasks placed on the migrant worker and the unpaid emotional labor that she provides to her own family and friends. Federici reinforces the need to understand production and reproduction as distinct categories to name and valorize the devalued reproductive labor that is necessary for capitalist accumulation.[46]

FILIPINX PAID DOMESTIC WORK IN CANADA

Let us consider the LCP. This program began in 1992 and was Canada-specific, making it mandatory for migrant workers to live with a family who would employ them for two years, at which point the worker could apply for permanent residency.[47] Instead of funding a universal national daycare program, the federal government used the LCP as a way to acquire "cheap" workers, creating a "market for low-paid, domestic labor."[48] This program initially relied on West Indian women from the Caribbean and then on Filipina women.[49] LCP work is insecure, non-unionized, de-valued, low-skilled, and poorly paid. It is also reminiscent of historical master-servant relations:

> many Third World domestic workers endure a minimum of two years of virtual bonded servitude, institutionalized through the federal government's foreign domestic worker program. The program

continues to attract applicants only because of the promise of gaining permanent residence status.[50]

In 2015 the Canadian government made it optional to "live in" as part of a massive overhaul of the Canadian immigration system.[51] The current program allows migrant women one of two options to gain permanent residency: (1) two years of live-in employment; or (2) 3,900 hours of full-time employment from a period of twenty-two months to four years. Each of these options excludes periods of unemployment and time spent outside Canada. We have yet to see the long-term repercussions of this reform. It is still possible, however, that migrant women who enter the LCP as live-out caregivers will endure exhausting labor conditions as any time spent unemployed if they choose to leave an overly demanding employer works against their application for permanent residency.

The number of live-in caregivers (LCG) in Quebec is disproportionately smaller in comparison to other Canadian provinces. One possible explanation is that there is a large and affordable public daycare system in Quebec.[52] Moreover, the Filipinx community in Montreal remains the most spatially concentrated in Canada. Filipinx tend to speak English; far fewer of them speak French. The combination of language barriers and the high number of Filipinx employed in British households as nannies and domestic workers or in hospitals may explain why they tend to live in one central neighborhood of Montreal, Côte-des-Neiges. Other racialized immigrant groups (such as Chinese, South Asian, and black) experience residential segregation to a smaller degree in Montreal.[53] Côte-des-Neiges is also adjacent to the upper-class anglophone neighborhood of Westmount, so women employed by Westmount families have shorter commute times. The concentration of the Filipinx community in Côte-des-Neiges suggests that an emotional and social sense of community is spatially bound.

THE SOCIAL REPRODUCTION NEEDS OF MIGRANT WORKERS: MIGRATION AND THE RELATIONSHIP BETWEEN SOCIAL REPRODUCTION AND PRODUCTION

While Silvia Federici considers the spatial overlap yet temporally distinct categories of home and work in paid domestic work,[54] a parallel argument is occurring in feminist economic geography. Barbara Ellen Smith and Jamie Winders argue against Katharyne Mitchell, Sallie

A. Marston, and Cindi Katz's position that the spheres of work and nonwork should be deconstructed.[55] Mitchell et al. use the examples of migrants who spend large amounts of time deciding on how to safely arrive at work and navigate intraurban movement.[56] In contrast, Smith and Winders argue that for working-class people, there is an increased distance between the temporal and spatial spaces of production and reproduction. This distancing is particularly noticeably for racialized and nonstatus members of the working class.[57] For instance, 2011 legislation in Alabama and Georgia criminalized many aspects of life, such as transporting, lodging or renting to nonstatus individuals, enforcing public schools to account for the legal status of their students, and allowing the police to stop any person believed to be nonstatus. When these laws were implemented after significant delays, there was a visible change in Alabama and Georgia. Notably there was a shortage of workers in agricultural production, migrant families left these two states and migrants were less likely to leave their homes and send their children to school out of fear of police profiling. Fewer people attended church, and churches cancelled events out of concern for their members' safety in public space. Indeed, these anti-immigration laws sharpened the distinction between public and private, work and home, and production and reproduction for migrant families in the southern United States.[58]

While Smith and Winders make a spatial and temporal argument against the blurring of the lines of work and nonwork, their methodology is not autonomist Marxist feminist, nor do the authors refer to autonomist Marxist feminism. Yet their argument extends Federici's emphasis on distinguishing between the spheres of reproduction and production. I build on Federici's theories as well as those of Smith and Winders to argue that even within paid domestic work that occurs in the space of the home—a form of work that spatially deconstructs the private sphere from the public—one can temporally and spatially separate the spheres of production and reproduction.

SETTING THE CONTEXT

This section uses the stories of Marie and Dawn, two Filipina women in Montreal, as vignettes to demonstrate the temporal and spatial stretching of their daily lives. These women were former live-in caregivers and are now permanent residents in Canada. They are shaped by their own past experiences with the LCP and harshly critique this program.[59] The use of these vignettes falls within the tradition of labor geography and feminist economics that rely on the experiences of an individual or a small number of individuals to provide a portrait of political-economic trends.[60] According to 2001 statistics, there were 25,000 domestic workers in Quebec: women constituted 87 percent, 80 percent were immigrants, and 80 percent of these immigrants were from the Philippines.[61]

Both Marie and Dawn requested that I interview them at their church in the neighborhood of Côte-des-Neiges. They attend the same church and are friends. Their church is predominantly Filipina women, many of whom are current or former live-in caregivers. I initially interviewed Marie, who then introduced me to Dawn. They invited me to join their church services on a few occasions, and each time I was the only white person in the space. Their church is located in Côte-des-Neiges, reflecting Balakrishnan, Ravanera, and Abada's findings about the spatial concentration of the Montreal Filipinx community.[62] Dawn also lives in Côte-des-Neiges with a roommate, while Marie lives in an eastern Montreal neighborhood with her white Québécois husband.

THE STRETCHING OF TIME

Marie is in her fifties and has been in Montreal for more than seven years. She works full-time as a domestic worker for a family, approximately forty-eight hours per week from Tuesday to Friday. On the side, she works two other part-time jobs that also involve cleaning and cooking. She is happy that she no longer lives as a caregiver with families:

> It's miserable when you are live-in. Because the employer, when you are live-in, tends to abuse your time. Any time they can wake you up, they can let you stay when they are outside, it's like working till seven [AM] until midnight. It's really hard. That's why I joined . . . an organization for caregivers.

Dawn moved to Montreal from Toronto in 2007 as an LCG and is now a permanent resident, working full-time as a domestic worker. Dawn tells me that, legally, domestic workers should only be working eight hours per day. If they work more, they should be paid overtime. In all of her work experience in Canada (with at least three employers), she's regularly worked one additional hour overtime without being paid. Despite Dawn's critique of unpaid overtime with these three employers, she tells me: "I always say yes, I don't complain." But she's never worked more than that one hour of unpaid overtime—that is where she draws the line. Many of the domestic workers that she knows in Montreal are frequently asked to work overtime; some work up to twelve-hour days (equaling four hours of unpaid overtime). Dawn knows the Quebec labor standards and has called the Labor Board to clarify her labor rights in the past. In all of the families she's worked for, she feels that people act superior. They say they love her and appreciate her, but Dawn feels that their comments are superficial.

In relation to one family for whom she worked for a month and a half, Dawn reflected: "they appreciate your work, but they don't seem sincere." For instance, this family never gave her breaks. They gave her leftover meals and secondhand clothes, yet would say, "You are family." The families, Dawn says, "think that you are a machine. I'm sorry to say that, but I experienced that." This treatment also lengthened her workday by not giving her the breaks to which she was entitled. After this family, she worked for another family for two years. For the first year, this family didn't give her any vacation days or holidays. She called the Quebec Labor Board to see if the family had to give her holidays; the second year they did.

Dawn and Marie's stories reflect the social reproduction research on migrant caregivers showing that employers frequently breach labor standards.[63] In a Montreal-based study that consisted of surveys with 148 live-in caregivers and focus groups with some of these caregivers, the focus-group participants reported that their contract outlined an eight-hour workday but that their daily workdays often exceeded eight hours. Even though a majority of the survey participants received lunch breaks, many worked "long hours without any respite"; almost half were not paid overtime. Slightly more than one-third of the survey participants mentioned occasions where they were not paid to watch their employers' children and 30 percent of the survey participants had used their own money to buy "items needed at work".[64]

The unpaid overtime of migrant caregivers reflects a temporal relation between the production-reproduction spheres. Let us recall Federici:[65] paid reproductive work in homes can be understood as a blurred site for the spheres of production and reproduction, but since women continue to perform the majority of unpaid household work, there is a rigid line between these spheres of production and reproduction.[66] Although one might argue that the overlap of the spaces of production and reproduction in the home is also temporal when employers breach labor standards and encroach on the unwaged socially reproductive time of paid domestic workers, I argue that workers themselves do not understand the violation of labor standards as a deconstruction of the lines between work and nonwork. Rather, Marie describes these occurrences as the abuse of her time; Dawn knows her labor rights, which affects the extent to which she performs unpaid overtime.

THE STRETCHING OF SPACE

One of the longstanding sources of support for Marie and Dawn is their church. Marie describes the emotional, social, and physical care that occurs through friendships at the church:

> If you are attached to a church, they will take care of you, especially when you are new. . . . Before, they take care of me. Now it's time for me to take care of the new ones. We give advice, whatever, from another employer to another employer so there's no employment [unemployment] in between, take care of them, food, whatever they want and need.

For Marie, the church plays an enormous role in social reproduction: Filipina women who arrived before her helped her to find work and cope with a new life in Montreal and gave her food and other things she needed. Now that she has been in Montreal for eight years, she has the knowledge, experience, and caring capacity to help newer women who arrive.

Dawn speaks in similar terms about the church but focuses on the emotional support that spirituality plays in her life. In addition to her full-time paid workweek, she spends twenty hours per week going to school to become an accountant. After her studies, she plans to leave domestic work to work in an office. When you work in the home, they treat you "like a slave." To cope with the stress, Dawn turns to her spiritual life: "Only God satisfies my heart." She has no family in Montreal, but has lots of friends here now who are her "spirit family." Sunday is her rest day; her relationship with the church and God is the "secret of my life." Similar to Marie, for Dawn the church plays a huge role in social reproduction, particularly through emotional support and family-like friendships to deal with work-related stress.

Marie and Dawn's relationships to the church reflect the scholarship on Filipinx caregivers in Canada that highlights the role of faith-based communities as a form of informal support.[67] Based on interviews with thirty domestic workers in southern Alberta, fifteen of whom are live-in, Glenda Bonifacio shows that domestic workers tend to rely on informal networks, not government programs, to care for themselves. In addition to faith-based communities, Filipina women also depend on Filipinx associations, friends, family members, and in some urgent cases recruitment agencies.[68] "Religion is inextricably linked with migration in the lives of Filipinx live-in caregivers in southern Alberta," Bonifacio writes. "Going to church gives them a sense of belonging and cultural familiarity of similar institutions found in the Philippines."[69] Church activities and spaces not only provide a sense of cultural inclusion for some Filipina women, but a way to experience caring labor that is not easily available for them as live-in caregivers.

I spatialize Bonifacio's argument that church activities provides an important source of informal care for caregivers by suggesting that the unpaid relationships between Filipina women at these churches provide the crucial support that women need to survive *socially* during their infrequent time away from work, *emotionally* amid difficult and exhausting work conditions, *physically* in situations when they must leave an employer's home and find immediate housing, and *materially* if they need financial support or a referral to a potential new employer during bouts of unemployment. Since the homes in which migrant caregivers live are sites of both employment and residence, churches can offer a safe and comforting space, something the workers do not necessarily receive in their own homes. Put simply, the physical location of the church means that spatial distance is crucial to the emotional, social, physical, and material well-being of migrant caregivers.

SITUATING A SENSE OF "HOME"

As live-in caregivers, Marie and Dawn did not find that the physical place of home felt like an emotional or spiritual home. Drawing on the Black feminist tradition, Doreen Massey tells us that "home" has not historically been a site of comfort and safety for enslaved African American women, but one of danger and exploitation:

> bell hooks argues that the very meaning of the term "home," in terms of a sense of place, has been very different for those who have been

> colonized, and that it can change with the experiences of decolonization and of radicalization. Toni Morrison's writing, especially in *Beloved*, undermines forever any notion that everyone once had a place called home which they could look back on, a place not only where they belonged but which belonged to them, and where they could afford to locate their identities. . . .
>
> There is, then, an issue of whose identity to which we are referring when we talk of a place called home and of the supports it may provide of stability, oneness, and security. There are very different ways in which reference to place can be used in the constitution of the identity of an individual, but there is also another side to this question of the relation between place and identity. For while the notion of personal identity has been problematized and rendered increasingly complex by recent debates, the notion of place has remained relatively unexamined.[70]

The feelings of danger, exploitation, and "slave"-like conditions in being tied to a work contract that is also one's home that emerge in Marie and Dawn's stories provide a contemporary analogy to the historical comparison of the slavery that Black women experienced. Indeed, the Black feminist tradition not only highlights that current domestic-worker employment relations are historically rooted in domestic slavery, but that an emotional sense of home is not necessarily located in a physical house.[71] Given the lack of safety and comfort in the home that migrant LCGs experience, they search for that emotional sense of home elsewhere. Church and faith-based friendships can provide this sense of home in a physical location outside the traditional boundaries of the home. While my argument builds on the need to distinguish between the spheres of production and reproduction[72] and the increasing spatial and temporal distances between places of home and work,[73] I externalize the location of unpaid social reproduction outside the home to church spaces. Indeed, for many migrant caregivers, their home is not a source of emotional support or safety, but one of workplace difficulty, danger, and exhaustion.

CONCLUSION

I have argued that despite the spatial overlap of the home as a place of employment and residence for migrant caregivers, there is a need to theorize the temporal and spatial aspects of the relationship between reproductive and productive work. Attention to the unpaid caring time and responsibilities of domestic workers illustrates that long work hours impede on the amount of time they can devote to their own social reproduction needs and that, when they do have time outside work tasks, they often attend church with other women friends. These faith-based friendship circles are significant to the giving and receiving of caring labor. While the paid employment of migrant workers in the service sector (particularly in domestic work) allows middle-class citizens to balance work and family obligations, migrant workers are not treated as having unpaid caring responsibilities and relationships of their own.[74] This chapter asks how migrant workers socially reproduce themselves and looks at faith-based spaces outside one's physical home as important sources of unpaid social reproduction.

It is worth interrogating the extent to which religious spaces outside one's physical home provide emotional, physical, material, and financial support for other groups of migrant women in Montreal. Let us take the example of Muslim migration. Montreal's immigration patterns differ from those in Toronto and Vancouver because French is its official language, meaning that there is a larger population from the Maghreb (Algeria, Morocco, and Tunisia).[75] Do mosques provide a level of socially reproductive support for women similar to that the Catholic church provides Filipina women? Cindi Katz is instructive for considering common points across difference.[76] Katz draws on the tradition of Marxist feminism to discuss the potential for political alliance across different places through her concept of countertopography. She reinterprets the traditional definition of topography, a cartographic term to describe physical landscapes; she then theorizes it as a multiscalar research method that examines the material world from the bodily level to the global. This materialist method of topography analyzes "natural" and social processes together to understand how both places and nature are produced.[77] The term *countertopography* uses the metaphor of a map's contour lines to link people in different places and to trace the connections between people under neoliberal globalization.[78]

Yet this countertopography is a politic, one that envisions the distinctiveness of a particular place while interrogating the shared capitalist processes that link these places. Katz asks, "What politics might work the contours connecting carceral California, sweatshop New York, maquiladora Mexico, and structurally adjusted Howa, and back again? . . . The prospects are tantalizing and the political stakes great."[79] Let us apply countertopography to the intraurban scale to consider the political contours that connect racialized migrants in Montreal as a way to not only link different groups of precarious workers, but to use social reproduction as a lens and as a way to connect people within the same city by focusing on religious spaces. Future research should compare religious spaces of both migrant and citizen populations to better assess the role of faith-based communities in providing social reproduction needs.

8
Pensions and Social Reproduction*

Serap Saritas Oran

INTRODUCTION

This essay aims to locate pensions in relation to the generational social reproduction of labor power. At first glance, pensions in the modern world appear as deferred wage payment to which the worker is to be entitled during retirement. Alternatively, pensions are accumulated in a fund as savings and returned to the beneficiary in their old age. Moreover, pensions are paid to people who are not entitled to any retirement scheme but are in need in old age. Finally, pensions are paid to relatives of the pension-scheme participant on the basis of kinship and dependency relations. These different pension arrangements show us that the structures, forms, and levels of pensions are diverse. This implies that they are not simply deferred wages or individual savings. In order to theorize pensions from a political economy perspective, we abstract them from different appearances and conceptualize them in relation to social reproduction processes and the value of labor power.

Marx defines *labor power* as a special commodity—the *capacity for labor*, which is found by the capitalist on the market and applied for production of surplus value.[1] According to Marx, this peculiar commodity, like all other commodities, has a value, and that value is determined "as in the case of every other commodity, by the labour-time necessary for the production of this specific article."[2] While, in this definition, the value of labor power is understood as the sum of use values that represent themselves in labor times, the other way to define it is by pointing out the correspondent value for sum of exchange values necessary for its reproduction: the wage.[3] However, none of these approaches is capable of explaining goods and services that have use value but not exchange value, such as reproductive household activities or state services, and those that do not have any use values but are

* This essay is dedicated to Nazenin.

part and parcel of modern daily life, such as art or luxury goods and services. In other words, labor power is not merely reproduced through goods and services that are produced within capitalist relations; it is also attached to noncapitalist provision and processes, such as state provisions and household labor. In this respect, we follow the argument that the value of labor power is attached to a *standard of living* that is necessary for the social reproduction of laborers outside the direct control, if not the influence, of production relations.[4] Therefore, one of the cruxes of the discussion here is the following idea: *The value of labor power is not merely the sum of labor time necessary for the reproduction of the individual worker's muscles and nerves. Rather, it is related to broader social reproduction processes that determine its value in relation to the capitalist class, the state, and the family.*

Marx mentions a "generational reproduction" aspect to the value of labor power, referring to children's expenses (including education) in terms of the reproduction of future generations of laborers. Yet, within value theory, what happens to the elderly (past workers) is mostly an overlooked aspect of the social reproduction of labor power. Clearly, pensions are neither a commodity nor a service that corresponds to labor time. Rather, pensions are old-age income used to exchange for sustaining materials after retirement. Thus, they are not directly part and parcel of *individual labor power* during the worker's career. In this regard, pensions are a component of the broader understanding of the value of labor power as a standard of living for the working class that consists of the payments and benefits necessary for generational social reproduction. These two positions—defining the value of labor power as a standard of living and placing pensions within it, in association with social reproduction processes—raise the questions of who is paying for pensions and out of which source pensions are paid.

My answer is that all pensions are paid out of surplus value produced by workers but appropriated by capitalists as a component of the total social product devoted to the social reproduction of the working class. In a nutshell, some of the total social product needs to be used to reproduce production relations, such as infrastructure, for future production processes. Some of this surplus value, on the other hand, is necessary for the reproduction of the working class: thus, social reproduction. To this end, I discuss Marx's insights in the *Critique of the Gotha Programme*, where he posits insurance funds in relation to the reproduction of the working class.[5] Here, Marx distinguishes between economic and social reproduction and places the "poor relief" of the time as a form of social reproduction of nonworkers. Extrapolating from this point of view, pensions are associated with the socialized costs of the means of consumption of the nonworking members of the working class. This understanding of pensions refers to the broad literature on social reproduction in the sense of biological reproduction, reproduction of the labor force, and caring activities in the household, as well as child and elder care, while the latter becomes increasingly important.[6]

Moreover, in light of the historical development of pensions, it is clear to see the diffusion of capitalism as the underlying mode of production that creates the necessary and sufficient conditions for the emergence of pension systems. In a similar vein, the role of class struggle in increasing living standards, including old-age security, is a substantial factor. In some contexts, the instrumental use of establishing pension schemes to attract political support has been a fundamental mechanism underlying the pension system. Thus, pensions' emergence as part of the working-class standard of living is an outcome of mixed historical developments and factors such as class struggle to sustain the living standards of the working period, at least partially, during retirement, as well as capitalists' effort to tie workers to production relations in a more stable and long-term fashion. By the same token, pensions are used as part of political arguments that favor capitalism as an ideal system and those that aim to prevent unrest, as in the case of Bismarck (discussed below).[7] In other words, as the historical development of capitalist relations shows us, the nonworking members of the proletariat have increased in significance in a way that requires systematic old-age income, resulting in the need to socialize the costs of social reproduction of the elderly. In this sense, the state's formation as a nation-state is one of the elements determining how the costs of social reproduction will be shared among many capitalists through taxes on surplus value; this is evident from the fact that the most prevalent pension provision structure is public pay-as-you-go (PAYG).

Looking from this angle enables us to understand the recent reforms in pensions. Increasingly, in the last three decades, with the involvement of the World Bank, the pension schemes of more than thirty countries have been altered to decrease the significance of the public-PAYG scheme, as opposed to increasing the importance of financialized schemes—that is, individual funded pensions. The main difference between these two pension arrangements is that the former uses the state (taxation) as the intermediary mechanism for sharing the costs of reproduction of the elderly, while the second scheme relies on financial markets. Most analyses recognize the potential effects of this alteration, though they limit their scope to discussing privatization. As a contribution to the literature, this study analyzes pension reforms in the context of financialization, which attaches ever more aspects of economic and social life to financial conduits. I argue that recent pension reforms signify the financialization of old-age income: that is, the penetration of finance into social reproduction processes.[8] In this regard, pension reforms should be understood in relation to the neoliberal attack on the funds necessary for the reproduction of the working class in general and generational social reproduction in particular. How much these funds are squeezed depends on the class struggle to preserve the living standards of active members of the labor market as well as retirees. Beyond the varying effects of financialized pension provision on different sections of the working class, it is an undeniable fact that integrating old-age income into the fictitious mechanisms of the financial sphere puts pensions at stake while providing new profit-making opportunities for finance capitalists. In a nutshell, the financial sphere, where money capital circulates, has a fictitious character, which means that financial instruments' values are regulated differently than the value of the real capital underlying the paper.[9]

First, I review the factors underlying the emergence and spread of pensions as a right. This historical background reveals the factors underpinning the systematization of old-age income: capitalists try to get rid of these costs even it is not for their sake in the long run. It is crucial to see the transformation of the state within neoliberalism and finance's increasing replacement for state mechanisms as a factor underlying recent pension reforms. In the next section, I scrutinize what the value of labor power means in relation to social reproduction processes. I introduce Marx's insight on the old-age income of his time in the context of pensions as part of generational social reproduction. I continue with a sketch of recent transformations in pension schemes that shrink the intergenerational financing mechanisms while advocating individual funded pension schemes. I conclude with the argument that the overall pension-reform campaign is part of the neoliberal attack on the working class.

HISTORY OF PENSIONS, WELFARE-STATE DISCUSSIONS, AND POSITING PENSIONS FROM A POLITICAL ECONOMY PERSPECTIVE

Pension systems emerged at the eve of the modern age; before then, elderly people who were unable to work were looked after by their families. In the absence of families or relatives, local solutions provided a modest old-age income for those in need: for instance, religious institutions, charities, and mutual benefit friendly societies provided help, including in cases of sickness and for funerals.[10] In ancient Greece and Rome there were some social aids, such as income for the families of slain warriors and modest income for those unable to work.[11] The Guild of St James in London is believed to have established the first medieval income scheme before 1375.[12] Local initiatives to help elderly in need took varied forms: in France, *mutualité*; in Britain, "friendly societies"; in the Ottoman Empire, *teavun sandigi* (helping foundations) or *orta sandigi* (center foundations).[13] General public aid to the elderly was not available until the enactment of the first English Poor Law in 1587.[14]

With modernization, the idea of a universal pension for all citizens emerged and found expression in the second part of *The Rights of Man*, by Thomas Paine, in 1792.[15] Occupational pensions were in progress as well, and the first examples were introduced as a very modest civil-service scheme with the 1834 Superannuation Act in England.[16] It is important to note that the emergence of pensions was not because of employers' humanitarianism, as argued by some authors.[17] Rather, the real underlying reason was labor's struggle for reliable, steady old-age income. For instance, the UK Trade Union Congress began pushing pension demands in the 1890s because elderly workers were accepting lower wages, and that decreased the power of the union in wage bargaining. In other words, the history of pension provision is full of strikes and protests for pension rights.[18]

What is crucial in this context is the diffusion of the capitalist mode of production and creation of the proletariat as a distinct class. This is because, by comparison with agricultural labor, industrial production is less likely to allow for elderly people to work.[19] Moreover, around the 1880s, friendly societies' actuarial tables fell into deficit because of the increased length of life under development of medicine. However, this was accompanied by chronic illnesses such as tuberculosis, cancer, and respiratory and circulatory diseases stemming from the impure air and dirt of industrial cities.[20] People were living longer than they could work, but desperately needed a systematic old-age income. The first known pension fund was established in 1862 by the Bank of South Wales in Australia. It was followed by the American Express Company in the United States.[21]

Pension provision remained uncommon until Otto von Bismarck established the first universal pension system in 1889 in the German Empire. It was not directly a product of capitalism but of fear of socialism. Bismarck saw social-insurance measures, including old-age pensions, as a way of convincing workers not to support the Social Democratic Party.[22] In a nutshell, his program relied on the contributions of workers and firms. The pension income was very modest, the retirement age was high (seventy), the contributions were invested in financial securities, and the scheme did not have any redistributive features.[23] Nevertheless, other countries followed the German example: Denmark in 1891, New Zealand in 1899, and Britain in 1908, when Lloyd George introduced the Old-Age Pension Act.[24] Asbjørn highlights the historical context of trade-union movements and welfare states, both novel phenomena that emerged from industrial capitalism for several reasons:

> Industrial capitalism led to the tools and the means of production being taken over by the factory owner, the capitalist, while the workers were left with only their labour power, which was thereby transformed into a commodity on a labour market. The workers responded to this in two ways: first, by organizing themselves so as to weaken or neutralize competition between them on the labour market, and second, by establishing and struggling to put collective insurance schemes in place which meant that people were financially compensated if they were not able to take part in measures designed to reduce the negative effects of labour having become a marketable commodity.[25]

Thus, the emergence of pension provision has been the result of a mix of factors: the diffusion of capitalism, which destroyed the family and property relations that enabled elderly people to survive; workers' class struggle of for higher living standards, including security for old age, and the struggle between different political parties that appealed to pensions as an instrument for gaining support. As a result, during the postwar era, pensions became a substantial element of social provisions in almost every country with developed capitalist relations.

The Great Depression of 1929 was a turning point for the spread of all kinds of social programs, not least pensions. Since the Depression led to massive unemployment, which necessitated social measures, establishing state-funded pension plans and expanding the existing pension benefits were part of these measures.[26] During the postwar era, most countries offered a mix of public and private systems, following Sir William Beveridge's argument for "the necessity of contributory principle for a sustainable pension provision" in his famous report in 1942.[27] The Beveridge Report favored maintaining the existing pattern of funding pensions by national insurance based on flat-rate contributions and benefits.[28] It aimed to systemize the costs of supporting working people by spreading those costs through intergenerational transfers.[29] Systematizing pensions alongside other welfare services' prevalence necessitated the delayed conceptualization of the welfare state.[30]

Heterodox scholars approach the concept of the welfare state from various perspectives.[31] One is the *logic of industrialism* approach, which argues that welfare states develop due to the underlying logic of industrialization; therefore its key determinants are the changing forces of production. This approach is useful for pointing out that, as the process of industrialization continues, it creates new needs for public spending by reducing the functions of the traditional family and by dislocating certain categories of individuals such as the young, the old, the sick, and the disabled. Since the traditional ways of caring for vulnerable individuals do not exist under capitalism, the state expands to fill the gaps. Thus, the demographic and bureaucratic outcomes of economic growth are regarded as underlying reasons for the emergence of welfare states.[32] This view, however, is overly simplistic in disregarding historical and cultural elements within individual countries. Focusing on "automatically developing processes" neglects the importance of the class struggle.

The *capitalist development* view argues that social policies are the responses of states to the social reproduction requirements of capitalism. According to this, welfare-state policies are imposed by the contradictory imperatives of the capitalist mode of production, which creates the conditions for capital accumulation but also provides social legitimation of ruling classes. In this context, the welfare state consists of two sets of activities: state provision of social services to individuals or families in certain circumstances (social security, welfare, health care) and state regulation of private activities that alter the conditions of individuals within the population, such as benefits to personnel in key positions, such as military forces. This school of thought posits that the welfare state developed on the basis of capitalist development and class conflict, thus moving beyond the simplistic logic of the industrialization approach.[33]

Last, *power-resource theory* emphasizes the role of distribution in capitalist democracies. The adherents of this view see social policies as being driven and shaped by representative structures and electoral processes under the influence of social parties.[34] They suggest the welfare state is an outcome of, and an arena for, conflicts between class-related socioeconomic interest groups such as political parties, trade unions, and employer organizations. Adherents of this approach mainly focus on the redistributive effects of the welfare state, while claiming conflicts between interest groups to create distributive processes in the sphere of market and decreasing inequality and/or poverty.[35] This approach places significant emphasis on the role of class struggle. Because after the 1980s working-class power decreased under the pressure of government attacks, its impact on the changes in welfare regimes is of key relevance given the role of class struggle in those regimes' development.[36]

History illustrates different appearances of pensions as part of the welfare state's services, generating social security during old age and basic income for elderly people in need. These functions are accompanied by several management structures and ways of financing, such as funding or intergenerational transfers (PAYG). In each case, to varying extents, pensions are determined by factors associated with wages, though they also depend on elements that go far beyond wages.[37] Moreover, pensions are not enjoyed by all retirees at the same level of living standards. They vary across the population according to certain groups' positions within labor markets.[38] Future or current pension income can be altered with changes to calculations of benefits and indexation methods as well as in taxation. In a similar vein, pensions change under different schemes according to wage level, as well as according to the contribution of employers, workers, and the state. Thus, they differ with inflation and other monetary and real factors that change standards of living irrespective of the wage level. The impact of a pension, as an income stream supporting life in old age, is embedded within other aspects of social and economic reproduction, such as provisions for health and housing. So, what *is* a pension when we strip away all of these different considerations? It is an element in the living standards of workers that is necessary to enable the generational social reproduction of labor power.

LABOR POWER, SOCIAL REPRODUCTION, AND PENSIONS

Labor power is a special commodity that workers sell and capitalists buy in order to apply within the production process.[39] As we have seen, Marx argues that the value of labor power is determined by the labor time required to produce the commodities necessary to reproduce labor power. However, not all commodities necessary for the reproduction of labor power are produced through capitalist relations and thus have values that can be measured in necessary labor time. Some are produced through noncapitalist relations, such as those of the family, or are provided by the state. Moreover, reproducing labor power is not an individual process; it includes generational reproduction—that is, future workers. When Marx refers to the replacement of "muscles and nerves," he does not only mean one individual's physical capabilities, but that these should be replaced intergenerationally through the social reproduction of future workers: children.[40]

In this sense, past workers' reproduction is also embedded in the conditions of reproduction of labor power. Thus, value of labor power cannot be defined as an individual wage level. Rather, it refers to a material standard of living related to the broader social reproduction of the working class, as Marx makes clear:

> Such primarily economic analysis needs to be complemented by a second aspect of the value of labour-power: the notion that the consumption bundle so provided suffices for *social reproduction* of the work-force. The work-force does not depend solely upon a wage but is engaged in activity outside the place of employment, thereby involving the *state, the household and other social relations*, structures and processes more generally.[41]

This interpretation of value of labor power and social reproduction relation is crucial to understanding how the state, society, and family relations form labor power in modern capitalist relations. It is thus urgent to specify what *social reproduction* means.

Social reproduction is a broad term mainly applied by the feminist political economy literature in order to analyze the biological reproduction of human beings and caring practices within the family and/or through social provisions. Since most of this literature emphasizes the role of female unpaid labor, it is the best way of understanding the reproduction of labor power as the broader implication of social reproduction processes, mechanisms, and institutions.[42] Biological reproduction consists of activities related to childbearing—the development of the labor force—with women deemed commodities to be consumed for procreation purposes. Another aspect of social reproduction is the reproduction of labor power through workers' daily maintenance as well as the education, training, and care of future workers.[43] The final aspect of social reproduction literature focuses on caring practices that go beyond the labor process but have their own intrinsic value: childbearing, but also elder care. All three aspects are important in terms of defining how the value of labor power is reproduced.

Marx explicitly indicated that value of labor power contains the expenses for future generation workers and for the reproduction of the labor force. From Marx's point of view, under capitalist relations, the value of labor power has to include the reproduction of the labor force: the costs of raising children. Otherwise, the future labor force will not be adequate, which will increase future wages and decrease surplus value.[44] Marx's understanding of the reproduction of future workers is related to the concept of the reserve labor army, which keeps the wage level under control. If the reproduction of the workforce becomes excessive, the reserve army of the workforce would be too crowded, so the wage level would decrease and the workforce would again shrink.[45] Thus, the reproduction of future workers has a significant role in determining the value of labor power.

By the same token, it can be argued that the costs of provisioning and caring activities determine the value of labor power. In the case of the one-breadwinner model (in which one member of the family, generally male, is the only one working outside the home, even though there are other adults present), the value of labor power has to sustain the rest of the family, generally women, who take care of the inside-family work. This has a dual impact on the value of labor power. It increases the wage levels of individual workers in a way that covers the costs of reproduction of the entire family, but decreases the wage level compared to the private sector. Obviously the influence of provisioning activities on the value of labor power depends on how much of this is undertaken by a family member who works outside the house and *also* undertakes unpaid reproduction activities in the household—as is widely discussed in the feminist political economy literature.[46]

In the case of pensions, the issue is more complicated because pensions are not directly part and parcel of the reproduction of labor power. However, in the absence of a systematic old-age income, elder care costs might be part and parcel of household expenses. Or, on the contrary, pensioners' income might be a mitigating mechanism for the rest of the household, especially in the case of a backslide in living standards due to a crisis, as in the case of Greece. Therefore, whether part of a family or not, the elderly require a certain level of pension that functions as a systematic distribution of the costs of social reproduction. Then the question is from which source these costs are generated. Pensions are paid from the total social product necessary for the social reproduction of the working class. I base this argument on Marx's discussion on fair distribution in the *Critique of the Gotha Programme*.[47] Marx highlights the costs of elder care as part of the social reproduction of the working class, which is paid through the total social product.[48] According to him, the total social product consists of three different parts: the replacement of expended means of production; : the replacement of labor power, and the surplus value appropriated by the capitalist class and implemented for the expansion of production. In this regard, what is allocated for the working class's needs depends on the necessities of the class as a whole. In other words, not only the reproduction of labor power but the reproduction of future generations as well as previous generations' survival are considered part of the reproduction of the class. Therefore, the fraction of the total product used for means of consumption is related to the social reproduction of the working class. Marx writes in *Critique of the Gotha Programme*:

> First, the general costs of administration not belonging to production. This part will, from the outset, be very considerably restricted in comparison with present-day society, and it diminishes in proportion as the new society develops. Secondly, that which is intended for the common satisfaction of needs, such as schools, health services, etc. From the outset, this part grows considerably in comparison with present-day society, and it grows in proportion as the new society develops. Thirdly, funds for those unable to work, etc., in short, for what is included under so-called *official poor relief today*.[49]

It is important that Marx brings forward the poor relief of the time, because those benefits are the ancestors of what we now call *social assistance pensions*. Therefore, it can be argued that pensions are part of the means of consumption provided to sustain social reproduction. Moreover, the only source of pensions can be the current total social product; the class struggle in the political sphere determines how much of the total social product will be devoted to social reproduction. That explains why in different times, according to different strengths of the working class, capitalists attack to decrease pension levels by changing the parametric rules for eligibility or indexation. Indeed, as we see in the next section, the recent pension-reform trend highlights the political success of the capitalist class in suppressing the costs of social reproduction through changing pension levels.

My position here contributes to and benefits from the political economy literature on pensions in relation to the reproduction of labor power and in the context of welfare-state provisions.[50] However, at the same time, my approach divorces from social wage and decommodification conceptualizations by analyzing welfare-state provisions, in both cash and services, in the context of the *social wage*, which not only enables the reproduction of labor power but also maintains the nonworking population.[51] However, the concept of the social wage has two contradictions with the Marxist political economy on which it claims to be based. The first is the relation between the social wage and the value of labor power. Gough argues that the value of labor power in the modern welfare state equals the social wage, which is the expanded wage that consists of welfare benefits in cash alongside individual wages. Therefore, the value of labor power is not equal to wages. Instead there is an exchange of nonequivalents: workers earn more than the value of their labor power. This approach is problematic because the value of labor power can only be exchanged for an equivalent wage, and the capitalist's payment of wages involves the money wage, which has equivalent value for the purchase of labor power.[52] Moreover, according to Gough, welfare services are financed by direct and indirect taxes to working-class population. In this regard, nonworking members pay taxes through consumption (indirectly), whereas workers pay income taxes out of their wages. Therefore, welfare services are horizontal income transfers from different groups of the working class, rather than being vertical, inter-class flows.[53] Gough uses this argument to show how different tax implementations can change whether or not the capitalist class or the working class undertakes the burden of the costs of welfare services. Despite good intentions, this position is open to dispute because, from a Marxist point of view, all taxes are a tax on capital. Workers cannot pay tax, as they are paid the equivalent of their value of labor power and a permanent divergence in wages from this level is not sustainable. Thus the "social wage" concept is far from adequately positing welfare provisions, including pensions, from a political economy perspective. The main advantage of this approach is its attempt to connect welfare services to a broad understanding of reproduction of labor power.[54]

Another significant attempt to relate welfare provisions to labor power is Esping-Andersen's concept of the decommodification of labor power.[55] The term *commodification* refers to workers' dependence on the sale of their labor power for survival. According to this, workers themselves become commodities when they must rely on their labor power for survival and compete with one another to sell their labor power. This pure commodification of workers is characteristic of capitalist relations, which create a working class that owns no means of production.[56] In this sense, the social rights granted through welfare services loosen this pure-commodity status by enabling workers to live without selling their labor power. Providing old-age income decommodifies elderly people in different ways. For instance, with social assistance pensions, rights are not attached to work performance but are granted on the basis of need. With social insurance pensions, on the other hand, there is a strong relation to employment status and rights. Thus, pension income is related to labor-market position of the worker during their career. Pension benefits can also be organized in the form of universal rights, which depend on citizenship rather than need or labor-market status. Esping-Andersen identifies all these implementations of old-age income provisions as different levels of decommodification in modern welfare regimes.

However, this approach also has a problematic relationship with the concept of labor power it applies. The value of labor power is analyzed as a concept related to the reproduction of individual workers. Accordingly, workers are decommodified for having old-age income during retirement because they are commodities during their careers. However, there are kinship and disability pensions in addition to universal pensions, which are separate from the individual commodification process. In other words, pensions are social rather than individual outcomes. Therefore, there is a need to relate them to labor power with an emphasis on social reproduction. In Esping-Andersen's framework, the concept of the value of labor power does not have any specificity; it refers to the value of labor power of the worker before and after retirement as well as the value of labor as an individual wage payment, but also some social provision benefits. That is why retirees who do not need to work are decommodified whether or not this is directly related to their commodity status during their careers. In a similar vein, if a woman gains the right to kinship (dependency) pensions on the basis of her husband's career earnings, this is not related to her reproductive contribution for all those years as an unpaid houseworker.[57]

In other words, pensions cannot be an individual decommodification mechanism and refer to social reproduction in a broader sense, because pensions are paid to the worker after she performs her reproduction and thus gains a certain standard of living during her career. This is an ex-post payment, from an individual worker's perspective. Although pension has a strong relationship to the worker's wage level during her career, it is also determined by factors that interact with broader issues of social reproduction, such as health, education, and housing. Let us consider, for the sake of illustration, a worker who is promised a very generous retirement income as part of wage negotiations while the working-class movement is strong. When the worker retires, a big financial crisis shakes the world and devaluates the generous pension pot promised to the worker thirty years before. Does this mean the value of this worker's labor power has decreased? No. It is paid while the worker, as an individual, is serving capitalist relations. However, a general change in pensioners' income might cause a reduction in working-class living standards. For instance, in Greece after the crisis, the main intention has been to decrease wages; comparatively high levels of pension income have become the main income source for households with a retired family member. However, after a while, those retirees' benefits were also decreased due to austerity measures. This does not mean that the value of their labor power has been altered; it signifies a deterioration in the living standards of the working class as a whole.

There are several advantages to political-economy discussions on welfare services, in particular pensions, such as how they associate these services with the reproduction of labor power. Moreover, considering commodification is significant in terms of pointing out the different positions of state-labor-market relations. However, these approaches are unsatisfactory when it comes to answering who exactly benefits from welfare services and who pays for them. In order to address these questions, social reproduction theory has developed a framework inspired by previous discussions but which brings forward a new perspective that defines pensions in relation to the social reproduction processes that affect the value of labor power, alongside other systemic factors. For this purpose, I posit the concept of social reproduction of the working class, which is broader than previous understandings of the reproduction of labor power. Then I specify why pensions with other social policy instruments influence the value of labor power.

My argument is based on two pillars. First, social reproduction is not only about current workers' daily reproduction. Rather, children, the sick, and the elderly are part of this process on the basis of the intergenerational principle. Therefore, the material living standard of the working class consists of both the value of labor power of workers and social reproduction, such as education, health, or housing benefits. The second pillar is that the resources used for social reproduction processes are not related to individual labor power's returns. Rather, they are part of the total surplus value produced by the workers and appropriated by the state from capitalists and used for providing means of consumption to the working class (alongside means of production for capitalists). In this regard, the generosity of welfare services is contingent upon current production of surplus value, class struggle over these funds, and political relations between the state and different classes. This framework sheds light on the recent transformations in pension schemes while considering the social reproduction implications of the involvement of financial actors in pension provision.

ANALYZING RECENT CHANGES

The recent trend in pensions is characterized by finance's increasing role. This trend started with Chile's pension privatization in 1980, on the advice of Milton Friedman's "Chicago Boys."[58] After the country's PAYG state scheme was completely replaced by compulsory funded schemes, the individual financial scheme spread around the rest of Latin America and into many post-Soviet countries.[59] The World Bank, along with other international financial institutions such as the International Monetary Fund, was predominantly influential in the pension reform campaign with its breakthrough 1994 report, *Averting the Old-Age Crisis*.[60] According to the report, the world population is aging; the best way to cope with budget deficits related to the increasing number of retirees (compared to workers) is to privatize state pensions and leave pension provision to the market, not least financial conduits.[61]

Following the World Bank's advice, more than thirty countries either introduced funded schemes or strengthened the existing financial component of their pension systems.[62] Moreover, in line with the argument that pension schemes are not financially sustainable, eligibility rules were tightened while the retirement age was increased and more contribution dates required for entitlement. The indexation of benefits and calculation methods for pension income were changed to decrease replacement rates so that future pension income would be much lower than current levels.[63] The reforms were achieved in a comparatively short period, mostly without significant opposition due to the complicated nature of pension rules, which make it difficult to foresee the results of such alterations.[64] As a consequence, pension income from the state PAYG schemes has shrunk while individual responsibility to invest in financial markets for old-age income has increased.[65] Therefore, government authorities and international financial actors recommend that individuals register for funded schemes in order to compensate for losses to the nonfinancial pension system.[66]

On the basis of this development, I argue that this change in pension schemes is underpinned by *financialization*, the intensifying integration of finance into ever more areas of economic and social life.[67] The financialization literature investigates the extensive and intensive growth of finance in the production and reproduction processes. Slow rates of economic growth, increasing significance of financial activity within national economies, and a rising proportion of financial profits within nonfinancial companies' revenues are some of the implications of the financialization of production processes, raised by several authors in the literature.[68] Nevertheless, moving beyond economic issues and addressing the social-reproduction-related outcomes of financialization, as Fine does, is a rare and vital approach:

> In particular, not only has the presence of finance grown disproportionately within the direct processes of capital accumulation for the purposes of production and exchange, it has also increasingly intervened in less traditional areas associated with what might be termed social as opposed to economic reproduction. This extends beyond housing (and mortgages) to an increasing range of elements previously provided by the state.[69]

The financialization of pensions is a significant example of this phenomenon, but it is also present in education, health, and other areas of daily life. Thus, while households increasingly reproduce themselves with the intermediation of financial mechanisms, financial actors redefine social reproduction areas as profit-making areas.[70] In this context, it can be argued that the allocation of a certain fraction of the total social product for the social reproduction of the working class is increasingly undertaken by financial actors rather than the state. Naturally, this has far-reaching consequences from the working class's point of view. The most important implication is that the concrete boundary between social product and social reproduction through taxes is loosened, while the social product is tied to the fictitious capital of the financial sphere. Therefore, the relation between the social reproduction of the working class and the production of value is stretched so that workers are not connected to their product through their class position. Rather, the return from pension contributions becomes dependent on the financial markets' profitability. In other words, regardless of what a worker puts into the pension pot, what she gets is an unknown outcome of financial market forces. For instance, while workers entitled to a pension during the 1990s (the heyday of the financial markets in the Anglophone countries) were lucky, those who retired after the massive 2008 crisis were unfortunate and lost much of their pension savings.

This is especially because, while the state was responsible for undertaking social reproduction activities through appropriating surplus value from capitalists, the political sphere was suitable for demands for better material living standards.[71] However, the same cannot be said for financialized intermediation. For instance, in the case of a funded scheme, even though the worker contributes for years, the return depends on the circumstances of the financial markets. Therefore, a pensioner who retires right after a huge financial crisis is just *unlucky* for accruing half of the pension benefit she was expecting before.[72] In this case, there is no one to blame for bad management and no platform to continue political struggle. This is a completely *individual* matter; the authorities might even accuse the pensioner of investing in risky assets. In this sense, having an adequate pension income depends on one's ability to cope with financial risks.

Moreover, individualization accompanied by financialization turns social rights into debts and beneficiaries into debtors, while rights are understood as securities.[73] This results in a crucial change in employees' and their unions' understanding of pension provision, now financialised and no longer a social right, but rather a sort of investment that is deeply contingent upon financial-market performance, as Deken notes:

> "Financialization" . . . expands the role of financial motives, financial markets and financial institutions in the operation of the pension system. It is a change in the funding of retirement that also has also far reaching repercussions in the way that pensions are governed. If the accumulated assets of pension schemes are invested through the intermediation of the financial services industry, the monitoring of the performance of those assets on financial markets becomes a "life strategy" for people from all walks of life. They are then led to adopt the identity of a "self-disciplined investor subject." "Financialization" of retirement provision thus leads employees and their trade union representatives to stake their long-term welfare on the ability of the finance industry to reap high returns on investment.[74]

Moreover, recent pension reforms have exacerbated the social-reproduction-related problems of disadvantaged groups within the working class, such as workers who are unemployed occasionally and those who are employed informally. These vulnerable groups benefited from the redistribution mechanisms of the PAYG state schemes in the past. However, with individual funded schemes, it is hard for these groups to gain access to an adequate pension income. They confront crucial difficulties in terms of contributing to funded pension schemes, which mostly appeal to middle- and high-income earners.[75]

Most significantly, women are worse off as a result of funded pension schemes compared to PAYG ones, which include many inter- and intragenerational redistribution mechanisms. Thus, while women with interrupted careers can compensate for their losses through maternal-leave subsidies or kinship pensions through the PAYG schemes, most of the funded pensions are gender-neutral and individualistic in a way that abolishes kinship rights.[76] Although some argue that financial pension provision is better for women because it pushes them to join the labor market, this fails to understand the real reasons women cannot benefit from an adequate pension income. In a nutshell, the structure of labor markets which do not welcome women or do not provide equal income for them are the main underlying reasons of lower pension benefits of female retirees. In effect, this problem even exacerbates with the funded schemes in which women almost always contribute less than men for earning less than male workers.[77]

All these developments have severe consequences for class struggle, as individualization abolishes the collective logic behind social reproduction processes.[78] Every worker has to negotiate privately for rights such as unemployment insurance and welfare assistance that were previously held collectively on the grounds of class interest.[79] Indeed, what party would even negotiate for an increase in pension funds? Authorities suggest that workers should contribute more and invest in riskier assets with higher returns. Unions are also very disadvantaged when it comes to negotiating for financialized social reproduction rights. For instance, occupational pension funds, which are often established or run by unions, can become a political instrument in the hands of financial capitalists, who can threaten workers with the loss of pension benefits if they go on strike, if their pension funds mostly invest in the employer's assets. This complicated ownership status harms class struggle by creating an illusion of tradeoff between current wages and future old-age income.[80]

Therefore, it can be argued that the financialization of social reproduction and pension income is related to the political struggle over means of consumption. The source of means for social reproduction is surplus value. However, how much of this surplus value is used for the needs of the working class depends significantly on political struggle. To be clear, I do not refer to class struggle as a way of shared ownership through pension funds in the sense of a "democratizing finance" agenda.[81] Consider the example of the Meidner Plan in Sweden, which ended up using employees' old-age savings as an instrument for prevailing neoliberal financial expansion.[82] Rather, I refer to class struggle to suggest that pension provision should be completely detached from any fictitious financial mechanisms.

This position is grounded on the literature on financialization, which shows that financialized pension schemes, through *pension funds*, play a substantial role in deepening the financialization of economies via three channels:

- With their dominance in capital markets as institutional investors that promote shareholder value and changing the way in which corporations are governed.[83]

- Through capital inflows to capital markets, which causes asset market inflation and results in increasing financial-market instability.[84]
- As a consequence of their logic of funding, which provides demand for speculative financial instruments.[85]

Indeed, case studies frequently refer to these mechanisms to explain the key function of pension funds in intensifying financialization. For instance, Macheda argues that pension funds played a decisive role in financializing the Icelandic economy through two conduits:[86] the money-capital flow into national and international markets, which resulted in inflation in asset prices, thus causing asset values to rise significantly; and the increasing demand for pension funds with short-term yields as a consequence of maturity. Thus, pension funds became involved in riskier speculative circuits. Theurillat et al. discuss the financialization of the property sector in the context of Swiss pension funds, which were involved in property as financial players between 1992 and 2005.[87] Decisions made by pension funds structured the property sector in a financialized way. Belfrage examines the impact of pension funds on workers in Sweden after the public pension reform in 1999,[88] when decommodification and solidarity principles were replaced with self-responsibility for pension income. The increasing complexity of the financial products puts at risk the target of securing a high material living standard during retirement.

In 2016, for example, the minimum wage in Turkey after taxes was increased by 30 percent. Yet, with the new level of income, minimum-wage earners would be classified in a higher income-tax group; thus the substantial amount of the wage increase would be repaid to the state as income tax. In addition to this development, the privately funded "individual pension system" was made mandatory; a certain percentage of the minimum wage is thus appropriated by the financial pension scheme. Hence, most of the raise will be taken back in the form of tax and financial pension scheme contribution. This point is important because it confirms approaching the value of labor power as a living standard rather than as welfare payments or cuts to social security. It shows that, whatever the amount paid to workers, their living standard only increases in relation to broader processes of social reproduction. This demonstrates the significance of class struggle for workers to improve their living conditions. In the absence of that, the value of labor power will be altered, explicitly or implicitly, by financial or nonfinancial interventions, as in the case of the financial pension schemes.

To sum up, my position on pension reforms in relation to financialization contributes to the social reproduction literature, which sheds light on deteriorating working-class living standards under the influence of neoliberal policies. In effect, the capitalist class's efforts to reshape pensions might not necessarily target abolishing old-age income, but they are doing so in a novel way that pushes certain groups within the working class to secure old-age income through financial conduits while also creating new profit-making opportunities for financial capitalists. Financialized pensions do not have the same impact on all groups of the working class; they sometimes benefit high-income workers through wealth effects, as in the 1990s United States.[89] Nevertheless, it is certain that for the growing bulk of workers with low-waged, flexible, and/or insecure work, financialized pension provision will result in much less income security in retirement. Hence, while workers' old-age savings create lucrative profit opportunities for financialized capitalists, the capitalist class in general enjoys the decreasing burden of social reproduction expenses in the form of either less tax or diminishing contributions to workers' retirement pots.

CONCLUSION

The reproduction of the working class takes place in different countries within varying structures, forms, and levels of provision,[90] depending on what Marx calls "moral and historical elements"[91] demonstrated in relations across capitalists, labor, and the state.[92] Pensions' emergence is systematic and internal to capitalist production relations, but pensions did not automatically develop out of capitalists' needs. Rather, they are part of social reproduction processes that are essential for and complementary to production relations. Pensions belong to a specific component of reproduction: the generational reproduction of labor power. As opposed to the generational reproduction of future workers (children), pensions, which constitute the generational reproduction of the previous generation of workers, might be seen less essential than other provisions. There are further important factors underlying pensions' emergence and spread to be found in their historical progress as one of the cornerstones of state provisions in general and welfare-state services in particular.

Pensions emerged as a basic human right due to working-class struggle which challenged capitalist dispossession relations for the right for security and sustenance for those no longer capable of working. Moreover, it is clear that systematizing pensions is closely related to the evolution of nation-states as an intermediate agency and relation for socializing the costs of capitalist production and social reproduction processes by taxing surplus value. Therefore, a pension income, which would be either uncommon or unsatisfactory if left to individual capitalists' own initiative, has become a prevalent and crucial element of social rights.

Indeed, when looking at recent developments within pension systems through this lens, we see that pension entitlement is being transformed. With the involvement of international financial institutions, not least the World Bank, solidarity and class-related gains are replaced by self-responsibility.[93] While longer contribution periods and lower pension benefits are projected for all workers, for nonworkers—particularly women confined to domestic labor—pensions based on kinship are rendered more vulnerable. Longer lifespans, one of the main reasons for pension income being adopted as a necessity (alongside the need to avoid social unrest, create political alliances, and tie workers to the workplace), has become the flagship argument of pension-reform advocates. However, this does not change the fact that the social reproduction of workers, including the generational reproduction of previous workers, is even more crucial than before. Pension reforms signify the capitalist class's endeavor to decrease their responsibility by putting the burden of retirement on the shoulders of the working class. This can be done only in one way: by decreasing the living standards of the working class while squeezing funds for social reproduction. This might result in currently working individuals taking responsibility for the care of previous workers by limiting the resources necessary for their own reproduction.

On top of this, financial conduits have become more important in pension provision. This is attached to the financialization of the social reproduction process, which is a specific example of the deeper integration of finance into more aspects of economic and social life. Recent pension reforms point to financial markets as the most efficient, reliable, and favorable way of delivering old-age income. For these reasons, approaching pensions from a social reproduction perspective is of paramount significance for shedding light on the class implications of the financialization of pension reforms.

While the structures of pension systems have changed with the international financial institutions' (IFIs') pension-reform campaign, their forms have also been altered; old-age income is now considered a financial investment. Pensions' relation to social reproduction, and thus capitalist production relations, is loosened, while old-age income becomes a matter of individual investment and a safety net for elderly people in poverty. One of the IFIs' main arguments during the reform campaign was that funded pension schemes would contribute to the extent and depth of capital markets, improving savings levels and accelerating economic growth.[94] This is a completely novel mission for pensions, which previously were not seen as functional for financial markets; the main concern was their role in providing for the elderly. Now pension-reform advocates are concerned with pensions' impact on capital markets, and thus the production sphere, rather than on social reproduction. In order to secure social rights for reproduction, social reproduction processes should be detached from financialization. For this purpose, strengthening the class struggle for the right to social reproduction is of crucial importance.

9
Body Politics: The Social Reproduction of Sexualities

Alan Sears

INTRODUCTION

Feminist, antiracist, anticolonial, and queer struggles since the 1960s have played an important role in transforming the social spaces of sexuality, though in different ways around the globe. These changes are so profound that they are casually referred to as the "sexual revolution." In Canada and some other places in the Global North, LGBTQ people have won equality rights and a new cultural prominence, women's sexual agency is more widely acknowledged, sexual assault and violence against women are publicly identified as social problems, eroticism is expressed more openly, and transgender people are winning greater rights.

Yet the reality of gendered and sexualized lives after the sexual revolution is not one of genuine emancipation. The real world of sexuality is framed by silence and violence. Breanne Fahs argues that real sexual liberation must include both freedom to engage in rich and mutually satisfying sexual relations *and* freedom from sexual coercion or violence.[1] We are still a long way from meeting either of those criteria.

The sexual revolution did not overturn the dominant normative sexualities but rather shifted their bounds. Heteronormativity has continued to shape acceptable sexual practices, but its bounds have shifted to include nonmarital heterosexual relations, same-sex couples, and some degree of trans rights. In this article I do not discuss the specifics of bisexuality or discuss the range of queer expressions of gender and sexuality in rich detail. The focus here is more on the general dynamics of sexuality in relation to capitalist reproduction, but this leaves a great deal of necessary discussion and inquiry outside the bounds of this chapter.

In this chapter, I argue that the social reproduction frame provides important tools for understanding the persistence of heteronormativity through the process of the sexual revolution. It locates sexuality within a broader set of social relations through which people make lives, specifically the organization of production and social reproduction. The barriers to full sexual liberation lie not only in the limited visions that guide movements toward equality rights as sufficient grounds for freedom, but also in the broader relations of life-making that frame our everyday work, household formation, leisure, and community activities.

The impoverished vision of sexual freedom that has been produced through the sexual revolution is grounded in the relations of "free" labor under capitalism. Members of the working class are free in that they own their own bodies, yet are subjected to systemic compulsion because they must sell their capacity to work in order to gain access to the basic requirement for subsistence. The combination of consent and compulsion that underlies basic labor relations under capitalism also shapes the realities of sexual freedom within the bounds of that system.

CAPITALISM AND HETERONORMATIVITY

Heteronormativity has been changed but not eliminated by the sexual revolution of the past sixty years. Berlant and Warner define *heteronormativity* as the "project of normalization that has made heterosexuality hegemonic."[2] It refers to the practices and ideas that frame a specific, institutionalized heterosexual orientation as normal, making it the reference point around which all forms of sex and intimacy are assessed. This institutionalized form of heterosexuality is represented as the pinnacle of human sexuality, "from which everything else remains a falling away."[3] Heteronormativity naturalizes and eternalizes culturally and historically specific forms of sexuality, framing particular household forms and divisions of labor as products of human nature and as necessary foundations for a healthy human society across time.

Jonathan Ned Katz describes the eternalization at the core of heteronormativity when he argues that heterosexuality is "constructed in a historically specific discourse as that which is outside time."[4] The term *heterosexual* was developed in specific social conditions in the late nineteenth century, and only after *homosexual* had been coined to name a same-sex orientation. The conceptual development of heterosexuality was one component of the development of heteronormativity as a mode of sexual regulation.

The development of new terms did not summon new ways of being sexual, but rather named ways of life that were already emerging. Katz wrote, "I *don't* think the invention of the word *heterosexual,* and the concept, created a different-sex erotic."[5] The naming of these forms of sexuality was connected to efforts to regulate the ways of life brought about by capitalist relations, specifically the social reproduction of "free" labor.

Sexuality is framed by the matrix of social relations that organize life-making in any society. The rise of capitalism brought about a fundamental restructuring in ways of work and life that transformed personal life in important ways. Indeed, the development of sexuality—the formation of identities around erotic preferences (such as "lesbian")—is a product of capitalist social organization. In noncapitalist societies, a variety of forms of sexual practice (whether same-sex or other-sex oriented) tended to be integrated into the dominant form of kinship relations, which was the basic mode of organizing human life-making activity. Under capitalism, as we will discuss below, human productive activity was dramatically reorganized in ways that created contradictory forms of sexual freedom connected to the emergence of "free" labor.

Foucault argued that sexuality, understood as a distinct realm of human activity separate from biological reproduction, appeared in the eighteenth century: "Between the state and the individual, sex became an issue, and a public issue no less; a whole web of discourses, special knowledges, analyses, and injunctions settled upon it."[6] The deployment of sexuality marked the rise of a new form of "bio-power" that combined "disciplines of the body" with "the regulation of populations" to form "the entire political technology of life."[7]

In Foucault's analysis, sexuality entered history when it was deployed as a strategy of ruling. The trajectory he traces for the deployment of sexuality corresponds in important ways to the rise of capitalism. Foucault focuses specifically on sexuality as a regulatory power from above. Here I will use the Marxist-feminist social reproduction frame to provide a different view of the rise of sexuality, seeing it as a contested response to the new social relations associated with the rise of capitalism. Sexuality developed as a set of practices as people made lives in the context of developing capitalist relations. The emergence of sexuality was both a product of strategies of ruling from above (for example, legal measures outlawing male homosexuality and prostitution) and mobilization from below (such as struggles around access to abortion and contraception, as well as the rights of sexual minorities). Sexuality is shaped around the relations of exploitation and oppression that characterize capitalism yet, at the same time, demonstrates the potential for liberation.

One of the important aspects of the rise of sexuality was the development of social identities based on the orientation of desire (homosexual or heterosexual). Gayle Rubin writes, "The idea of a type of person who is homosexual is a product of the nineteenth century."[8] It was only after the homosexual, the person who specialized in same-sex desire, was named that it became necessary to name the taken-for-granted dominant form of desire as "heterosexuality."[9]

John D'Emilio developed an influential explanation for the connection between capitalism and the rise of the homosexual as a type of person. This explanation fits well with the basic focus of the social reproduction frame: "Only when individuals began to make their living through wage labor, instead of as parts of an interdependent family unit, was it possible for homosexual desire to coalesce into a personal identity—an identity based on the ability to remain outside the heterosexual family and to construct a personal life based on attraction to the one's own sex."[10]

Peter Drucker developed this understanding further with his important conception of same-sex formations within capitalism. One of the most important features of capitalism as a mode of production is its dynamism. Drucker links processes of capitalist restructuring to the development of a succession of different same-sex formations, each grounded in a particular organization of work, community, and politics at the local, national, and global levels. A *same-sex formation* is "a specific hierarchy of different same-sex patterns (like transgender, intergenerational and lesbian/gay patterns) in which one pattern is culturally dominant (if not necessarily more prevalent)."[11] The restructuring of capitalism in the Global North has created the conditions for the development of three different same-sex formations: the *invert-dominant* (roughly 1870-1940), the *gay-dominant* (roughly 1940-1990) and the *homonormative-dominant* (roughly 1990 to the present).

The invert-dominant mode was characterized by a tendency toward homosexual relationships organized around polarized identities, such as gender (e.g., butch/femme), class (e.g., working class and bourgeois), or racialized/imperialized status (e.g., colonizer and "native"). It was only the gender non-conformists (feminine men and masculine women) who tended to identify as members of a sexual minority in these relations, while gender conformists often fit in to the dominant ("normal") order. The gay-dominant mode saw the more culturally influential model of relationships shift to a less polarized form: for example, two women or men with roughly similar gender identities. It also saw gay and lesbian identities grounded in sexual orientation begin to separate off from transgender identities based on gender nonconformity. This separation has become even more established in the homonormative mode, where the recognition of partnership and/or marriage rights has begun to create an important distinction between socially acceptable forms of lesbian, gay, and (to a lesser degree) trans identities and other forms of same-sex or gender nonconforming practice that were highly stigmatized.

At the core of Drucker's work is the argument, "the correspondence between regimes of accumulation and same-sex formations provides evidence for a basic historical materialist assertion: the material relations of production and reproduction constitute the fundamental matrix underlying all of social reality."[12] This matrix of relations of production and reproduction frames our experiences of sexuality and of our bodies. The social reproduction frame provides crucial tools for locating sexuality within this matrix of social relations.

"FREE" LABOR AND SEXUAL FREEDOM

Capitalism prepared the ground for the rise of forms of sexuality that combine freedom with compulsion. Freedom of sexuality under capitalism is based on the social reproduction of "free" labor, as the working class under capitalism is distinguished from other subordinated classes through history in that workers can lay claim to formal ownership of their own bodies. Yet the freedom of labor based on self-ownership is necessarily combined with forms of compulsion. Workers do not own or control the means of production and therefore must sell their laboring capacities to those who do in order to gain access to the necessities of life. Further, free labor itself does not replace, but develops in relation to, forms of unfreedom including slavery, colonization, incarceration, and statelessness or undocumented status.

In each form of class society, the ruling class uses specific methods of domination to control the living labor of the toiling classes. Landowners in tributary modes of production control peasants through extra-economic means, such as armed force and mobility/employment restrictions that tie the toilers to the land.[13] In this mode, the members of ruling and subordinated classes are seen almost as different species bound by very different rules. In contrast, members of the working class in capitalist societies own their own bodies and therefore live in apparent freedom and formal equality.

This freedom, however, is far more limited than it seems. Members of the working class may control their own bodies, but they have no immediate access to subsistence requirements. It is the capitalist who own and control the *means of production*, the technical term to describe the key productive resources in society such as land, patents, mineral rights, and workplaces ranging from factories to mines to offices. Members of the working class can obtain food, shelter, and other subsistence requirements only if someone in the household can get a wage (or equivalent) by selling their capacity to work. Marx described this as a paradoxical double freedom:

> The worker must be free in the double sense that as a free individual he can dispose of his labor-power as his own commodity, and that, on the other hand . . . he is free of all the objects needed for the realization . . . of his labor-power.[14]

Sexuality in capitalist societies is organized around this paradoxical double freedom, in which control over one's own body is always combined with forms of compulsion. We have to be dispossessed of our control over our bodies in order to comply with the requirements of exploitation through selling our capacities to work for less than the value of what we produce. This dispossession has two key dimensions. First, it requires that the key productive resources be taken from our control. Marx saw this as a violent process of expropriation that created the working class, who were stripped of control over any productive resources aside from their own bodies:

> These new freedmen became sellers of themselves only after they had been robbed of all their own means of production. . . . And this history, the history of their expropriation, is written in the annals of mankind in letters of blood and fire.[15]

The history of blood and fire meant that people starved after being kicked off the land or died in the genocidal colonizing projects associated with capitalism and slavery. This process, which Marx dubbed *primitive accumulation*, produced a class of "free, unprotected and rightless proletarians."[16] Marx saw this as a historical process that created the working class in the first place, occurring at different times around the globe. Once workers were expropriated, Marx believed the economic need to obtain their subsistence by selling their capacity to work would discipline workers: "The silent compulsion of economic relations set their seal on the domination of the capitalist over the worker. Direct extra-economic force is still of course used, but only in exceptional cases."[17]

However, extra-economic force has proven to be a more resilient characteristic of capitalist societies than Marx might have anticipated. Despite being brutally separated from control over the means of production through a process of primitive accumulation, workers necessarily get their hands on these means of production in order to labor and reproduce. This creates a potential challenge to the control of the ruling class that is actualized as workers develop capacities for counterpower. The process of dispossession must therefore be ongoing to reestablish effective control over the means of production for those who formally own them. Dispossession is therefore connected to ongoing contestation and resistance from below. As Geoff Bailey writes, "Dispossession is not something separate from, but part of, the process of expansion and exploitation, and the struggles against them are not separate spheres that need to be bridged but struggles that are deeply interlinked."[18]

Further, the working class is not a single flat category of potential toilers who own their own bodies while being dispossessed from control over the means of production. Feminist and antiracist writers have understood dispossession as an ongoing and differentiated process, producing a working class that is organized around gender, colonization, and racialization. Divisions of labor are grounded in differentiating processes of dispossession and subordination.

Italian Marxist-feminist Sylvia Federici has developed an approach to dispossession that emphasizes its continuous and differentiated character. It is not enough to deprive workers of ownership over key productive resources; it is also necessary to take away effective control of their bodies on an ongoing basis. As part of this subordination, the gendered division of labor works through specific processes to deprive women of control over their bodies and compel them to socially reproduce free laborers. She argues against the idea of primitive accumulation as a one-time event that established the grounds for the modern capital-labor relationship, positing instead that it was an ongoing feature of class formation:

> A return of the most violent aspects of primitive accumulation has been accompanied in every phase of capitalist globalization, including the present one, demonstrating that the continuous expulsion of farmers from the land, war and plunder on a world scale, and the degradation of women are necessary conditions for the existence of capitalism in all times.[19]

Federici argues that dispossession produced "a new sexual division of labor subjugating women's labor and women's reproductive function to the reproduction of the work-force."[20] This was accomplished through specific forms of violence, silencing, and debasement that created vulnerability and dependence among women. Thus dispossession produced not only a new working class but also "a new patriarchal order, based upon the exclusion of women from waged work and their subordination to men."[21]

Rosemary Hennessey argues that this patriarchal order is produced, in part, through processes of abjection that systematically devalue certain categories of human and certain kinds of work: "In devaluing some bodies, abjection helps to produce subjects who are worth less—that is, subjects who forfeit more of themselves in the labor relations that produce capital."[22] These devalued humans perform and are identified with degraded forms of labor. In capitalist societies, for example, caregiving tends to be systematically devalued. Hennessey defines *caregiving work* as "the both paid and unpaid care work of feeding, child care, elder care, and housework that enables the predication of the wage worker."[23] Rather than being highly valued as crucial to human being, caregiving—whether paid or unpaid—is taken for granted and under-recognized. This has much to do with the way it is privatized in capitalist societies and seen as a personal concern of working-class families. This has a huge impact on the lives of women, who bear most of the weight of caregiving. For women, "motherwork and housework have a negative bearing upon their relationship to paid labor."[24]

The orientation of women's work disproportionately around caregiving has a lot to do with the way production and social reproduction are organized in capitalist societies as different moments in the cycle of life-making. In other modes of production, social reproduction and production are bound together in a single set of social relations organized around kinship. In contrast, in capitalist societies there is a separation between household and workplace.

Members of the working class own their own bodies, and therefore the responsibility for sustaining themselves and their households falls on their shoulders. This responsibility is essentially privatized and separated from the public sphere of social production. Working-class women are thus dispossessed both as members of the working class and as reproductive workers. Even in paid work, women's wages will tend to be depressed due to the devaluation of caregiving labor (where rates of pay are pulled down through association with unpaid labor in the home), presumptions of bounded competence, and the responsibilities of the domestic sphere, whose worth is connected to the unpaid character of much of their labor.

Dispossession is thus differentiated within the working class. Different categories of workers are not simply interchangeable units, but will tend to be located differently in terms of divisions of labor and paid in relation to the degree of their dispossession.[25] This differentiated dispossession is racialized as well as gendered and has been produced through histories of colonization, racialization, and slavery.

Angela Davis argued that histories of slavery have meant African American women are more likely to be pushed into paid work and heavier forms of manual labor than white women: "During the post-slavery period, most Black women workers who did not toil in the fields were compelled to become domestic servants."[26] This is a form of differentiated dispossession that had a profound impact on the character of social reproduction. African American families tended to look different and did not conform with the heteronormative standards established through the lens of whiteness. Roderick Ferguson notes, "As racial differences in how people make a living affected domestic life, producing increasingly diverse forms of family, family became an index of those differences."[27]

The social reproduction frame, with its broad view of life-making, provides important insights into differentiated dispossession. Marxist feminists put a particular emphasis on the analysis of social reproduction, as too often Marxists have emphasized the realm of paid employment and virtually ignored relations in the household. Many Marxists thus have not put much importance on the unpaid work done mainly by women to keep the working class alive and raise children. As Johanna Brenner argues, "Marxists have focussed their attention almost entirely on the production of things. Marxist feminists have broadened this notion of necessary labor to include the care and nurturing of people—we use the term 'social reproduction.'"[28]

Social reproduction is a crucial feature of ongoing cycles of interchange with nature—the process of replenishing what is used up in the activity of production. People need rest, food, leisure activities, and social engagement to sustain their ability to work. Children and those who are not well need caregiving. Lise Vogel points out that the reproduction of labor power is a crucial element of social reproduction: "Some process that meets the ongoing personal needs of the bearers of labor power as human individuals is therefore a condition of social reproduction, as is some process that replaces workers who have died or withdrawn from the active work force."[29]

SEXUALITY AND ALIENATION

The social reproduction frame casts light on the specific ways life-making processes are organized under capitalism. People do this work on nature in very different ways depending on how their society is organized and the specific environmental circumstances in which they find themselves. Some humans have lived in relatively small bands that harvested nature through hunting and gathering to meet their needs. The ways of life of those who plant seeds and domesticate animals tends to be very different than that of foragers; for example, they can form larger communities and are generally less compelled to move for fresh resources.

At the most basic level, all life forms derive sustenance from their environment, and higher life forms work in various ways on their surroundings to get what they need. The work humans do to survive has much in common with the work that bees, giraffes, or dolphins do, but also one important difference: humans plan this work and make deliberate choices about the ways we transform nature and meet our needs. Beehives may be much more beautiful than certain structures humans build, but "what distinguishes the worst architect from the best of bees is that the architect builds the cell in his mind before he constructs it in wax."[30]

Humans base their production on intention and choice in a way that no other species does, as far as we know. These deliberate choices make an enormous difference in our life-making work compared to that of other species. Other species interact with their environments in ways that are basically set, through a combination of instinct and a limited repertoire of learned responses. Human work is potentially much more open-ended; we make numerous choices along the way in our engagement with nature. Hunger is a biological drive and we work on nature to satisfy those requirements, but, unlike other species, we do so in many different ways. Some humans are vegetarians and others eat meat, even at times in the same household. This kind of variation is not present in the same way in other species.

Each nonhuman animal produces “only in accordance with the standard and the need of the species to which it belongs,” while humans produce creatively, “in accordance with the standards of every species” and applying “the inherent standard to the object.” Humans, therefore, “also form objects in accordance with the laws of beauty.”[31] Other species may produce more beautiful things, but only humans develop specific goals for taste, appearance, and feel. Our work on nature not only satisfies our needs but generates new needs. Marx and Engels distinguished between primary sustenance needs, such as nutrition, and secondary ones produced through our work on nature, writing that “the satisfaction of the first need, the action of satisfying, and the instrument of satisfaction which has been acquired, leads to new needs; and this production of new needs is the first historical act.”[32]

We realize our humanity through our work on the world, understanding work in the broadest sense of the mental and physical transformation of nature to create things, concepts, and interactions. People make their life activity “the object of [their] will and of [their] consciousness.”[33] While other animals only produce to meet immediate needs, “man produces even when he is free from physical need and only truly produces in freedom therefrom.”

This labor is not separate from nature but part of it. Marx argues that the laboring human “sets in motion the natural forces which belong to his own body, his arms, legs, head and hands, in order to appropriate the materials of nature in a form adapted to his own needs.”[34] As people transform nature to meet their needs, they also change themselves: “Through this movement, he acts upon external nature and changes it, and in this way he simultaneously changes his own nature.” Thus planning, choice, and deliberate decisions play a particularly important role in human work: “He develops the potentialities within nature, and subjects the play of its forces to his own sovereign power.”[35]

Human nature is thus dynamic, the product of the interaction between people and their environment. Our behavior is neither socially nor biologically determined, but produced by the interaction between the two. Richard Levins and Richard Lewontin put this at the core of their conception of *dialectical biology*: "organism and environment as interpenetrating so that both are at the same time subjects and objects of the historical process."[36] While it is possible to think of the nature of other species as relatively set at any moment until changed by processes of evolution, "the evident fact about human life is the incredible diversity in individual life histories and in social organization across space and time."[37]

The work humans do on nature is necessarily social; it is organized through society in very specific ways. As Marx and Engels put it:

> The production of life, both of one's own in labor and of fresh life in procreation now appears as a twofold relation: on the one hand as a natural, on the other as a social relation—social in the sense that it denotes the co-operation of several individuals.[38]

In many human societies, this cooperation is organized around social classes, a social relationship in which those in the ruling classes extract some of the proceeds of the labor of those in the toiling classes.

Some human societies do not have social classes. In forager societies, everyone contributes to the basic work on nature and receives a share of the collective production. In contrast, in contemporary capitalist society there is a distinction between those who own and/or control the workplace and those who are employed by those in control. The rise of social classes fundamentally restructures this work on nature. The work of society is organized primarily around meeting the needs of the most powerful. Slaveowners, aristocrats, and capitalists use their control over production to orient society around their interests and not those of the toilers.

For example, in contemporary capitalist society, workers are hired by employers to do work that yields a profit to corporations, rather than working for the inherent satisfaction of accomplishment and to meet their needs. The work is a means to end—to gain a wage—rather than an end in itself. Marx describes such work as *alienated labor*, where workers neither control the product nor the process of production, and thus do not fulfill their human potential or establish bonds of mutuality through the process of work. It is the character of alienated labor that "life itself appears only as a means to life."[39]

The worker feels used up and dehumanized by this. Bodies and minds are destroyed through work, not developed. The worker, "in his work, therefore . . . does not affirm himself but denies himself, does not feel content but unhappy, does not develop freely his physical and mental energy but mortified his body and ruins his mind."[40] Thus, in our most distinctively human function, purposive labor, people feel demeaned. Assembly-line workers often say that "a trained monkey could do my work." Marx wrote that the worker "only feels himself freely active in his more animal functions—eating, drinking, procreating, or at most in his dwelling and in dressing-up, etc.; and in his human functions he no longer feels himself to be anything but an animal."[41] Employers and teachers, for example, have to monitor toilet use because it seems to be a welcome relief from the grind of work.

It would follow from this discussion that human sexuality is different from that of other animals. Heteronormativity naturalizes sexuality and erases the ways humans make deliberate choices about sexuality that are social and aesthetic. Our sexuality is natural, but at the same time it is social. Sexual practices vary tremendously across human societies, and even the definition of what constitutes sex is highly contentious. Even within established social patterns, there are important individual variations.

Sexuality is part of the way we realize our humanity; it is part of the work on nature (internal and external) through which we make our mark on the world. It is an aesthetic, personal, and societal expression of who we are. Alienated life conditions link sex to compulsion and make it a means to an end rather than an end in itself. This is fairly obvious in the case of paid sex work, but we are often put in the position of using sexuality to meet our life goals, including companionship, sustenance, and escape from misery and meaning in a life in which other activity feels empty. Sexuality is deeply shaped by alienation in class society.

THE SOCIAL REPRODUCTION OF CONSENT AND COERCION

Heteronormativity developed as a form of sexual regulation tied to alienation and dispossession that reinforced the specific organization of social reproduction at a particular moment in the development of capitalism. It is not static but has changed with the restructuring of relations of social reproduction.

Hegemonic heterosexuality is institutionalized in the form of monogamous couples who cohabitate and raise children in a household. Before the sexual revolution, this couple relationship was organized primarily through marriage. The sexual revolution expanded this normative realm in certain ways, so that in some locations cohabitation by unmarried couples, single parenthood, and the engagement of mothers in paid work are much more accepted than they were before the 1960s. Further, the parameters of sexual normativity have been expanded to include homonormativity, a new lesbian and gay normality that presumes that same-sex couples live much as heterosexual couples do.[42]

The lens of heteronormativity grounded in an analysis of social reproduction provides useful tools for understanding sexual assault in terms of relations of coercion and consent. Mobilization around issues of sexual assault has been a prominent theme of "second wave" feminism since the 1970s. Recent years have seen an important increase in activism around sexual assault, on campuses and more broadly in society. There is widespread recognition that, even with the important gains won since the 1970s, the system is not working. Indeed, the system is *not working* so badly that one could believe it *is* working to normalize sexual assault and trivialize women's experiences.[43]

Sexual assault is not the product of a few men gone rogue; it is systemic and indeed normalized. Nicola Gavey argues that the "everyday taken-for-granted normative forms of heterosexuality work as a cultural scaffolding for rape."[44] Specifically, she argues that heterosex is based on gendered norms of "women's passive, acquiescing (a)sexuality and men's forthright, urgent pursuit of sexual 'release.'"[45] Action against sexual assault must undermine this cultural scaffolding by "the 'queering' of sex and sexuality in the broadest of ways."[46] This queering is to be accomplished through a combination of education, cultural critique, and social activism. One of its crucial dimensions is developing "opportunities for girls and women to experience and develop physical strengths, pleasures, and acumen necessary for an embodied agency."[47]

The social reproduction frame provides an approach to sexuality and life-making that can contribute to deepening this conception of the cultural scaffolding of rape. Heteronormativity is grounded in practices of life-making within a matrix of power relations. We develop a sense of embodied agency, or the absence thereof, through our engagement in various forms of paid and unpaid work, as well as leisure practices organized around divisions of labor based on sexualized class, gender, and racialized hierarchies in the context of an exploitative world order grounded in histories of colonialism and imperialism.

The attitudes of men toward their own bodies, those of women, and those of other men is in part based on experiences of labor (and of preparing for certain forms of labor, even in play). Gendered norms are not simply a discourse but a set of everyday practices framed by a matrix of power relations that structure production and reproduction in capitalist societies. Men develop their sense of embodiment in part through engagement in particular forms of work in the context of specific power relations. For example, in the early twentieth century, as mass production developed, the Ford Motor Company developed management strategies organized specially around masculine pride grounded in providing for dependent family members and the ability to endure difficult, painful, and tedious work.[48] This relationship of work and household creates a certain sense of embodied agency that is very different than the one women might develop through unpaid labor in the household, which creates very real economic dependence. The masculine pride of the professor, the miner, and the taxi driver differ in important ways, yet are all tied to a particular configuration of work and household and a specific location within divisions of labor.

Women are more likely to engage in practices of caregiving labor, whether paid or unpaid, that develop a different sense of one's body than working in a mine or in heavy industry. Carolyn Steedman reflected on her work as a schoolteacher of young children: "My body died during those years, the little fingers that caught my hand, the warmth of a child leaning and reading her book to me somehow prevented all the other meeting of bodies."[49] Dorothy Smith argues that women and men tend to know the world differently because they are engaged in different everyday practices of work. Given prevalent divisions of labor, men often know more abstractly as their work often "depends upon the alienation of subjects from their bodily and local existence." This way of life is only possible for a man because of the work of a woman in the domestic sphere "who keeps house for him, bears and cares for his children, washes his clothes, looks after him when he is sick, and generally provides for the logistics of his bodily existence."[50]

This abstract way of knowing, established in part through specific practices of labor and leisure, plays out in the sphere of sexuality in terms of understandings of sexual activity that are abstracted from the whole matrix of human embodied interactions forged around mutuality. Gavey argues that one underpinning of the cultural scaffolding of rape is the conception of heterosexual sex in terms of a *coital imperative* that "constructs the main point of heterosex as the penetration of the vagina by the penis."[51] This narrow definition of sex abstracts one moment in the complex relations of bodies and lives that shape actual sexual engagement and makes it the pinnacle of heterosex. This imperative is so fundamental to heteronormativity that it is assumed to be a biological drive, yet we know that eroticism is far more complex and varied than this hydraulic model of pressure buildup and release. The coital imperative is connected to the abstract mode associated with masculinity in the dominant division of labor, where bodily and social engagement between people seeking mutual pleasure is subordinated to the abstraction of the coital imperative, the image of the crowning moment or the "money shot." Women, whose life-making labor is more likely to include caregiving, are less likely to know sexuality through this narrow abstraction.

Social reproduction is organized around divisions of labor, power relations, and constructions of dependence and independence that frame questions of sexual consent and coercion. Gavey points out that the simple framing of consent and coercion does not do justice to the reality of women's reflections, in which many sexual experiences fit in a grey area somewhere in between. Women sometimes have sex that they do not necessarily desire when they "didn't feel like they had a choice; when the sense of obligation and pressure is too strong."[52] Gavey discusses experiences where the "man applied pressure that fell short of actual or threatened physical force, but which the women felt unable to resist."[53] Women reported going along with sex that was not coerced but was unwanted "because she did not feel it was her right to stop it or because she did not know how to refuse."[54]

The social reproduction frame provides important tools for understanding men's entitlement and women's lack of a sense of agency that go beyond the cultural forms of heteronormativity. Unequal power relations create senses of vulnerability and agency while divisions of labor created specific expectations of embodiment. Tithi Bhattacharya sketches this clearly, beginning with the image of

> a naked white man pursuing a low-wage Black female asylum seeker down the corridors of an expensive Manhattan hotel in order to force

> her to have sex with him. The man, of course, is the then-director of the International Monetary Fund, French politician Dominique Strauss-Kahn, and the woman, thirty-three-year-old Nafissatou Diallo, a housekeeper at Strauss-Kahn's hotel who was also at the time seeking asylum in the United States from her native Guinea, a former colony of France.[55]

Bhattacharya points out that "a veritable cartography of dispossession extends between these two figures."[56]

The social reproduction frame contributes to mapping this "cartography of dispossession" by contributing to an understanding of the relation between consent and coercion in forms of sexuality organized around alienation and dispossession. Participation in sexual activity is organized around unequal wage structures, the hectic scheduling of precarious work, histories of gendered embodiment through work and leisure, lack of access to quality affordable childcare, histories of slavery and colonialism, the erosion of social assistance, violence against women and gender nonconformists, the vulnerability of migrants without full status, the gendered expectation that women will be mothers and wives, gendered and racialized sexual scripts, lack of access to contraception and abortion, and many other factors. In this discussion, I focus on rape in relation to violence against women. It is important to note that men and people who are gender nonbinary also get raped, and that this is integrated into to the same relations of gendered domination. There is much more to be said about the variety of forms and meanings of sexual assault; however, here I am focusing specifically on one dimension.

The cultural scaffolding of rape is nested in broader relations of domination and subordination that both naturalize sexual coercion and are sustained by it. Angela Davis writes that "sexual coercion was . . . an essential dimension of the social relations between slavemaster and slave."[57] This "rape culture," as it is now commonly known, outlasted the specific conditions of slavery: "The pattern of institutionalized sexual abuse of Black women became so powerful that it managed to survive the abolition of slavery."[58] Racism underpins rape culture and is bolstered by it: "Racism has always drawn strength from its ability to encourage sexual coercion."[59]

The idea of sex as conquest associated with heteronormative masculinity is integrally connected with the sexualization of domination. Military conquest has often been associated with sexual coercion, as

Angela Davis notes: "It was the unwritten policy of the US Military Command [Vietnam] to systematically encourage rape, since it was an extremely effective weapon of mass terrorism."[60] The Japanese army in World War II enslaved Chinese, Korean, Taiwanese, and other women from occupied nations as sex slaves (euphemistically called "comfort women"). Yoshimi Yoshiaki argues that "an attitude privately acknowledging rape as a 'wartime benefit' permeated all ranks of the Japanese military."[61] Today, Israeli prisons use sexual assault and humiliation against Palestinian political prisoners: "Sexual harassment and humiliation in all forms, including attempted rape and rape, are used to deter women from participating in the struggle."[62]

Sexual assault reinforces power relations by marking the conquest by the dominant and the abjection of the subordinated. It is deeply connected to existing forms of power and vulnerability. Kimberlé Crenshaw notes that rape-crisis services for women of color necessarily allocate significant resources to meeting needs that are not directly associated with a specific sexual assault. She quotes a rape-crisis service worker:

> For example, a woman may come in or call in for various reasons. She has no place to go, she has no job, she has no support, she has no money, she has no food, she's been beaten, and after you finish meeting all those needs, or try to meet all those needs, then she may say, by the way, during all this, I was being raped. So that makes our community different than other communities. A person wants their basic needs first. It's a lot easier to discuss things when you are full.[63]

Relations of domination and subordination thus frame sexual consent and coercion. Carol Pateman argues that the idea of sexual consent as we understand it is already founded on women's relative unfreedom rather than freedom:

> The "naturally" superior, active, and sexually aggressive male makes an initiative, or offers a contract, to which a "naturally" subordinate, passive woman "consents." An egalitarian sexual relationship cannot rest on this basis; it cannot be grounded in "consent." Perhaps the most telling aspect of the problem of women and consent is that we lack a language through which to help constitute a form of personal life in which two equals freely agree to create a lasting association together.[64]

The basic labor contract between employer and employee is similarly an example of consent grounded in inequality. The worker and employer meets as formal equals, one purchasing the capacity to work that the other is selling. Yet the worker is ultimately compelled to sell to gain access to the necessities of life, so that "the relation of capitalist exploitation is mediated through the form of contract."[65] The struggle against sexual assault must be about consent, but also about understanding the way pervasive inequalities frame interactions and make consent more complicated. As Bhattacharya argues, "Management of sexuality and management of labor, then, are braided chains of discipline that bind the most vulnerable sections of global labor."[66]

SOCIAL MOVEMENTS AND EMBODIED AGENCY

In many ways, anticapitalist activism seems to meet some of Gavey's criteria for queering heteronormativity and developing the embodied agency of women. Women who participated in the often militant activism of Women Against Pit Closures during the 1984–85 miners' strike in Britain, for example, experienced rich opportunities for the development of agency:

> The discovery of individual talents and skills and the excitement of living the protest to the full shine through in the narratives of every woman. The bonds that were formed were strong in many cases, particularly where the women relied on one another for emotional and practical support.[67]

These women also faced tensions and a sense of exclusion from the inner workings of the union. While their sense of themselves changed, they still "had to confront the masculine culture of the trade unions during the strike."[68]

That "masculine culture" and the threat of sexual assault can undercut the positive opportunities of activism as a place to challenge the heteronormative matrix. For example, women were sexually assaulted in activist spaces during the 2012 Quebec student strike and the 2015 strike by CUPE 3903 at York University.[69] Mobilization often has a contradictory impact, both undermining and reinforcing heteronormativity. Activism can create openings for new ways of interacting, yet militancy in the current social structure often foregrounds practices grounded in aggressive masculinity. Steve Meyer argues that militant auto workers in America in the 1930s often "employed a militant and heroic manhood in resistance to the challenges to masculinity that resulted from the eras of mechanization and unemployment."[70]

Practices of aggressive masculinity have often served activists well in confronting the power of the employer and the state. The classic union song "Which Side are You On?" (interestingly, written by a woman, Florence Reece) asks, "Will you be a lousy scab or will you be a man?" The masculinity of struggle often draws on the same repertoire of behaviors that is fundamental to the perpetuation of rape culture. The struggle against sexual assault means finding new resources of militancy and challenging the toxic heteronormativity often sustained in activist spaces because of the usefulness of masculine aggression in militancy.

There are other ways of being militant. Organizing in unions, student unions, and other movements is tremendously important to women. The trajectory of women's mobilization is often somewhat different than that of men. Linda Briskin argues that "women enter unions differently from men because of their workplace locations and their household/family responsibilities."[71] Anne Forrest found, in interviews with women who formed a union at an auto parts plant in Windsor Ontario, that they had organized to seek respect, dignity, an end to sexual harassment, and scheduling responsive to their needs as workers and mothers.[72]

Women have often drawn on different resources and experiences to support militancy. A strike wave in Eastern Tennessee in 1929 was largely fueled by women's activism. Community strike mobilization provided women with an opening to take public space that was often closed to them. Young women were in a position to engage in confrontational activism:

> Once in motion, their daughters might outdo men in militancy, perhaps because they had fewer dependents than their male co-workers and could fall back more easily on parental resources, perhaps because the peer culture and increased independence encouraged by factory labor stirred boldness and inspired experimentation.[73]

The strike provided women with opportunities for transgressing heteronormative gender codes. Hall mines the transcript of a trial of two female picket leaders who were charged with violating an injunction to capture some of their transgressive actions:

> Using words that, for women in particular, were ordinarily taboo, they refused deference and signaled disrespect. Making no secret of their sexual experience, they combined flirtation with fierceness on the picket line and adopted a provocative courtroom style.[74]

Indeed, the intense, festive, and experimental atmosphere of the strike created a situation in which there was an erotic freedom. "Romance and politics comingled in the excitement of the moment, flowering in a spectrum of behavior—from the outrageousness of Trixie Perry [who had a reputation for sexual activity] to a spate of marriages among other girls."

Activist spaces that are not structured around deliberate antirape activism are likely to include both a joyous exploratory opening to the erotic and an aggressive masculinity tied to heteronormative patterns associated with sexual assault that is quite possibly freed from some everyday inhibiting constraints. This is a toxic combination if rape culture is not deliberately disrupted.

CONCLUSION

The struggle for sexual liberation is an important dimension of broader transformative mobilizations. Sexual liberation will not be an automatic outcome of other changes in social life, nor can it be accomplished apart from struggles against capitalism, racism, colonialism, and gender inequality. The social reproduction frame provides important conceptual tools for understanding the ways sexuality is nested into broader social relations. The challenge of sexual liberation is ultimately that of democratizing our everyday lives by building power from below.

10

From Social Reproduction Feminism to the Women's Strike

Cinzia Arruzza

In the fall of 2016, Polish activists called for a massive women's strike, which managed to stop a bill in Parliament that would have banned abortion. They were inspired by the historic women's strike against wage inequality in Iceland. The Argentinian activists of Ni Una Menos also adopted this tactic in October 2016 to protest male violence. Following the mass participation in these strikes, feminist grassroots organizations started coordinating internationally to promote an international day of mobilization in November 2016, on the occasion of the International Day for the Elimination of Violence against Women. On November 26, 300,000 women took to the streets in Italy. The call for an international women's strike on March 8 grew organically from these struggles: it was initiated by the Polish activists who had organized the women's strike in September and, over the course of the months, managed to extend to around fifty countries.

In the United States, the idea of organizing a women's strike originated from a specific set of considerations.

The mass nature of the Women's March on January 21, 2017, indicated that the conditions for the rebirth of a feminist mobilization were perhaps in place. At the same time, the march also exposed the structural limitations of the kind of liberal feminism that has become hegemonic over the past decades. This brand of feminism showed its true face during the Democratic Party primaries, when the Bernie Sanders campaign became the target of a constant attack from liberal feminists supporting Hillary Clinton, who argued that it would be antifeminist to vote for Sanders and that women should unite under the banner of the "women's revolution" embodied by Clinton. At the presidential election, however, a majority of white women who voted preferred to vote for an openly misogynistic candidate rather than the alleged champion of women's rights.[1]

While plain racism may explain part of this vote, it does not tell the whole truth, for it still fails to explain why Clinton's alleged feminism didn't appeal to these women. One way to address this issue is to raise a very simple question: Who has concretely benefitted from the kind of liberal feminism Hillary Clinton represents?

According to the sociologist Leslie McCall, a woman with a college education in the 1970s, on average, earned less than a man without a college education. In the decade from 2000 to 2010, the situation changed dramatically: while the average income of working-class women and men stayed flat, elite women's earnings increased faster than those of elite men; in 2010 a high-earning woman made, on average, more than 1.5 times as much as a middle-class man. This transformation was the outcome of progressive legislation such as the Equal Pay Act of 1963, which eliminated the most blatant forms of gender discrimination in the workplace. This kind of legislation, however, took place within a context of fast-growing economic inequality within society as a whole. The result was the growth of economic and social inequality among women, with upper-class women successfully decreasing the wage gap while working-class women were entirely left behind.[2]

In a piece that appeared in the *Nation* in early 2017, Katha Pollitt wondered what should count as a feminist issue and concluded that, while reproductive rights and the fight against gender discrimination are clearly identifiable as feminist demands, war, poverty, environmental crisis, and perhaps even the fight against racism extend beyond the scope of feminism.[3] Pollitt here is echoing a very important and central argument of this brand of liberal feminism—a juridical and rights-based definition of feminism. It is thus not surprising that this articulation of feminism failed to appeal to millions of working-class women. Equal pay and the end of gender discrimination in the workplace, for example, are certainly worthy causes, but as McCall's data show, they have little tangible effect on the lives of working-class women if decoupled from demands for a minimum wage or for income redistribution.

The outcome of the US presidential election marked an impasse for liberal feminism, one that not even the immense participation in the January women's marches could fully overcome. The call for a women's strike came from awareness of this impasse, which opened a political space for an alternative feminist politics, and from awareness of the existence in the United States of dozens of grassroots collectives, networks, and national organizations that were already developing an alternative to liberal feminism: a class-based, antiracist feminism, inclusive of trans women and queer and nonbinary people. The strike call came, therefore, from the awareness that another feminism was already there: the call served the purposes of creating a national network of organizations and individuals, of making this other feminism visible on a national level, of challenging the hegemony of the kind of corporate feminism embodied by Clinton and her supporters, and, finally, of opening up a national conversation about empowering working-class, migrant, and black women.

Adopting the term *strike* was meant to emphasize the work that women perform not only in the workplace but outside it, in the sphere of social reproduction. It also had an additional function, which can be better understood by taking into consideration the US labor situation.

From 1983 to 2016 the rate of unionization in the United States dropped from 20.1 percent to 10.7 percent. The situation is even more depressing in the private sector, where unionization dropped in the same period from 16.8 percent to 6.4 percent. If we look at data on formal strikes, from 1947 to 2016 the number of strike days involving more than a thousand workers dropped from 25,720,000 to 1,543,000; 2016 even saw a small surge in strike days, due in particular to the Chicago teachers' and Verizon workers' strikes. This situation is the outcome of antiunion legislation and the political orientation and practice of business unionism. Class struggle, however, should not be conflated with labor struggle in the workplace: class struggle takes many forms. Important manifestations of the class as a political actor and an agent of conflict often take place in the sphere of social reproduction, where these struggles have the potential to attack capitalist profitability. In recent years we have seen a number of important labor mobilizations organized by nontraditional labor organizations and networks: for example, the Fight for Fifteen campaign or the mobilizations organized by the Restaurant Opportunities Centers (ROC); movements such as Black Lives Matter, the migrants' strikes, and the mobilizations against the wall at the border with Mexico; and the near-spontaneous mobilizations against the "Muslim Ban." Instead of seeing all these forms of mobilization as alternatives to labor organizing in the workplace, it is more useful to see them as all various forms that class struggle is currently taking, forms that potentially empower each other and can create the conditions for organizing work stoppages in the workplace. The women's strike was part of this process: it contributed to politically relegitimizing the term "strike" in the United States, it caused nonconventional work stoppage in three school districts, and it gave visibility to labor organizations where the majority of workers are women, such as the ROC and the New York State Nurses Association, and to instances of local labor organizing and workplace struggles led by women and queer people.

The concrete experience of the women's strike, as well as the social reproduction theory that inspired some of its organizers, made the question of whether class struggle should take priority over "identity-based" struggles not only obsolete but ultimately misleading. If we think of the class as a political agent, gender, race, and sexuality should be recognized as intrinsic components of the way people concretize their sense of self and their relation to the world, and therefore are part of the way people become politicized and engage in struggle. In lived reality, class, race, and gender inequality are not experienced as separate and compartmentalized phenomena that intersect in an external way: their separation is merely the outcome of an analytical thought process, which should not be mistaken as a reflection of experience.

This is a key insight for political organizing, for political strategies, tactics, and organizational forms should always have their roots in people's concrete experience. Abstracting from experience leads to replacing materialism with rationalism—namely, conflating analytical categories and subjective reality and projecting bookish blueprints about what class struggle means (or should mean) onto people's lived realities. On the other hand, if feminism and antiracism want to be projects of liberation for all humanity, then the question of capitalism is unavoidable. The problem of the replacement of class struggle with identity-based struggles should therefore be reformulated as a political problem arising from the hegemony of the liberal articulation of feminist discourse. This articulation turns feminism into a project of self-promotion for elite women by erasing the key issue of the structural relation between gender oppression and capitalism. How to break this hegemony is what we should discuss now, and the women's strike was a first important step in this direction.

While not all the organizers of and participants in the women's strike had a theoretical commitment to social reproduction feminism, the women's strike can legitimately be seen as a political translation of social reproduction theory. Recent mobilizations are showing a new and increasing awareness of the need to rebuild solidarity and collective action as the only way to defend ourselves against continuous attacks on our bodies, freedom, and self-determination, as well as against imperialist and neoliberal policies. Moreover, they act as an antidote to the liberal decline of feminist discourse and practice.

At the same time, overcoming this understanding of feminism does not mean reverting to economic reductionism or to a universalistic politics based on abstraction from differences. In recent decades we have acquired a greater awareness of the stratification of the social condition of cis and trans women, according to class, ethnicity, race, age, ability, and sexual orientation. The challenge that the new feminist movement must face is articulating forms of action, organization, and demands that do not make these differences invisible but—on the contrary—take them into serious account. This diversity must become our weapon, rather than an obstacle or something that divides us. To make this happen, it is necessary to show the internal relations between various forms of oppression and to combine the differences these oppressions generate in a more encompassing critique of capitalist social relations. In this process, each political subjectivation based on a specific oppression can provide us with new insights on the various ways capitalism, racism, and sexism affect our lives.

Notes

CHAPTER 1: INTRODUCTION

1. Susan Ferguson, "Capitalist Childhood, Anti-Capitalist Children: The Social Reproduction of Childhood," unpublished paper, 2015.
2. Meg Luxton, "Feminist Political Economy in Canada and the Politics of Social Reproduction," in *Social Reproduction: Feminist Political Economy Challenges Neoliberalism*, edited by Kate Bezanson and Meg Luxton (Montréal: McGill-Queen's University Press, 2006), 36.
3. "Marx Is Back" was the headline for *Foreign Policy* (January 21, 2014), while the *Guardian* led with "Why Marxism Is on the Rise Again" (July 4, 2012), the *New York Times* with "Marx Rises Again" (April 19, 2014), and Salon.com "Believe It or Not: Karl Marx Is Making a Comeback" (June 22, 2014).
4. These include, among others: Elmar Altvater, *Marx neu entdecken* (Rediscovering Marx) (Hamburg: VSA Verlag, 2012); David Harvey's *A Companion to Marx's Capital* (New York: Verso, 2010) and *A Companion to Marx's Capital Volume 2* (New York: Verso, 2013), Wolfgang Fritz Haug, *Das Kapital lesen—aber Wie? Materialien* (Reading *Capital*—But How? Materials) (Hamburg: Argument-Verlag/Ariadne, 2013), the English translation of Michael Heinrich's introductory book to *Capital*: *An Introduction to the Three Volumes of Marx's* Capital (New York: Monthly Review Press, 2012), originally published in German in 2004; Fredric Jameson, *Representing Capital: A Reading of Volume One* (New York: Verso, 2011); Alex Callinicos, *Deciphering Capital* (London: Bookmarks, 2014).
5. This literature is too vast to be reported in its entirety here, but some key representational texts are: Veronica Beechey, *Unequal Work* (New York: Verso, 1987); Dorothy Smith, "Feminist Reflections on Political Economy," *Studies in Political Economy* 30 (1987); Johanna Brenner, *Women and the Politics of Class* (New York: Monthly Review Press, 2000); Antonella Picchio, *Social Reproduction: The Political Economy of the Labor Market* (Cambridge: Cambridge University Press, 1992); and work by Canadian Marxists such as Heather Jon Maroney, Bonnie Fox, Kate Bezanson, and Isabella Bakker.
6. György Lukács, *History and Class Consciousness: Studies in Marxist Dialectics* (Cambridge, MA: MIT Press, 1971), 181.
7. Cinzia Arruza, *Dangerous Liaisons* (London: Merlin, 2013), 128.
8. Shahrzad Mojab, ed., *Marxism and Feminism* (London: Zed Books, 2015), 5–6.

9. Nancy Holmstrom, ed., *The Socialist Feminist Project: A Contemporary Reader in Theory and Politics* (New York: Monthly Review Press, 2002), 7.
10. Kate Benzanson and Meg Luxton, eds., *Social Reproduction* (Montreal: McGill-Queen's University Press, 2006), 37, emphasis mine.
11. Johanna Brenner and Barbara Laslett, "Gender, Social Reproduction, and Women's Self-Organization: Considering the US Welfare State." *Gender & Society* 5, no. 3 (1991): 314.
12. Karl Marx, *Capital,* Vol. 1 (Washington, DC: Gateway Editions, 1996), 139.
13. Ben Fine and Alfredo Saad-Filho, *Marx's 'Capital,'* 6th ed. (London: Pluto, 2017), 60.
14. Karl Marx, *Capital,* Vol. 3 (London: Penguin, 1981), 959.
15. John Holloway, *Crack Capitalism* (London: Pluto Press, 2010).
16. V.I. Lenin, "A Great Beginning," *Collected Works,* Vol. XXIX (London: Lawrence & Wishart, 1965 [March–August 1919]), 429.
17. As Ollman points out, given that Marx variously described capitalist labor "as 'torment,' a 'sacrifice of life' and 'activity as suffering,' it is not to be wondered at that no one in capitalism works unless he is forced." Bertell Ollman, *Alienation* (Cambridge: Cambridge University Press, 1977), 141.
18. Karl Marx, *Economic and Philosophic Manuscripts of 1844* (Moscow: Progress Publishers, 1959), 69.
19. Bertell Ollman, *Alienation: Marx's Conception of Man in Capitalist Society* (Cambridge: Cambridge University Press, 1971), 141.
20. Ibid.
21. For more details, see Bonnie Fox, ed., *Hidden in the Household: Women's Domestic Labor Under Capitalism* (New York: Women's Press, 1980); Maxine Molyneux, "Beyond the Domestic Labor Debate," *New Left Review* 116 (1979).
22. In which money (M) is exchanged for commodities (C), that is, a combination of means of production (M_p) and labor power (L_p). The two elements combine through capitalist production (P) to produce new commodities and surplus value (C') to be then exchanged for a greater amount of money (M').
23. For details, see George Caffentzis, "On the Notion of a Crisis of Social Reproduction," in *In Letters of Blood and Fire: Work, Machines and the Crisis of Capitalism* (Oakland, CA: PM Press, 2013).
24. Philip J. Kain, *Marx and Ethics* (Oxford: Oxford University Press, 1988), 160.
25. Ben Fine and Laurence Harris, *Rereading Capital* (London and Basingstoke: McMillan Press, 1983), 6.
26. Patricia Hill Collins, *Black Sexual Politics: African Americans, Gender and the New Racism* (New York: Routledge, 2004), 65.
27. Quoted in M. Dobb, "Introduction," in Karl Marx, *Appendix to A Contribution to the Critique of Political Economy* (Moscow: Progress Publishers, 1970 [1857]), 206.
28. Marx, *Capital,* Vol. 1, 284.

CHAPTER 2: CRISIS OF CARE?

1. An earlier version of this essay appeared under the title "Contradictions of Capital and Care" in *New Left Review* 100 (July/August 2016): 99–117, portions of which are reprinted here with permission. A French translation was delivered in Paris on June 14, 2016, as the thirty-eighth annual Marc Bloch Lecture of the École des hautes études en sciences sociales, and is available on the École's website . I gratefully thank Pierre-Cyrile Hautcoeur for the lecture invitation, Johanna Oksala for stimulating discussions, Mala Htun and Eli Zaretsky for helpful comments, and Selim Heper for research assistance.
2. Ruth Rosen, "The Care Crisis," *Nation*, February 27, 2007; Cynthia Hess, "Women and the Care Crisis," Institute for Women's Policy Research Briefing Paper, IWPR C#401, April 2013, http://www.iwpr.org/publications/pubs/women-and-the-care-crisis-valuing-in-home-care-in-policy-and-practice. Daniel Boffey, "Half of All Services Now Failing as UK Care Sector Crisis Deepens," *Guardian*, September 26, 2015. For "time poverty," see Arlie Hochschild, *The Time Bind: When Work Becomes Home and Home Becomes Work* (New York: Henry Holt, 2001); Heather Boushey, *Finding Time: The Economics of Work-Life Conflict* (Cambridge, MA: Harvard University Press, 2016). For "family/work balance," see Heather Boushey and Amy Rees Anderson, "Work-Life Balance: 5 Ways To Turn It From The Ultimate Oxymoron Into A Real Plan," *Forbes*, July 26, 2013, https://www.forbes.com/sites/amyanderson/2013/07/26/work-life-balance-the-ultimate-oxymoron-or-5-tips-to-help-you-achieve-better-worklife-balance/#7af10a775841; Martha Beck, "Finding Work-Life Balance: How To Keep Your Job And Home Lives Separate And Healthy," *Huffington Post*, March 10, 2015, http://www.huffingtonpost.com/2013/04/10/work-life-balance-job-home-strategies-for-women_n_ 3044764.html. For "social depletion," see Shirin M. Rai, Catherine Hoskyns, and Dania Thomas, "Depletion: The Cost of Social Reproduction," *International Feminist Journal of Politics* 16, no. 1 (2013): 1–20.
3. For a critique of the view of capitalism as an economy and a defense of the "enlarged" view, see Nancy Fraser, "Behind Marx's 'Hidden Abode': For an Expanded Conception of Capitalism," *New Left Review* 86 (2014): 55–72.
4. For an account of the necessary political background conditions for a capitalist economy, see Nancy Fraser, "Legitimation Crisis? On the Political Contradictions of Financialized Capitalism," *Critical Historical Studies* 2, no. 2 (2015): 157–89. For the necessary ecological conditions, see James O'Connor, "Capitalism, Nature, Socialism: A Theoretical Introduction," *Capitalism, Nature, Socialism* 1, no. 1 (1988): 1-22; and Jason W. Moore, *Capitalism in the Web of Life* (New York: Verso, 2015).
5. Many feminist theorists have made versions of this argument. For Marxist-feminist formulations, see Lise Vogel, *Marxism and the Oppression of Women: Toward a Unitary Theory* (Chicago: Haymarket Books, 2013); Silvia Federici, *Revolution at Point Zero: Housework, Reproduction, and*

Feminist Struggle (Oakland, CA: PM Press, 2012); and Christine Delphy, *Close to Home: A Materialist Analysis of Women's Oppression* (New York: Verso, 2016). Another powerful elaboration is Nancy Folbre, *The Invisible Heart: Economics and Family Values* (New York: New Press, 2002). For social reproduction theory, see Barbara Laslett and Johanna Brenner, "Gender and Social Reproduction: Historical Perspectives," *Annual Review of Sociology* 15 (1989): 381–404; Kate Bezanson and Meg Luxton, eds., *Social Reproduction: Feminist Political Economy Challenges Neo-Liberalism* (Montreal: McGill–Queen's University Press, 2006); Isabella Bakker, "Social Reproduction and the Constitution of a Gendered Political Economy," *New Political Economy* 12, no. 4 (2007): 541–56; Cinzia Arruzza, "Functionalist, Determinist, Reductionist: Social Reproduction Feminism and its Critics," *Science and Society* 80, no. 1 (2016): 9–30.

6. For boundary struggles, see Fraser, "Behind Marx's 'Hidden Abode.'"
7. Louise A. Tilly and Joan W. Scott, *Women, Work, and Family* (London: Routledge, 1987).
8. Karl Marx and Friedrich Engels, "Manifesto of the Communist Party," in *The Marx-Engels Reader*, ed. Robert C. Tucker (New York: Norton, 1978), 487–88; Friedrich Engels, *The Origin of the Family, Private Property and the State* (New York: Penguin, 2010), 106–114.
9. Nancy Woloch, *A Class by Herself: Protective Laws for Women Workers, 1890s-1990s* (Princeton, NJ: Princeton University Press, 2015).
10. Karl Polanyi, *The Great Transformation* (Boston: Beacon Press, 2001), 87, 138–39, 213.
11. Ava Baron, "Protective Labor Legislation and the Cult of Domesticity," *Journal of Family Issues* 2, no. 1 (1981): 25–38.
12. Maria Mies, *Patriarchy and Accumulation on a World Scale* (London: Zed Books, 2014), 74.
13. Eli Zaretsky, *Capitalism, the Family and Personal Life* (New York: HarperCollins, 1986); Stephanie Coontz, *The Social Origins of Private Life: A History of American Families 1600–1900* (London: Verso, 1988).
14. Judith R. Walkowitz, *Prostitution and Victorian Society: Women, Class, and the State* (Cambridge: Cambridge University Press, 1980); Barbara Hobson, *Uneasy Virtue: The Politics of Prostitution and the American Reform Tradition* (Chicago: University of Chicago Press, 1990).
15. Angela Y. Davis, "Reflections on the Black Woman's Role in the Community of Slaves," *Massachusetts Review* 13, no. 2 (1972): 81–100.
16. David Wallace Adams, *Education for Extinction: American Indians and the Boarding School Experience, 1875–1928* (Lawrence: University Press of Kansas, 1995); Ward Churchill, *Kill the Indian and Save the Man: The Genocidal Impact of American Indian Residential Schools* (San Francisco: City Lights, 2004).
17. Gayatri C. Spivak, "Can the Subaltern Speak?" in *Marxism and the Interpretation of Culture*, ed. Cary Nelson and Lawrence Grossberg (Urbana-Champaign, University of Illinois Press, 1988), 305.

18. For the concept of the triple movement, see Nancy Fraser, "Marketization, Social Protection, Emancipation: Toward a Neo-Polanyian Conception of Capitalist Crisis," in *Business as Usual: The Roots of the Global Financial Meltdown*, edited by Craig Calhoun and Georgi Derluguian (New York: New York University Press, 2011), 137–58; and Nancy Fraser, "A Triple Movement? Parsing the Politics of Crisis after Polanyi," *New Left Review* 81 (2013): 119–32.
19. Michel Foucault, "Governmentality" in *The Foucault Effect*, edited by Graham Burchell, Colin Gordon, and Peter Miller (Chicago: University of Chicago Press, 1991), 87–104; Michel Foucault, *The Birth of Biopolitics: Lectures at College de France 1978–1979* (New York: Picador, 2010), 64.
20. Kristin Ross, *Fast Cars, Clean Bodies: Decolonization and the Reordering of French Culture* (Cambridge, MA: MIT Press, 1996; Dolores Hayden, *Building Suburbia: Green Fields and Urban Growth* (New York: Vintage, 2003); Stuart Ewen, *Captains of Consciousness: Advertising and The Social Roots of the Consumer Culture* (New York: Basic Books, 2008).
21. In this era, state support for social reproduction was financed by tax revenues and dedicated funds to which both metropolitan workers and capital contributed, in different proportions, depending on the relations of class power within a given state. But those revenue streams were swollen with value siphoned from the periphery through profits from foreign direct investment and through trade based on unequal exchange. Raúl Prebisch, *The Economic Development of Latin America and its Principal Problems* (New York: United Nations, 1950); Paul A. Baran, *The Political Economy of Growth* (New York: Monthly Review Press, 1957); Geoffrey Pilling, "Imperialism, Trade and 'Unequal Exchange': The Work of Aghiri Emmanuel," *Economy and Society* 2, no. 2 (1973): 164–85; Gernot Köhler and Arno Tausch, *Global Keynesianism: Unequal Exchange and Global Exploitation* (New York: Nova Science, 2001).
22. Jill Quadagno, *The Color of Welfare: How Racism Undermined the War on Poverty* (Oxford: Oxford University Press, 1994; Ira Katznelson, *When Affirmative Action Was White: An Untold History of Racial Inequality in Twentieth-Century America* (New York: Norton, 2005).
23. Jacqueline Jones, *Labor of Love, Labor of Sorrow: Black Women, Work, and the Family, from Slavery to the Present* (New York: Basic Books, 1985); Evelyn Nakano Glenn, "From Servitude to Service Work: Historical Continuities in the Racial Division of Paid Reproductive Labor," *Signs* 18, no. 1 (1992): 1–43; Evelyn Nakano Glenn, *Forced to Care: Coercion and Caregiving in America* (Cambridge, MA: Harvard University Press, 2010).
24. Nancy Fraser, 'Women, Welfare, and the Politics of Need Interpretation,' in Nancy Fraser, *Unruly Practices: Power, Discourse, and Gender in Contemporary Social Theory* (Minneapolis: University of Minnesota Press, 1989), 144–60; Barbara J. Nelson, "Women's Poverty and Women's Citizenship: Some Political Consequences of Economic Marginality," *Signs* 10, no. 2 (1985): 209–31; Diana Pearce, "Women, Work and Welfare: The Feminization of Poverty," in *Working Women and Families*, edited by

Karen Wolk Feinstein (Thousand Oaks, CA: Sage, 1979), 103–24; Johanna Brenner, "Gender, Social Reproduction, and Women's Self-Organization: Considering the U.S. Welfare State," *Gender and Society* 5, no. 3 (1991): 311–33.

25. Hilary Land, "Who Cares for the Family?" *Journal of Social Policy* 7, no. 3 (1978): 257–84; Harriet Holter, ed., *Patriarchy in a Welfare Society* (Oxford: Oxford University Press, 1984); Mary Ruggie, *The State and Working Women: A Comparative Study of Britain and Sweden* (Princeton, NJ: Princeton University Press, 1984; Birte Siim, "Women and the Welfare State: Between Private and Public Dependence," in *Gender and Caring*, edited by Clare Ungerson (New York: Prentice-Hall, 1990), 93–96. A.S. Orloff, "Gender and Social Rights of Citizenship: The Comparative Analysis of Gender Relations and Welfare States," *American Sociological Review* 58, no. 3 (1993): 303–28; A.S. Orloff, J.S. O'Connor, and S. Shaver, *States, Markets, Families: Gender, Liberalism and Social Policy in Australia, Canada, Great Britain and the United States* (Cambridge: Cambridge University Press, 1999); Diane Sainsbury, ed., *Gender and Welfare State Regimes* (Oxford: Oxford University Press, 2000); F. Williams, R. Lister, A. Anttonen, J. Bussemaker, U. Gerhard, J. Heinen, S. Johansson, and A. Leira, *Gendering Citizenship in Western Europe: New Challenges for Citizenship Research in a Cross-National Context* (Bristol, UK: Policy Press, 2007); Ann S. Orloff, "Gendering the Comparative Analysis of Welfare States: An Unfinished Agenda," *Sociological Theory* 27 (2009): 317–43.
26. Adrienne Roberts, "Financing Social Reproduction: The Gendered Relations of Debt and Mortgage Finance in Twenty-First Century America," *New Political Economy* 18, no. 1 (2013): 21–42.
27. The fruit of an unlikely alliance between free-marketeers and "new social movements," the new regime is scrambling all the usual political alignments, pitting "progressive" neoliberal feminists like Hillary Clinton against authoritarian nationalist populists like Donald Trump.
28. Nancy Fraser, "Feminism, Capitalism, and the Cunning of History," *New Left Review* 56 (2009): 97–117.
29. Elizabeth Warren and Amelia Warren Tyagi, *The Two-Income Trap: Why Middle-Class Parents are (Still) Going Broke* (New York: Basic Books, 2003).
30. Arlie Hochschild, "Love and Gold," in *Global Woman: Nannies, Maids and Sex Workers in the New Economy*, edited by Barbara Ehrenreich and Arlie Hochschild (New York: Henry Holt, 2002), 15–30; Brigitte Young, "The 'Mistress' and the 'Maid' in the Globalized Economy," *Socialist Register* 37 (2001): 315–27.
31. Saskia Sassen, "Women's Burden: Counter-Geographies of Globalization and the Feminization of Survival," *Journal of International Affairs* 53, no. 2 (2000): 503–24; Jennifer Bair, "On Difference and Capital: Gender and the Globalization of Production," *Signs* 36, no. 1 (2010): 203–26.
32. "Apple and Facebook Offer to Freeze Eggs for Female Employees," *Guardian*, October 15, 2014. Importantly, this benefit is no longer reserved

exclusively for the professional-technical-managerial class. The US Army now makes egg-freezing available gratis to enlisted women who sign up for extended tours of duty. "Pentagon to Offer Plan to Store Eggs and Sperm to Retain Young Troops," *New York Times*, February 3, 2016. Here the logic of militarism overrides that of privatization. To my knowledge, no one has yet broached the looming question of what to do with the eggs of a female soldier who dies in conflict.

33. Courtney Jung, *Lactivism: How Feminists and Fundamentalists, Hippies and Yuppies, and Physicians and Politicians Made Breastfeeding Big Business and Bad Policy* (New York: Basic Books, 2015), especially 130–31. The Affordable Care Act ("Obamacare") now mandates that health insurers provide such pumps free to their beneficiaries. So this benefit too is no longer the exclusive prerogative of privileged women. The effect is to create a huge new market for manufacturers, who are producing the pumps in very large batches in the factories of their Chinese subcontractors. See Sarah Kliff, "The Breast Pump Industry Is Booming, Thanks to Obamacare," *Washington Post*, January 4, 2013.
34. Lisa Belkin, "The Opt-Out Revolution," *New York Times*, October 26, 2003; Judith Warner, *Perfect Madness: Motherhood in the Age of Anxiety* (New York: Riverhead Books, 2006); Lisa Miller, "The Retro Wife," *New York*, March 17, 2013; Anne-Marie Slaughter, "Why Women Still Can't Have It All," *Atlantic* (July–August 2012); Anne-Marie Slaughter, *Unfinished Business: Women Men Work Family* (New York: Random House, 2015); Judith Shulevitz, "How to Fix Feminism," *New York Times*, June 10, 2016.

CHAPTER 3: WITHOUT RESERVES

1. See, for example, Charlie Post, "We're All Precarious, Now," *Jacobin*, April 20, 2015, https://www.jacobinmag.com/2015/04/precarious-labor-strategies-union-precariat-standing; Jefferson Cowie, *The Great Exception: The New Deal and the Limits of American Politics* (Princeton, NJ: Princeton University Press, 2016).
2. See, for example, Aaron Benanav, "Precarity Rising," *Viewpoint*, June 15, 2015, https://www.viewpointmag.com/2015/06/15/precarity-rising.
3. William Appleman Williams, *The Contours of American History* (London: Verso, 2011 [1961]), 19.
4. The concept of *social reproduction* has generally come to signify at least three distinct levels. First, the reproduction of individual labor power, or how the commodity labor power is produced and reproduced. Second, the reproduction of the total workforce of a given capitalist social formation, a level that necessarily involves a discussion of generational replacement, immigration, colonization, and enslavement. Third, the reproduction of the capitalist system itself. In this text, we touch on all three levels but focus primarily on the first. For other, sometimes opposed definitions of social reproduction, see Leopoldina Fortunati, *The Arcane of Reproduction:*

Housework, Prostitution, Labor and Capital (New York: Autonomedia, 1995 [1981]; Lise Vogel, *Marxism and the Oppression of Women: Toward a Unitary Theory* (Chicago: Haymarket Books, 2013 [1983]); Barbara Laslett and Johanna Brenner, "Gender and Social Reproduction," *Annual Review of Sociology* 15 (1989): 381–404; Kate Bezanson and Meg Luxton, eds., *Social Reproduction: Feminist Political Economy Challenges Neoliberalism* (Montreal: McGill–Queen's University Press, 2006); Silvia Federici, *Revolution at Point Zero: Housework, Reproduction, and Feminist Struggle* (Oakland, CA: PM Press, 2012); Tithi Bhattacharya, "How Not to Skip Class: Social Reproduction of Labor and the Global Working Class," *Viewpoint Magazine* 5 (October 2015) and in the following chapter of this volume; Cinzia Arruzza, "Functionalist, Determinist, Reductionist," *Science and Society* 80, no. 1 (January 2016): 9–30. For the trajectory of social reproduction theory, see Sue Ferguson, "Building on the Strengths of the Socialist Feminist Tradition," *Critical Sociology* 25, vol. 1 (January 1999): 1–15.

5. Sue Ferguson and David McNally, "Capital, Labor-Power, and Gender-Relations: Introduction to the Historical Materialism Edition of Marxism and the Oppression of Women," in Vogel, *Marxism and the Oppression of Women*, xxv.
6. Immanuel Wallerstein and Joan Smith, "Households as an Institution of the World-Economy," in *Creating and Transforming Households: The Constraints of the World-Economy*, edited by Joan Smith and Immanuel Wallerstein (Cambridge: Cambridge University Press, 1992), 13.
7. Fred A. Shannon, *The Farmer's Last Frontier: Agriculture, 1860–1897* (New York: Farrar & Rinehart, 1945), 357–59; Alan Kulikoff, *The Agrarian Origins of American Capitalism* (Charlottesville: University Press of Virginia, 1992), 34–59; Thomas Summerhill, *Harvest of Dissent: Agrarianism in Nineteenth-Century New York* (Chicago: University of Illinois Press, 2005).
8. Richard White, *It's Your Misfortune and None of My Own: A New History of the American West* (Norman: Oklahoma University Press, 1991), 241–42.
9. White, *It's Your Misfortune*, 115; C. Joseph Genetin-Pilawa, *Crooked Paths to Allotment: The Fight over Federal Indian Policy after the Civil War* (Chapel Hill: University of North Carolina Press, 2012); Cathleen D. Cahill, *Federal Fathers and Mothers: A Social History of the United States Indian Service, 1869–1933* (Chapel Hill: University of North Carolina Press, 2011).
10. Steven Hahn, "Hunting, Fishing, and Foraging: Common Rights and Class Relations in the Postbellum South," *Radical History Review* 26 (1982): 37–64.
11. White, *It's Your Misfortune*, 237–241.
12. Michael W. Fitzgerald, *Urban Emancipation: Popular Politics in Reconstruction Mobile, 1860–1890* (Baton Rouge: Louisiana State University Press, 2002), 255–56; Brett Mizelle, "Unthinkable Visibility:

Pigs, Pork, and the Spectacle of Killing and Meat," *Rendering Nature: Animals, Bodies, Places, Politics,* edited by Marguerite S. Shaffer and Phoebe S.K. Young (Philadelphia: University of Pennsylvania Press, 2015), 269–70; Henry Hartog, "Pigs and Positivism," *Wisconsin Law Review* 4 (July 1985): 899–935.

13. Aaron D. Anderson, *Builders of a New South: Merchants, Capital, and the Remaking of Natchez, 1865–1914* (Jackson: University Press of Mississippi, 2013), 79–81; Harold D. Woodman, *New South, New Law: The Legal Foundations of Credit and Labor Relations in the Postbellum Agricultural South* (Baton Rouge: Louisiana State University Press, 1995); Steve Hahn, *The Roots of Southern Populism* (Oxford: Oxford University Press, 1983), 155–56; Roger L. Ransom and Richard Sutch, *One Kind of Freedom: The Economic Consequences of Emancipation* (New York: Cambridge University Press, 1977), 120–30; Jonathan Wiener, *Social Origins of the New South: Alabama, 1860–1885* (Baton Rouge: Louisiana State University Press, 1978), 36–47, 66–69; Nancy Bercaw, *Gendered Freedoms: Race, Rights, and the Politics of Household in the Delta, 1861–1875* (Gainesville: University of Florida Press, 2003), 46, 108–9. For an overview of debates about how to characterize the social relations of sharecropping, see Scott P. Marler, "Fables of the Reconstruction: Reconstruction of the Fables," *Journal of the Historical Society* 4, no. 1 (Winter 2004): 113–37.
14. Jeanne Boydston, *Home and Work: Housework, Wages, and the Ideology of Labor in the Early Republic* (Oxford: Oxford University Press, 1990), 20. See also, Stephanie McCurry, *Masters of Small Worlds: Yeoman Households, Gender Relations, and the Political Culture of the Antebellum South Carolina Low Country* (New York: Oxford University Press, 1995), 37–92.
15. To be sure, many wage-earning women organized to challenge these arrangements: in the 1860s, for example, working women in Boston circulated petitions for "garden homesteads," which would redistribute land to unmarried women and allow them to grow foodstuffs independently. See Lara Vapnek, *Breadwinners: Working Women and Economic Independence, 1865–1900* (Chicago: University of Illinois Press, 2009), 19–20.
16. Thomas Dublin, "Women and Outwork in a Nineteenth-Century New England Town," in *The Countryside in the Age of Capitalist Transformation: Essays in the Social History of Rural America,* eds. Steven Hahn and Jonathan Prude (Chapel Hill: University of North Carolina Press, 1985), 51–69; Christine Stansell, *City of Women: Sex and Class in New York, 1789–1860* (Chicago: University of Illinois Press, 1987), 15.
17. Mignon Duffy, "Doing the Dirty Work: Gender, Race, and Reproductive Labor in Historical Perspective," *Gender and Society* 21, no. 3 (June 2007): 320; Daniel Sutherland, *Americans and Their Servants: Domestic Service in the United States from 1800 to 1920* (Baton Rouge: Louisiana State University Press, 1981).
18. While many feminists initially limited social reproduction to unpaid domestic work, some scholarship has tried to expand the concept to bridge

the waged and unwaged division. See, for example, Evelyn Nakano Glenn, "From Servitude to Service Work: Historical Continuities in the Racial Division of Paid Reproductive Labor," *Signs* 18, no. 1 (Autumn 1992): 1–43; Duffy, "Doing the Dirty Work," 313–36.

19. This number varied by region. See Glenn, "From Servitude to Service Work," 7–11. See also Nancy Folbre, "The Unproductive Housewife: Her Evolution in Nineteenth-Century Economic Thought," *Signs* 16, no. 3 (Spring 1991): 465; Lynn Y. Weiner, *From Working Girl to Working Mother: The Female Labor Force in the United States, 1820–1980* (Chapel Hill: University of North Carolina Press, 1985), 27; Duffy, "Doing the Dirty Work," 320.
20. Alice Kessler-Harris, "Women's Wage Work as Myth and History," *Labor History* 19 (Spring 1978): 287–307; Mimi Abramovitz, "Poor Women in a Bind: Social Reproduction without Social Supports," *Affilia* 7, no. 2 (Summer 1992): 26.
21. Evelyn Nakano Glenn, *Issei, Nisei, War Bride: Three Generations of Japanese American Women in Domestic Service* (Philadelphia: Temple University Press, 1986), 4; Matthew Sobek, "Female Labor Force Participation Rate, by Race, Marital Status, and Presence of Children: 1880–1990," in Susan B. Carter, Scott Sigmund Gartner, Michael R. Haines, Alan L. Olmstead, Richard Sutch, and Gavin Wright, eds., *Historical Statistics of the United States, Earliest Times to the Present: Millennial Edition* (New York: Cambridge University Press, 2006), 425–69.
22. Faye Dudden, *Serving Women: Household Service in Nineteenth-Century America* (Middletown, CT: Wesleyan University Press, 1983), 224–25; Tera W. Hunter, "Domination and Resistance: The Politics of Wage Household Labor in New South Atlanta," *Labor History* 34, no. 2–3 (1993): 208.
23. Weiner, 84–87; Jacqueline Jones, *Labor of Love, Labor of Sorrow: Black Women, Work, and the Family, from Slavery to the Present* (New York: Basic Books, 2010), 105, 156; Stansell, 156–58; Glenn, "From Servitude to Service Work," 8. On Irish-born women in domestic service in the earlier part of the nineteenth century, see Faye Dudden, *Serving Women*, 59–65.
24. Lawrence Glickman, *A Living Wage: American Workers and the Making of Consumer Society* (Ithaca, NY: Cornell University Press, 1997).
25. Jenna Weissman Joselit, "The Landlord as Czar: Pre–World War I Tenant Activity," in *The Tenant Movement in New York City, 1904–1984*, edited by Ronald Lawson and Mark Naison (New Brunswick: Rutgers University Press, 1986); Paula E. Hyman, "Immigrant Women and Consumer Protest: The New York Kosher Meat Boycott of 1902," *American Jewish History* 70, no. 1 (September 1980): 91–105; Annelise Orleck, *Common Sense and a Little Fire: Women and Working-Class Politics in the United States, 1900–1965* (Chapel Hill: University of North Carolina Press, 1995), chapter 1.
26. William Freiburger, "War Prosperity and Hunger: The New York Food Riots of 1917," *Labor History* 25 (Spring 1984): 217–39.
27. Dana Frank, "'Food Wins All Struggles': Seattle Labor and the Politicization of Consumption," *Radical History Review* 50 (1991): 68–71.

28. Tera Hunter, *To 'Joy My Freedom: Southern Black Women's Lives and Labors After the Civil War* (Cambridge, MA: Harvard University Press, 1997), 88–97.
29. Ibid., 97.
30. Alexander Keyssar, *Out of Work: The First Century of Unemployment in Massachusetts* (New York: Cambridge University Press, 1986), 50.
31. Herbert G. Gutman, "The Failure of the Movement by the Unemployed for Public Works in 1873," *Political Science Quarterly* 80 (June 1965): 255, 257, 261.
32. David Huyssen, *Progressive Inequality: Rich and Poor in New York, 1890–1920* (Cambridge: Harvard University Press, 2014), 141.
33. Barry J. Kaplan, "Reformers and Charity: The Abolition of Public Outdoor Relief in New York City, 1873–1890," *Social Service Review* 52, no. 2 (June 1978): 202–14; Mimi Abramovitz, *Regulating the Lives of Women: Social Welfare Policies from Colonial Times to the Present* (Boston: South End Press, 1996), 137–71; Michael Katz, *In the Shadow of the Poorhouse: A Social History of Welfare in America* (New York: Basic Books, 1996), chapter 3; Katz *The Undeserving Poor: From the War on Poverty to the War on Welfare* (New York: Pantheon Books, 1989).
34. Katz, *In the Shadow of the Poorhouse*, 117.
35. Alan Derickson, "From Company Doctors to Union Hospitals: The First Democratic Health Care Experiments of the United Mine Workers of America," *Labor History* 33 (Summer 1992): 325–42; Alan Derickson, *Workers' Health, Workers' Democracy: The Western Miners' Struggle, 1891–1925* (Ithaca, NY: Cornell University Press, 1988); Twenty-Third Annual Report of the Commissioner of Labor, 1908: Workmen's Insurance and Benefit Funds in the United States, *House Congressional Documents*, 60th Cong., 2nd sess., doc. no. 1565 (Washington, D.C.: Government Printing Office, 1909).
36. Antonio Gramsci, "Americanism and Fordism," in *The Gramsci Reader*, edited by David Forgacs (New York: New York University Press, 2000), 275–99; Mariarosa Dalla Costa, *Family, Welfare, and the State: Between Progressivism and the New Deal*, translated by Rafaella Capanna (New York: Common Notions, 2015), 8–9. For Ford, see Richard Snow, *I Invented the Modern Age: The Rise of Henry Ford* (New York: Scribner, 2013), chapters 13 and 14.
37. David Montgomery, *The Fall of the House of Labor: The Workplace, the State, and American Labor Activism, 1865–1925* (Cambridge: Cambridge University Press, 1987); Christopher J. Cyphers, *The National Civic Federation and the Making of a New Liberalism, 1900–1915* (Westport, CT: Praeger, 2002); Jonathan Weinstein, *The Corporate Ideal in the Liberal State, 1900–1918* (Boston: Beacon Press, 1968); Seth Koven and Sonya Michel, "Womanly Duties: Maternalist Politics and the Origins of Welfare States in France, Germany, Great Britain, and the United States, 1880–1920," *American Historical Review* 95, no. 4 (October 1990): 1076–108; Kathy Peiss, *Cheap Amusements: Working Women and Leisure*

in Turn-of-the-Century New York (Philadelphia: Temple University Press, 1986), 42–43.

38. Katz, *In the Shadow of the Poor House*, 134–37, 215–17; Coontz, *The Social Origins of Private Life*, 274; Mimi Abramovitz, *Regulating the Lives of Women*, 185–87; Linda Gordon, *Pitied but Not Entitled: Single Mothers and the History of Welfare, 1890–1935* (New York: Free Press, 1994); David Wallace Adams, *Education for Extinction: American Indians and the Boarding School Experience, 1875–1928* (Lawrence: University Press of Kansas, 1995).
39. Barbara Young Welke, *Recasting American Liberty: Gender, Race, Law, and the Railroad Revolution, 1865–1920* (New York: Cambridge University Press, 2001), 351–52; Gary Gerstle, *Liberty and Coercion: The Paradox of American Government from the Founding to the Present* (Princeton, NJ: Princeton University Press, 2015), 80–82; Theda Skocpol, *Protecting Soldiers and Mothers: The Political Origins of Social Policy in the United States* (Cambridge, MA: Harvard University Press, 1992).
40. Skocpol, *Protecting Soldiers and Mothers*, 471–472.
41. Frances Fox Piven and Richard A. Cloward, *Poor People's Movements: Why They Succeed, How They Fail* (New York: Vintage Books, 1979), 47–48; Dalla Costa, *Family, Welfare, and the State*, 27–35.
42. Robert Angell Cooley, *The Family Encounters the Great Depression* (New York: Scribner, 1936).
43. Joan M. Crouse, *The Homeless Transient in the Great Depression: New York State, 1929–1941* (Albany: State University of New York Press, 1986), 48.
44. Ibid., 97–102. The classic sociological study of hobos remains Nels Anderson, *The Hobo: The Sociology of the Homeless Man* (Chicago: University of Chicago Press, 1961). For a broader history of hobos in the United States, see Todd Depastino, *Citizen Hobo: How a Century of Homelessness Shaped America* (Chicago: University of Chicago Press, 2003).
45. For struggles of the unemployed, see Piven and Cloward, *Poor People's Movements*, chapter 2.
46. Randi Storch, *Red Chicago: American Communism at its Grassroots, 1928–1935* (Urbana-Champaign: University of Illinois Press, 2009), 102.
47. Dalla Costa, *Family, Welfare, and the State*, chapter 3.
48. Mary E. Triece, *On the Picket Line: Strategies of Working-Class Women during the Depression* (Urbana-Champaign: University of Illinois Press, 2007), 64–69.
49. Irving Bernstein, *The Lean Years: A History of the American Worker, 1920–1933* (Baltimore: Penguin Books, 1970), 421–23.
50. Piven and Cloward, *Poor People's Movements*, 53–55.
51. For surveys of the concept of "class composition" in English, see Red Notes, *Working Class Autonomy and the Crisis: Italian Marxist Texts of the Theory and Practice of a Class Movement, 1964–79* (London, CSE Books); Kolinko, "Paper on Class Composition," September 2001, https://www.nadir.org/nadir/initiativ/kolinko/engl/e_klazu.htm; Steve Wright, *Storming Heaven:*

Class Composition and Struggle in Italian Autonomist Marxism (London: Pluto Press, 2002); and Salar Mohandesi, "Class Consciousness or Class Composition?," *Science and Society* 77, no. 1 (January 2013): 72–97.

52. Mark Naison, *Communists in Harlem during the Depression* (New York: Grove Press, 1984); Susan Ware, *Holding Their Own: American Women in the 1930s* (Boston: Twayne Publishers, 1982), chapter five; Robert Shaffer, "Women and the Communist Party, USA, 1930–1940," *Socialist Review*, no. 8 (1979): 73–118; Triece, *On the Picket Line*; Danny Lucia, "The Unemployed Movements of the 1930s: Bringing Misery out of Hiding," *International Socialist Review* 71 (May 2010), http://isreview.org/issue/71/unemployed-movements-1930s; Dalla Costa, *Family, Welfare, and the State*, 79–83.
53. The idea that the terrain of social reproduction could operate as a site of class recomposition derives from the work of Italian feminists in the workerist tradition. Although formulated to think through struggles in the present, this insight also animated a wealth of historical writing, and not just about Italy. In *Family, Welfare, and the State*, for example, Mariarosa Dalla Costa explicitly argues that just such a process of class recomposition took place in the United States during the Great Depression.
54. Frances Fox Piven and Richard A. Cloward, *Regulating the Poor: The Functions of Public Welfare* (New York: Pantheon Books, 1972), part 1.
55. Helen Seymour, unpublished report of December 1, 1937 to the Committee on Social Security of the Social Science Research Council, 15, quoted in Piven and Cloward, *Poor People's Movements*, 57.
56. Naison, *Communists in Harlem*, 76.
57. Lizabeth Cohen, *Making a New Deal: Industrial Workers in Chicago, 1919–1939* (Cambridge: Cambridge University Press, 1990), chapter 6; Dalla Costa, *Family, Welfare, and the State*, 62, 73–75.
58. Quoted in Harvey Klehr, *The Heyday of American Communism: The Depression Decade* (New York: Basic Books, Inc, 1984), 50.
59. Quoted in Lucia, "Unemployed Movements of the 1930s."
60. Klehr, *The Heyday of American Communism*, 52–53.
61. For the state's role in reproducing social cohesion, see, among others, Louis Althusser, *On the Reproduction of Capitalism: Ideology and Ideological State Apparatuses*, trans. G.M. Goshgarian (London: Verso, 2014); Nicos Poulantzas, *Political Power and Social Classes*, trans. Timothy O'Hagan (London: New Left Books, 1973)); and Nicos Poulantzas, *State, Power, Socialism*, trans. Patrick Camiller (London: New Left Books, 1978).
62. For the New Deal, see Ira Katznelson, *Fear Itself: The New Deal and the Origins of Our Time* (New York: Liveright Publishing, 2013).
63. Silvia Federici and Mario Montano [Guido Baldi, pseud.], "Theses on the Mass Worker and Social Capital," *Radical America* 6, no. 3 (May–June 1972): 3–21.
64. Ibid., 16.
65. For a good overview of these programs, see Katz, *In the Shadow of the Poorhouse*, chapter 8.

66. Piven and Cloward, *Regulating the Poor*, 75.
67. Quoted in Cohen, *Making A New Deal*, 271.
68. "Coal Ordered for Needy," *New York Times*, December 15, 1933.
69. "Relief Foods Total 692,228,274 Pounds," *New York Times*, October 18, 1934.
70. Emily D. Cahan, *Past Caring: A History of U.S. Preschool Care and Education for the Poor, 1820–1965* (New York: National Center for Children in Poverty, 1989), 26–27.
71. Eric Foner, *Give Me Liberty! An American History*, Vol. 2 (New York: W.W. Norton, 2012), 811.
72. Jeff Wiltse, *Contested Waters: A Social History of Swimming Pools in America* (Chapel Hill: University of North Carolina Press, 2007), chapter 4.
73. Ware, *Holding Their Own*, 28; Alice Kessler-Harris, "In the Nation's Image: The Gendered Limits of Social Citizenship in the Depression Era," *Journal of American History* 86 (December 1999): 1251–79.
74. Dalla Costa, *Family, Welfare, and the State*, 94. See also Linda Gordon, *Pitied but Not Entitled*; Alice Kessler-Harris, "In the Nation's Image."
75. Foner, *Give Me Liberty!*, 820–26.
76. Jefferson Cowie has recently made this point in *The Great Exception: The New Deal and the Limits of American Politics* (Princeton, NJ: Princeton University Press, 2016). See also Ira Katznelson, *Fear Itself*.
77. Gavin Wright, *Old South, New South: Revolutions in the Southern Economy Since the Civil War* (Louisiana State University Press, 1996), 226–38; William G. Robbins, *Colony and Empire: The Capitalist Transformation of the American West* (Lawrence: University Press of Kansas, 1994), 158–61.
78. Cahan, *Past Caring*, 27–30.
79. Jason Scott Smith, "The Fair Deal," in *A Companion to Harry S. Truman*, edited by Daniel S. Margolies (Malden MA: Blackwell, 2012), 210–21.
80. Katz, *In the Shadow of the Poor House*, 260.
81. Francis Fox Piven, "Ideology and the State: Women, Power, and the Welfare State," in *Women, the State, and Welfare*, edited by Linda Gordon (Madison: University of Wisconsin Press, 1990), 257.
82. Piven and Cloward, *Regulating the Poor*, 320–40; Premilla Nadasen, *Welfare Warriors: The Welfare Rights Movement in the United States* (New York: Routledge, 2005); Premilla Nadasen, *Household Workers Unite: The Untold Story of African American Women Who Built a Movement* (Boston: Beacon Press, 2015); Annelise Orleck, *Storming Caesar's Palace: How Black Mothers Fought their Own War on Poverty* (Boston: Beacon Press, 2005); Felicia Ann Kornbluh, *The Battle for Welfare Rights: Politics and Poverty in Modern America* (Philadelphia: University of Pennsylvania Press, 2007).
83. Katz, *In the Shadow of the Poor House*, 269–76.
84. For an articulation of this perspective, see Linda Gordon, "Family, Violence, and Social Control," and Piven, "Ideology and the State," in *Women, the State, and Welfare*.

85. Lyndon B. Johnson: "Remarks Upon Signing the Food Stamp Act," August 31, 1964, http://www.presidency.ucsb.edu/ws/?pid=26472.
86. Silvia Federici, "Wages against Housework," in *Revolution at Point Zero: Housework, Reproduction, and Feminist Struggle* (Oakland, CA: PM Press, 2012).
87. Louis Massiah, "Interview with Huey P. Newton," May 1989, http://digital.wustl.edu/e/eii/eiiweb/new5427.0458.119hueypnewton.html.
88. David Hilliard, ed., *The Black Panther Party: Service to the People Programs* (Albuquerque: University of New Mexico Press, 2008).
89. Cedric Johnson, "Between Revolution and the Racial Ghetto: Harold Cruse and Harry Haywood debate Class Struggle and the Negro Question, 1962–1968," talk presented at the 11th annual Historical Materialism conference, London, November 7, 2014; Cedric Johnson, *Revolutionaries to Race Leaders: Black Power and the Making of African American Politics* (Minneapolis: University of Minnesota Press, 2007); Robert O. Self, *American Babylon: Race and the Struggle for Postwar Oakland* (Princeton, NJ: Princeton University Press, 2003), especially chapters 5 and 6; Joshua Bloom and Waldo E. Martin Jr., *Black Against Empire: The History and Politics of the Black Panther Party* (Berkeley: University of California Press, 2013), 36–37, 48.
90. Mimi Abramovitz, "Women, Social Reproduction and the Neo-Liberal Assault on the US Welfare State," in *The Legal Tender of Gender: Welfare, Law, and the Regulation of Women's Poverty*, edited by Shelley A.M. Gavigan and Dorothy E Chunn (Portland, OR: Hartland Publishing), 19.
91. Frances Fox Piven and Richard A. Cloward, *The New Class War: Reagan's Attack on the Welfare State and its Consequences* (New York: Pantheon Books, 1982), 15.
92. Lyndon B. Johnson: "Remarks at the City Hall in Buffalo," October 15, 1964, http://www.presidency.ucsb.edu/ws/?pid=26606.
93. Katz, *In the Shadow of the Poor House*, 266.
94. James H. Herbert, *Clean Cheap Heat: The Development of Residential Markets for Natural Gas in the United States* (New York: Praeger, 1992), 145; The National Center for Policy Analysis, "Technology and Economic Growth in the Information Age," *Policy Backgrounder* no. 147, March 12, 1998, 7; Sue Bowden and Avner Offer, "Household Appliances and the Use of Time: The United States and Great Britain since the 1920s," *Economic History Review* 47, no. 4 (1994): 725–48.
95. Christine E. Bose, Philip L. Bereano and Mary Malloy, "Household Technology and the Social Construction of Housework," *Technology and Culture* 25, no. 1 (January 1984): 53–82.
96. Ruth Schwartz Cowan, *More Work for Mother: The Ironies of Household Technology from the Open Hearth to the Microwave* (New York: Basic Books, 1983), 99, 202.
97. Glenn, "From Servitude to Service Work," 20.
98. Karl Marx, "Results of the Immediate Process of Production," in *Capital*, Vol. 1, translated by Ben Fowkes (London: Penguin, 1990). The literature

on this concept is as contentious as it is voluminous, with various writers appropriating the idea of subsumption for their own ends. Rather than taking sides in these debates, here we wish only to add to and enrich the discussion by suggesting that subsumption should be understood as involving social reproduction as well as the labor process at point of production. It should go without saying that despite their interrelationship, the histories of each process cannot be reduced to one another. For example, even when real subsumption is obtained at the point of production, in some places the subsumption of social reproduction may have only been formal.

99. Bhattacharya, "How Not to Skip Class"; Piven and Cloward, *New Class War.*
100. For neoliberalism as a political, state-driven response to the crisis, see Leo Panitch and Sam Gindin, *The Making of Global Capitalism* (New York: Verso, 2012), 14–15; Nicos Poulantzas, *State, Power, Socialism*, translated by Patrick Cammiler (London: New Left Books, 1978), part 4.
101. For mass incarceration, see, among many others, Joy James, ed., *States of Confinement: Policing, Detention Prisons* (New York: St. Martin's Press, 2000); Michelle Alexander, *The New Jim Crow* (New York: New Press, 2001); Angela Y. Davis, *Are Prisons Obsolete?* (New York: Seven Stories Press, 2003); Ruth Wilson Gilmore, *Golden Gulag: Prisons, Surplus, Crisis, and Opposition in Globalizing California* (Berkeley: University of California Press, 2007).
102. Mimi Abramovitz, *Under Attack, Fighting Back: Women and Welfare in the United States* (New York: Monthly Review Press, 2000), 29.
103. Mimi Abramovitz, "Poor Women in a Bind: Social Reproduction without Social Supports," *Affilia* 7, no. 2 (Summer 1992): 37.
104. Abramovitz, *Under Attack*, 28–32, 36–37.
105. Kenneth J. Neubeck and Noel A. Cazenave, *Welfare Racism: Playing the Race Card Against America's Poor* (New York: Routledge, 2001).
106. Abramovitz, *Under Attack*, 18.
107. Silvia Federici, "Permanent Reproductive Crisis: An Interview with Silvia Federici," *Mute*, March 7, 2013; Nancy Fraser, "Contradictions of Capital and Care," *New Left Review* 100 (July–August 2016): 99–117.
108. See, for example, the fifth issue of *Viewpoint* magazine, especially Asad Haider and Salar Mohandesi, "Making A Living"; Bue Rübner Hanser, "Surplus Population, Social Reproduction, and the Problem of Class Formation"; and Bhattacharya, "How Not to Skip Class." Bhattacharya, in particular, very convincingly shows how the framework of social reproduction forces us to rethink our understanding of the "economy," the working class, and the processes of class formation, especially on a global scale.
109. On financialization and the detachment from production, see David Graeber, *Debt: The First 5,000 Years* (New York: Melville House, 2011), 375–76; David M. Kotz, *The Rise and Fall of Neoliberal Capitalism* (Cambridge, MA: Harvard University Press, 2015).

110. Bronwyn Bailey, *Long-Term Commitments: The Interdependence of Pension Security and Private Equity* (Washington, DC: Private Equity Growth Council, 2013); Christopher Matthews, "Why Pension Funds Are Hooked on Private Equity," *TIME*, April 15, 2013.
111. Susan Ferguson and David McNally, "Precarious Migrants: Gender, Race, and the Social Reproduction of a Global Working Class," *Socialist Register* 51 (2015): 1–23.
112. Though the literature on surplus populations is growing, there is still a desperate need for direct inquiries. For some general theoretical reference points, see Mike Davis, *Planet of Slums* (London: Verso, 2006); Michael Denning, "Wageless Life," *New Left Review* 66 (November–December 2010): 79–97; Aaron Benanav and Endnotes, "Misery and Debt: On the Logic and History of Surplus Populations and Surplus Capital," *Endnotes* 2 (2010); Bue Rübner Hansen, "Surplus Population, Social Reproduction, and the Problem of Class Formation," *Viewpoint* 4 (October 2015).

CHAPTER 4: HOW NOT TO SKIP CLASS

1. Thanks are due to Charles Post, Colin Barker, Andrew Ryder, and Bill Mullen for reading draft versions of this essay and making extensive comments. All errors remain mine.
2. Many foundational Marxist concepts, of course, inhere to and derive from this proposal. The questions of the apparent separation between, say, economics and politics or the state and civil society are implicated in this question of appearance. For more details, see Ellen Meiksins Wood, "The Separation of the 'Economic and the 'Political' in Capitalism" in *Democracy Against Capitalism: Renewing Historical Materialism* (Cambridge: Cambridge University Press, 1995); Peter D. Thomas, *The Gramscian Moment: Philosophy, Hegemony and Marxism* (Leiden, Netherlands: Brill, 2009).
3. Ellen Meiksins Wood, *The Retreat from Class: A New 'True Socialism'* (London: Verso, 1986), 111.
4. Karl Marx, *Capital: A Critique of Political Economy*, vol. 1, translated by Ben Fowkes (New York: Penguin Books, 1976), 280.
5. Ibid., 274.
6. Ibid., 270.
7. "Labor-power was not always a commodity (merchandise). Labor was not always wage-labor, i.e., free labor. The slave did not sell his labor-power to the slave-owner, any more than the ox sells his labor to the farmer. The slave, together with his labor-power, was sold to his owner once and for all. He is a commodity that can pass from the hand of one owner to that of another. He himself is a commodity, but his labor-power is not his commodity. The serf sells only a portion of his labor-power. It is not he who receives wages from the owner of the land; it is rather the owner of the land who receives a tribute from him. The serf belongs to the soil, and to the lord of the soil he brings its fruit. The free laborer, on the other hand,

sells his very self, and that by fractions. He auctions off eight, 10, 12, 15 hours of his life, one day like the next, to the highest bidder, to the owner of raw materials, tools, and the means of life—i.e., to the capitalist. The laborer belongs neither to an owner nor to the soil, but eight, 10, 12, 15 hours of his daily life belong to whomsoever buys them." From "Wage-Labor and Capital" in *Marx and Engels Collected Works*, Vol. 9 (New York: International Publishers, 1986), 203. This, however, is not the whole story. Jairus Banaji has convincingly shown that "wage labor," that is, "the commodity labor power, was known under various forms of social production *before* the capitalist epoch." What distinguished capitalism from all other modes of production was that wage labor "in this simple determination as the commodity labor-power, was the necessary basis of capitalism as the *generalized form of social production*." (Emphasis mine.) The specific role that wage labor played under capitalism was that it was "capital-positing, capital-creating labor." See Banaji, *Theory as History: Essays on Modes of Production and Exploitation* (Chicago: Haymarket Books, 2011), 54.

8. Marx, *Capital*, vol. 1, 272.
9. Ibid., 274.
10. Ibid.
11. Ibid., 275.
12. For more details, see Lise Vogel, *Marxism and the Oppression of Women: Towards a Unitary Theory* (Chicago: Haymarket Books, 2014 [1983]).
13. Karl Marx, "Outlines of the Critique of Political Economy (Rough Draft of 1857–58)," in *Marx and Engels Collected Works*, Vol. 28 (New York: International Publishers, 1986), 215.
14. There is a rich literature and debate on the status of housework as value-producing labor. For arguments in favor of housework as producing surplus value, see the work of activist-theorists such as Selma James, Mariarosa Dalla Costa, and Silvia Federici. For example: Mariarosa Dalla Costa, "Women and the Subversion of the Community," *Radical America* 6, no. 1 (January–February 1972), originally published in Italian as "Donne e sovversione sociale," in *Potere femminile e sovversione sociale* (Padova: Marsilio, 1972); Selma James, "Wageless of the World," in *All Work and No Pay*, edited by Wendy Edmonds and Suzie Fleming (Bristol, UK: Falling Wall Press,1975). For the position that domestic labor does not produce surplus value, to which I subscribe, see Paul Smith, "Domestic Labor and Marx's Theory of Value" in *Feminism and Materialism: Women and Modes of Production*, edited by Annette Kuhn and Annmarie Wolpe (Boston: Routledge and Kegan Paul, 1978). While I disagree with the argument that domestic work is unpaid productive labor, it is important to emphasize here that we owe the wages-for-housework feminists of the 1970s a great analytical debt for theorizing questions of domestic labor in an effort to overcome the lacuna in Marx.
15. Karl Marx, *Grundrisse* (London: Penguin Classics, 1993), 776ff.
16. Marx, *Capital*, vol. 1, 711.

17. Michael A. Lebowitz, *Beyond Capital: Marx's Political Economy of the Working Class*, 2nd ed. (Basingstoke, UK: Palgrave Macmillian, 2003), 65. Emphasis in the original.
18. Marx, *Capital*, vol. 1, 724.
19. Ibid., 280.
20. Ibid., 724.
21. Karl Marx, *Value, Price, Profit: Speech by Karl Marx to the First International Working Men's Association* (New York: International Co., 1969), chapter 6.
22. Marx, *Capital*, vol. 1, 275.
23. Lebowitz, *Beyond Capital*, 31.
24. Marx, *Theories of Surplus Value*, quoted in Lebowitz, *Beyond Capital*, 32.
25. Ibid., 31.
26. Ibid., 110.
27. Ibid., 127.
28. Marx, "Wage-Labor and Capital," 216.
29. Marx, *Capital*, vol. 1, 711.
30. Marx, *Grundrisse*, 287.
31. Lebowitz, *Beyond Capital*, 69.
32. Karl Marx, *Wages, Price and Profits* (Beijing: Foreign Language Press, 1975), 74.
33. Marx, "Wage-Labor and Capital," 203.
34. Lebowitz, *Beyond Capital*, 96.
35. E.P. Thompson, *The Making of the English Working Class* (Harmondsworth, UK: Penguin, 1963), 347.
36. Redcliffe N. Salaman, quoted in Thompson, *Making of the English Working* Class, 348.
37. Sandra Halperin, *War and Social Change in Modern Europe: The Great Transformation Revisited* (Cambridge: Cambridge University Press, 2004), 91–92.
38. Lebowitz, *Beyond Capital*, 96.
39. Karl Marx, "Instructions for the Delegates of the Provisional General Council. Different Questions," in *Minutes of the General Council of the First International*, quoted in Lebowitz, *Beyond Capital*, 97.
40. Karl Marx, *Capital*, vol. III (Moscow: Progress Publishers, 1971), 791.
41. Raymond Williams, *Towards 2000* (London: Chatto & Windus, 1983), 172.
42. Ibid., 255.
43. Raymond Williams, *Towards 2000* (London: Chatto & Windus, 1983), 132–33.
44. Tithi Bhattacharya, "Explaining Gender Violence in the Neoliberal Era," *International Socialist Review* 91 (Winter 2013–14): 25–47.
45. Arman Sethi, "India's Young Workforce Adopts New Forms of Protest," *Business Standard*, May 5, 2014, http://www.business-standard.com/article/current-affairs/india-s-young-workforce-adopts-new-forms-of-protest-114050500049_1.html.

46. Karl Marx, "Trades' Unions: Their Past, Present and Future," in *Instructions for the Delegates of the Provisional General Council: The Different Questions* (London: International Workingmen's Association, 1886), https://www.marxists.org/history/international/iwma/documents/1866/instructions.htm#06.
47. For details on urban slums and gendered violence in India, see Tithi Bhattacharya, "India's Daughter: Neoliberalism's Dreams and the Nightmares of Violence," *International Socialist Review* 97 (Summer 2015): 53–71.
48. Karl Marx, "Address of the Central Authority to the League," in *Marx and Engels Collected Works*, Vol. 10 (New York: International Publishers, 1986), 282–83.

CHAPTER 5: INTERSECTIONS AND DIALECTICS

1. G.W.F. Hegel, *Phenomenology of Spirit*, translated by A V. Miller (Oxford: Oxford University Press, 1977), 22, 27.
2. Kimberlé Crenshaw, "Mapping the Margins: Intersectionality, Identity Politics and Violence against Women of Color," paper presented at the World Conference Against Racism, Durban, South Africa, 2001. This paper was based on one of the same title published in *Stanford Law Review* 43 (1993), 1241–99, available at: http://socialdifference.columbia.edu/files/socialdiff/projects/Article__Mapping_the_Margins_by_Kimblere_Crenshaw.pdf.
3. Christine Bose, "Intersectionality and Global Gender Inequality," *Gender and Society* 26, no. 1 (2012): 67–72; Helma Lutz, "Intersectional Analysis: A Way Out of Multiple Dilemmas?" paper presented to the International Sociological Association, Brisbane, July 2002; Bunch's paper is described by Nira Yuval-Davis, "Intersectionality and Feminist Politics," *European Journal of Women's Studies* 13, no. 3 (2006): 203.
4. Patricia Hill Collins, *Black Feminist Thought* (London: HarperCollins, 1990), 276, 24–25.
5. Sherene Razack, *Looking White People in the Eye: Gender, Race and Culture in Courtrooms and Classrooms* (Toronto: University of Toronto Press, 1998), 13.
6. Rita Kaur Dhamoon, "Considerations on Mainstreaming Intersectionality," *Political Research Quarterly* 64, no. 1 (2011): 232.
7. Floya Anthias, "Hierarchies of Social Location, Class and Intersectionality: Towards a Translocational Frame," *International Sociology* 28, no. 1 (2012): 129.
8. Yuval-Davis, "Intersectionality and Feminist Politics," 195, 200–201.
9. Isaac Newton, *The Principia: Mathematical Principles of Natural Philosophy*, translated by I. Bernard Cohen and Anne Whitman (Berkeley: University of California Press, 1999), 408.
10. See David McNally, *Political Economy and the Rise of Capitalism: A Reinterpretation* (Berkeley: University of California Press, 1988), 180–92.

11. Daniel Bensaïd, *Marx for Our Times*, translated by Gregory Elliot (London: Verso, 2002), 301.
12. Ludwig von Bertalanffy, *General Systems Theory* (Harmondsworth, UK: Penguin, 1973), 198–99.
13. For one explicit example, see Richard Levins and Richard Lewontin, *The Dialectical Biologist* (Cambridge, MA: Harvard University Press, 1985).
14. Anthias, "Hierarchies of Social Location," 130, 133. Note that the idea of multiple social strata was a liberal-pluralist response to critical theories of social class.
15. G.W.F. Hegel, *Science of Logic*, translated by A.V. Miller (London: George Allen & Unwin, 1969), 728, 731.
16. Himani Bannerji, "Building from Marx: Reflections on Class and Race," *Social Justice* 32, no. 4 (2005): 147.
17. Hegel, *Science of Logic*, 711, 713, 714, 722.
18. Ibid., 728, 731.
19. Gabriele Winker and Nina Degele, "Intersectionality as Multi-Level Analysis: Dealing with Social Inequality," *European Journal of Women's Studies* 18, no. 1 (2011): 54.
20. On interconnectivities, see Francisco Valdes, "Sex and Race in Queer Legal Culture: Ruminations on Identities and Inter-connectivities," in *Critical Race Theory: The Cutting Edge*, edited by R. Delgado and J. Stefancic (Philadephia: Temple University Press, 1995), 334–39. Dhamoon (232) gestures toward a more dialectical formulation when she argues that "processes of differentiation dynamically function through one another and enable each other." But her analysis regularly retreats toward a liberal pluralism, perhaps in part because of her concern with "mainstreaming intersectionality," i.e., making it part of the toolkit of mainstream social science.
21. It is interesting that one of the most eloquent theorists in this idiom was the Scottish philosopher David Hume, whose conventionalist empiricism remains the basis of much pragmatism and certain variants of postmodern theory.
22. This fourfold account of causation is of course derived from Aristotle, *The Metaphysics*.
23. Here the limits of Hegel's bourgeois horizon come into play, both in his naturalization of the heterosexual household and his incapacity to transcend the horizon of the nation-state.
24. Hegel, *Phenomenology of Spirit*, 161.
25. Ibid., 22, 20.
26. As Songsuk Susan Hahn points out, the priority of life for thought warrants Hegel's introduction of ontological categories such as "life," "organics," "being," and "becoming" into his *Logic* in a manner entirely foreign to formal logic. See Hahn, *Contradiction in Motion: Hegel's Organic Concept of Life and Value* (Ithaca, NY: Cornell University Press, 2007), 62–63.
27. Hegel, *Phenomenology of Spirit*, 22.
28. Ibid., 31, 37.

29. Friedrich Engels, "Preface," in Karl Marx, *Capital*, vol. 2, translated by David Fernbach (Harmondsworth, UK: Penguin, 1981), 103.
30. "Marx conceives of things as Relations": see Bertell Ollman, *Alienation: Marx's Conception of Man in Capitalist Society* (Cambridge: Cambridge University Press, 1971), 27.
31. Bannerji, "Building from Marx," 144.
32. Bannerji, "But Who Speaks for Us?" in *Thinking Through: Essays on Feminism, Marxism and Anti-Racism* (Toronto: Women's Press, 1995), 83.
33. Bannerji, "Building from Marx," 146.
34. Hegel, *Science of Logic*, 769.
35. Karl Marx, *Grundrisse*, translated by Martin Nicolaus (Harmondsworth, UK: Penguin, 1973), 101.
36. István Mészáros, *Lukács' Concept of Dialectic* (London: Merlin Press, 1972), 63.
37. Hegel, *Science of Logic*, 748.
38. Bannerji, "Building from Marx," 149.
39. See, for instance, Iris Young, "Beyond the Unhappy Marriage: A Critique of Dual Systems Theory," in *Women and Revolution*, edited by Lydia Sargent (Boston: South End Press, 1981), 43–70; and, especially, Lise Vogel, *Marxism and the Oppression of Women: Toward a Unitary Theory* (Chicago: Haymarket Books, 2013 [1983]), and the Introduction to the new edition of Vogel's text by Susan Ferguson and me.
40. See Susan Ferguson, "Canadian Contributions to Social Reproduction Feminism, Race and Embodied Labor," *Race, Gender and Class* 15, nos. 1–2 (2008): 42–57; Susan Ferguson and David McNally, "Precarious Migrants: Gender, Race and the Social Reproduction of a Global Working Class," *Socialist Register 2015* (London: Merlin Press, 2014).
41. Ferguson, "Canadian Contributions," 45.
42. Angela Davis, *Women, Race and Class* (New York: Vintage Books, 1983), 5, 87–98, 129, 143–44, 224, 237–38. Here, Davis's book converges with the lines of analysis to be found in Evelyn Nakano Glenn, "Racial Ethnic Women's Labor: The Intersection of Race, Gender and Class Oppression," *Review of Radical Political Economics* 17, no. 3 (1985): 86–108. Notwithstanding the use of the term *intersection* in the title, this article too operates with one foot inside a social reproduction approach.
43. Ibid., 7–8, 18, 23, 91.
44. Ibid., 66.
45. Ibid., 243.
46. I would suggest that this is evident in the social and political program developed in tandem with the Black Lives Matter movement. See *A Vision for Black Lives: Policy Demands for Black Power, Freeedom, and Justice* (2016): https://policy.m4bl.org/.

CHAPTER 6: CHILDREN, CHILDHOOD, AND CAPITALISM

1. For example, Joel Bakan, *Childhood under Siege* (Toronto: Allen Lane, 2011); Sharon Beder, *This Little Kiddy Went to Market* (London: Pluto,

2009; David Buckingham, *Childhood and Consumer Culture* (New York: Palgrave Macmillan, 2011); John O'Neill, *The Missing Child in Liberal Theory* (Toronto: University of Toronto, 2004); Tim Kasser and Susan Linn, "Growing Up under Corporate Capitalism: The Problem of Marketing to Children, with Suggestions for Policy Solutions," *Social Issues and Policy Review* 10, no. 1 (2016): 122–50.

2. This is acknowledged in some cultural studies accounts (e.g., Daniel Thomas Cook, *The Commodification of Childhood* (Durham, NC: Duke University Press, 2004), and partially explored in others: for example, Beryl Langer, "Consuming Anomie: Children and Global Commercial Culture," *Childhood* 12, no. 2 (2005): 259–71; Kate Cairns, "The Subject of Neoliberal Affects: Rural Youth Envision their Futures," *Canadian Geographer* 57, no. 3 (2013): 337–44; Valerie Walkerdine, *Daddy's Girl: Young Girls and Popular Culture* (Cambridge, MA: Harvard University Press, 1997). My goal here is to contribute to these efforts by developing a theoretical framework that situates experiences of children and childhood more explicitly in relation to the social reproduction of capitalism.
3. They do this insofar as capital expropriates the means of production—and with it, the means of subsistence or reproduction—from workers. See Susan Ferguson, "Intersectionality and Social Reproduction Feminisms: Toward an Integrative Ontology," *Historical Materialism* 24, no. 2 (2016): 52.
4. See Raymond Williams, *Marxism and Literature* (Oxford: Oxford University Press, 1977), 83–89, for a discussion of determination in terms of exerting pressures and setting limits on social relations.
5. See Lise Vogel, *Marxism and the Oppression of Women: Toward a Unitary Theory* (Chicago: Haymarket Books, 2013).
6. I am not suggesting here that children are born outside of history. See below for a fuller discussion.
7. Craig Heron, *Lunch-Bucket Lives: Remaking the Workers' City* (Toronto: Between the Lines 2015), 127.
8. Steven Mintz, *Huck's Raft: A History of American Childhood* (Cambridge Harvard University Press, 2004), 207.
9. Gabriel Thompson, "Leaves of Poison," *Nation*, November 1, 2013.
10. Craig Kielburger and Marc Kielburger, "Child Labor Is Canada's Invisible Crisis," *Huffington Post*, November 14, 2011; Bob Barnetson, *Illegal and Injurious: How Alberta Has Failed Teen Workers* (Edmonton: Parkland Institute, 2015); B.C. Lee, S.S. Gallagher, A.K. Liebman, M.E. Miller, and B. Marlenga, eds., *Blueprint for Protecting Children in Agriculture: The 2012 National Action Plan* (Marshfield, WI: Marshfield Clinic, 2012); Stephen McBride and John Irwin, "Deregulating Child Labour in British Columbia," in *Lost Kids: Vulnerable Children and Youth in Twentieth-Century Canada and the United States*, edited by Mona Gleason, Tamara Myers, Leslie Paris and Veronica Strong-Boag (Vancouver: University of British Columbia Press, 2010).

11. Jane Humphries, *Childhood and Child Labour in the British Industrial Revolution* (Cambridge: Cambridge University Press, 2010). See also Mintz, *Huck's Raft*, and Susan Campbell Bartoletti, *Kids on Strike* (Boston: Houghton Mifflin, 1999).
12. Savage charts this trend beginning in the early 1900s: Jon Savage, *Teenage: The Creation of Youth Culture* (New York: Penguin, 2007), 118).
13. See, for example, Jeremy Seabrook, "Children of the Market," *Race and Class* 39, no. 4 (1998): 37–48.
14. See Tracey Skelton, "Children, Young People, UNICEF and Participation," *Children's Geographies* 5, nos. 1–2 (February–May 2007: 165–81.
15. Nicola Ansell, "Childhood and the Politics of Scale: Descaling Children's Geographies?" *Progress in Human Geography* 33, no. 2 (2009): 193.
16. Alan Prout, "Introduction. Childhood Bodies: Construction, Agency and Hybridity," in *Childhood Bodies*, edited by Alan Prout (New York: St. Martin's Press, 2000), 1–18; Allison James, "Embodied Being(s): Understanding the Self and the Body in Childhood," in Prout (ed.) *Childhood Bodies*, 19–37; Cindi Katz, *Growing Up Global: Economic Restructuring and Children's Everyday Lives* (Minneapolis: University of Minnesota Press, 2004). The history of children's sociology is reviewed in the 2010 issue of *Current Sociology* (volume 58, number 2).
17. Katz, *Growing Up Global*; Fernando J. Bosco, "Play, Work or Activism? Broadening the Connections between Political and Children's Geographies," *Children's Geographies* 8, no. 4 (2010): 381–90; Harriot Beazley, "Voices from the Margins: Street Children's Subcultures in Indonesia," *Children's Geographies* 1, no. 2 (2003): 181–200. Space, of course, is never neutral, and children's geographers are generally attentive to the wider power relations that position the child as relatively powerless. See Stuart Aitkin, "Placing Children at the Heart of Globalization," in *World Minds: Geographical Perspectives on 100 Problems*, edited by D.G. Janelle, B. Warf, and K. Hansen (Dordrecht, Netherlands: Kluwaer, 2004), 579–83, and James, "Embodied Beings." There is a tendency in this literature, however, to focus on the immediate socio-historic context over the wider power relations of the social totality (see Ansell, "Childhood and the Politics of Scale").
18. Philippe Ariès, *Centuries of Childhood: A Social History of Family Life*, translated by Robert Baldick (New York: Random House Vintage, 1962); Anne Higonnet, *Pictures of Innocence: The History and Crisis of Ideal Childhood* (London: Thames and Hudson, 1998).
19. Marjorie Lorch and Paula Hellal, "Darwin's 'Natural Science of Babies,'" *Journal of the History of Neuroscience* 19 (2010): 140–57.
20. For example, Artin Gőncü and Suzanne Gaskins, eds., *Play and Development: Evolutionary, Sociocultural, and Functional Perspectives* (Mahwah, NJ, and London: Lawrence Erlbaum Associates, 2007); Heather Montgomery, *An Introduction to Childhood: Anthropological Perspectives on Children's Lives* (Chichester, West Sussex: Wiley-Blackwell, 2009); J.L. Frost, *A History of Children's Play and Play Environments: Toward a*

Contemporary Child-saving Movement (Abingdon UK: Taylor & Francis, 2010); Y. Gosso, "Play in Different Cultures," in *Children and Play*, edited by P.K. Smith (New York: Wiley, 2010), 80–98; Jean Piaget, *Play, Dreams, and Imitation in Childhood*, transalated by C. Gattegno and F.M. Hodgson (London: Routledge, 1951). (The exception is children in situations of extreme deprivation.)

21. As Karl Marx emphasizes in his *Theses on Feuerbach* (in *Marx/Engels Selected Works*, vol. I, Moscow: Progress Publishers, 1969 [1845], 13–15).
22. Thomas Henricks, *Play Reconsidered: Sociological Perspectives on Human Expression* (Urbana-Champaign: University of Illinois Press, 2006), 1. Henricks and others caution against romanticizing play, as it can also have an aggressive or mean-spirited quality.
23. Lev S. Vygotsky, "Play and its Role in the Mental Development of the Child," *Soviet Psychology* 5, no. 3 (1967): 6–18; Orwain Jones, "Melting Geography: Purity, Disorder, Childhood and Space," in *Children's Geographies: Playing, Living, Learning*, edited by Sarah L. Holloway and Gill Valentines (London and New York: Routledge, 2000), 25–53; William Corsaro, *Friendship and Peer Culture in the Early Years* (Norwood, NJ: Ablex Publishing, 1985). Joanne L. Thomson and Chris Philo, "Playful Spaces? A Social Geography of Children's Play in Livingston, Scotland," *Children's Geographies* 2, no. 1 (February 2004): 111–30 reminds us that play is not necessarily a discrete activity so much as it is a matter of children "just existing, just *being*" (111). Neither is it always a happy and harmonious state. Johan Huizinga, *A Study of the Play Element in Culture* (London: Routledge and Kegan Paul, 1949), draws attention to plays internal tensions and seriousness.
24. Giorgi Hadi Curti and Christopher M. Moreno, Institutional Borders, Revolutionary Imaginings and the Becoming-Adult of the Child," *Children's Geographies* 8, no. 4 (2010): 416.
25. David McNally, "The Dual Form of Labour in Capitalist Society and the Struggle over Meaning: Comments on Postone," *Historical Materialism* 12, no. 3 (2010), 191–92.
26. See John Holloway, "From Scream of Refusal to Scream of Power: The Centrality of Work," in *Emancipating Marx*, vol. 3, edited by Werner Bonefeld, Richard Gunn, John Holloway, and Kosmas Psychopedis (London: Pluto, 1995), 170.
27. Even aggressive, mean-spirited play is enacted by the player's pleasure.
28. So-called "playbor" and the integration of playfulness into some workplaces is no exception insofar as it subsumes play to the law of value's temporal and spatial regime (see below).
29. This is not to say that childhood represents a victory of the working class. It is better seen in terms of an ambivalently embraced accommodation of the working class to middle class norms and values. See Viviana A. Zelizer, "From Useful to Useless: Moral Conflict over Child Labor," in (ed.), *The Children's Culture Reader*, edited by Henry Jenkins (New York and London:

New York University Press, 1998), 81–94. On the struggle for time more generally, see Jonathan Martineau, *Time, Capitalism and Alienation: A Socio-Historical Inquiry into the Making of Modern Time* (Chicago: Haymarket Books, 2016), 132–39, and E.P. Thompson, "Time-Work Discipline and Industrial Capitalism," in *Customs in Common* (New York: New Press, 1993).

30. On the rule of abstract time, see Martineau, *Time, Capitalism and Alienation*. All unpaid social reproductive labor is separated from the space and time of the law of value, but to varying degrees.
31. Ursula Huws, *Labor in the Global Digital Economy: The Cybertariat Comes of Age* (New York: Monthly Review Press, 2014), 110–11.
32. McNally, "Dual Form of Labour," 198.
33. John Holloway, "Cracks and the Crisis of Abstract Labor," *Antipode* 42, no. 4 (2010): 914. To acknowledge this point does not require us to subscribe to Holloway's political conclusions which suggests the labor movement comprises a "struggle of abstract labour against capital" whereas living itself is "a struggle against the capitalist forms of activity" (916 and 921).
34. There is no hard and fast rule about which social reproductive activities are more or less subject to the time/work discipline, but the conditions of social reproductive labor clearly do matter in this regard. We can fairly safely presume that the more impoverished or oppressive the conditions, the more work-like and less play-like the labor.
35. In fact, in affluent societies with large middle classes, so-called free or unstructured play is arguably seen as essential to a child's learning and development, especially to their capacity to "problem solve."
36. Karl Marx, *Grundrisse: Outline of the Critique of Political Economy* (New York: Penguin, 1973 [1857–61]), 544.
37. Clearly, this is truer of privileged (white, middle-class, settler) children's lives than others, but the hegemony of middle-class childhood has resulted in some protection for working-class and oppressed children too.
38. Lorna F. Hurl, "Restricting Child Factory Labour in Late Nineteenth Century Ontario," *Labour/Le Travail* 21 (1988), 91; see also Bryan Palmer, *Working-Class Experience: Rethinking the History of Canadian Labour, 1800–1991* (Toronto: McClelland and Stewart, 1992).
39. Mintz, *Huck's Raft*, 178; Hurl, "Restricting Child Factory Labour," 115; David Nasaw, *Children of the City: At Work and at Play* (New York: Random House, 1985), 49.
40. Hurl, "Restricting Child Factory Labour"; Mintz, *Huck's Raft*; Heron, *Lunch-Bucket Lives*.
41. Vicky Lebeau, *Childhood and Cinema* (London: Reaktion Books, 2008), 66 and 84.
42. Mintz, *Huck's Raft*, 154–84; Margrit Shildrick, *Leaky Bodies and Boundaries: Feminist, Postmodernism, and (Bio)ethics* (London: Routledge, 1997). This fear and anxiety are directed with the greatest intensity at black and indigenous children. See Robin Bernstein, *Racial Innocence:*

Performing American Childhood from Slavery to Civil Rights (New York: New York University Press, 2011).

43. Heron, *Lunch-Bucket Lives,* 139–43.

CHAPTER 7: MOSTLY WORK, LITTLE PLAY

1. Margaret Reid, *Economics of Household Production* (New York: J. Wiley & Sons, 1934). See Lourdes Benería, *Gender, Development, and Globalization: Economics as If All People Mattered* (New York): Routledge, 2003); Marilyn Waring, *If Women Counted: A New Feminist Economics* (London: Macmillan, 1989).
2. Mariarosa Dalla Costa and Selma James, *The Power of Women and the Subversion of the Community* (Bristol, UK: Falling Wall Press, 1975); Silvia Federici, *Wages against Housework* (Bristol, UK: Falling Wall Press, 1975); Paul Smith, "Domestic Labour and Marx's Theory of Value," in *Feminism and Materialism*, edited by Annette Kuhn and AnnMarie Wolpe, 198–219 (Boston: Routledge and Kegan Paul, 1978); Lise Vogel, *Marxism and the Oppression of Women: Toward a Unitary Theory* (Leiden: Brill, 2013); Margaret Benston, *Political Economy of Women's Liberation* (New York: Monthly Review, 1969). In Marxist terms, commodities have a use value and an exchange value. *Use value* refers to the practical utility of an object, and *exchange value* refers to the rate for which an object can be bought or sold in the capitalist labor market. See Karl Marx, *Capital*, vol. I, translated by Ben Fowkes (London: Penguin, 1990); Harry Braverman, *Labor and Monopoly Capital: The Degradation of Work in the Twentieth Century* (New York: Monthly Review Press, 1974).
3. Cindi Katz, "Vagabond Capitalism and the Necessity of Social Reproduction," *Antipode* 33, no. 4 (2001): 709–28; Isabella Bakker, "Social Reproduction and the Constitution of a Gendered Political Economy," *New Political Economy* 12, no. 4 (2007): 541–56; Isabella Bakker and Rachel Silvey, eds., *Beyond States and Markets: The Challenges of Social Reproduction* (New York: Routledge, 2008); Eleonore Kofman and Parvati Raghuram, *Gendered Migrations and Global Social Reproduction* (New York: Palgrave Macmillan, 2015); Meg Luxton, "Feminist Political Economy in Canada and the Politics of Social Reproduction," in *Social Reproduction: Feminist Political Economy Challenges Neo-Liberalism* (Montreal: McGill-Queen's University Press, 2006), 11–44; Katie Meehan and Kendra Strauss, eds., *Precarious Worlds: Contested Geographies of Social Reproduction* (Athens, Georgia: University of Georgia Press, 2015).
4. Sedef Arat-Koç, *Caregivers Break the Silence: A Participatory Action Research on the Abuse and Violence, Including the Impact of Family Separation, Experienced by Women in the Live-in Caregiver Program* (Toronto: INTERCEDE, 2001); Evelyn Nakano Glenn, "From Servitude to Service Work: Historical Continuities in the Racial Division of Paid Reproductive Labor," *Signs* 18, no. 1 (1992): 1–43; Adelle Blackett, "Introduction: Regulating Decent Work for Domestic Workers," *Canadian*

Journal of Women and the Law 23, no. 1 (2011): 1–45; Jane Wills, *Global Cities at Work: New Migrant Divisions of Labour* (London: Pluto Press, 2010).

5. bell hooks, *Ain't I a Woman: Black Women and Feminism* (Cambridge, MA: South End Press, 1981); Patricia Hill Collins, *Black Feminist Thought: Knowledge, Consciousness, and the Politics of Empowerment* (London: Routledge, 2009); Hazel V. Carby, "White Women Listen! Black Feminism and the Boundaries of Sisterhood," in *Materialist Feminism: A Reader in Class, Difference and Women's Lives,* edited by Rosemary Hennessy and Chrys Ingraham (New York: Routledge, 1997), 110–28; Rose M. Brewer, "Theorizing Race, Class, and Gender: The New Scholarship on Black Feminist Intellectuals and Black Women's Labor," in *Materialist Feminism: A Reader in Class, Difference and Women's Lives,* edited by Rosemary Hennessy and Chrys Ingraham (New York: Routledge, 1997), 236–47.
6. The study's parameters excluded participants who were full-time permanent workers, students, and nonstatus individuals. Interviews were conducted in both English and French. All names are pseudonyms and consent was achieved prior to conducting interviews. Most interviews were audio-recorded, but some participants preferred that I take notes, in which case I transcribed notes from the interview immediately afterward.
7. The two other paid domestic workers I interviewed never lived with their employers. I discuss the workplace experiences of all four paid domestic workers and political organizing around paid domestic work in Montreal elsewhere; see Carmen Teeple Hopkins, "Work Intensifications, Injuries and Legal Exclusions for Paid Domestic Workers in Montreal, Quebec, *Gender, Place and Culture* 24, no. 2 (2017): 201–12.
8. Silvia Federici, "Precarious Labour: A Feminist Viewpoint," 2008, http://inthemiddleofthewhirlwind.wordpress.com/precarious-labor-a-feminist-viewpoint; Barbara Smith and Jamie Winders, "Whose Lives, Which Work? Class Discrepancies in Life's Work," in *Precarious Worlds: Contested Geographies of Social Reproduction,* edited by Katie Meehan and Kendra Strauss (Athens: University of Georgia Press, 2015).
9. Cindi Katz, "On the Grounds of Globalization: A Topography for Feminist Political Engagement," *Signs* 26, no. 4 (2001): 1213–34.
10. Harry Cleaver, *Reading Capital Politically* (Austin: University of Texas Press, 1979), 51.
11. Tronti developed the term "social factory" in the article "Capital's Plan" in the Italian leftist journal *Quaderni Rossi* (1963). Cited in Cleaver, *Reading Capital Politically*, 57.
12. Ibid., 57.
13. It is worth mentioning that immaterial labor theorists Antonio Negri, Michael Hardt, Mauricizio Lazzarato, and Paulo Virno interpret the concept of the social factory differently than the autonomist Marxist feminists. I explore the immaterial labor tradition and their theoretical differences from feminists elsewhere; see Carmen Teeple Hopkins, *Precarious Work in Montreal: Women, Urban Space, and Time*, doctoral

dissertation, Toronto: University of Toronto: 2015. See Michael Hardt and Antonio Negri, *Empire* (Cambridge, MA: Harvard University Press, 2000); Michael Hardt and Antonio Negri, *Multitude: War and Democracy in the Age of Empire* (New York: Penguin, 2004); Maurizio Lazzarato, "Immaterial Labour," in *Radical Thought in Italy*, edited by Michael Hardt and Paulo Virno (Minneapolis: University of Minnesota Press, 1996), 132–46; Paolo Virno, *A Grammar of the Multitude: For an Analysis of Contemporary Forms of Life* (Los Angeles: Semiotext(e), 2003).

14. Cleaver, *Reading Capital Politically*, 59.
15. Selma James, *Sex, Race, and Class: The Perspective of Winning, a Selection of Writings 1952–2011* (Oakland, CA: PM Press, 2012).
16. Ibid., 51–52, emphasis in original.
17. Silvia Federici, *Revolution at Point Zero: Housework, Reproduction, and Feminist Struggle* (New York: Autonomedia, 2012) 7–8.
18. Ibid., 8.
19. Benston, *Political Economy of Women's Liberation*; Susan Himmelweit and Simon Mohun, "Domestic Labour and Capital," *Cambridge Journal of Economics* 1, no. 1 (1977): 15–31; Paul Smith, "Domestic Labour and Marx's Theory of Value," in *Feminism and Materialism*, edited by Annette Kuhn and AnnMarie Wolpe (Boston: Routledge and Kegan Paul, 1978), 198–219; Vogel, *Marxism and the Oppression of Women*. See Luxton, "Feminist Political Economy in Canada," for a review of the domestic labor debate and social reproduction theory.
20. Benería, *Gender, Development, and Globalization*; Benston, *Political Economy of Women's Liberation*; Veronika Bennholdt-Thomsen, "Subsistence Production and Extended Reproduction," in *Of Marriage and the Market*, edited by Kate Young, Carol Wolkowitz, and Rosalyn McCullagh (London: CSE Books, 1981); Ester Boserup, *Women's Role in Economic Development* (London: George Allen and Unwin, 1971); Jane L. Collins and Martha Gimenez, eds., *Work without Wages: Comparative Studies of Domestic Labor and Self-Employment* (Albany: State University of New York Press, 1990).
21. Susan Himmelweit, "The Discovery of 'Unpaid Work': The Social Consequences of the Expansion of 'Work,'" *Feminist Economics* 1, no. 2 (1995): 15–16.
22. Paul Smith, "Domestic Labour and Marx's Theory of Value."
23. Ibid., 215.
24. Ibid., 204.
25. Hill Collins, *Black Feminist Thought*, 47; hooks, *Ain't I a Woman*, 23, cited in Carmen Teeple Hopkins, "Introduction: Feminist Geographies of Social Reproduction and Race," *Women's Studies International Forum* 48 (January 2015): 136.
26. Mignon Duffy, "Doing the Dirty Work: Gender, Race, and Reproductive Labor in Historical Perspective," *Gender and Society* 21, no. 3 (2007): 313–36; Jules Falquet, "La Règle Du Jeu. Repenser La Co-Formation Des Rapports Sociaux de Sexe, de Classe et de 'Race' Dans La Mondialisation

Néoliberale," in *Sexe, Race, Class, Pour Une Epistemologie de La Domination,* edited by Elsa Dorlin (Paris: Presses Universitaires de France, 2009), 91–110; Glenn, "From Servitude to Service Work"; Linda Peake, "Toward an Understanding of the Interconnectedness of Women's Lives: The 'Racial' Reproduction of Labor in Low-Income Urban Areas," *Urban Geography* 16, no. 5 (1995): 414–39.

27. Peake, "Toward an Understanding," 420.
28. Blackett, "Regulating Decent Work for Domestic Workers"; Adelle Blackett, "The Decent Work for Domestic Workers Convention and Recommendation 2011," *American Journal of International Law* 106, no. 4 (2012): 778–94; Glenn, "From Servitude to Service Work"; Bridget Anderson, *Doing the Dirty Work? The Global Politics of Domestic Labour* (London: Zed Books, 2000).
29. Duffy, "Doing the Dirty Work."
30. Ronaldo Munck, Carl Ulrik Schierup, and Raúl Delgado Wise, "Migration, Work, and Citizenship in the New World Order," *Globalizations* 8, no. 3 (2011): 249–60; Brenda S. Yeoh and Shirlena Huang, "Transnational Domestic Workers and the Negotiation of Mobility and Work Practices in Singapore's Home Spaces," *Mobilities* 5, no. 2 (2010): 219–36.
31. Munck, Schierup, and Wise, "Migration, Work, and Citizenship," 255.
32. Patricia R. Pessar and Sarah J. Mahler, "Transnational Migration: Bringing Gender In," *International Migration Review* 37, no. 3 (2003): 812–46; Geraldine Pratt and Brenda Yeoh, "Transnational (Counter) Topographies," *Gender, Place & Culture* 10, no. 2 (2003): 159–66; Yeoh and Huang, "Transnational Domestic Workers."
33. Munck, Schierup, and Wise, "Migration, Work, and Citizenship," 256.
34. Pessar and Mahler, "Transnational Migration"; Pratt and Yeoh, "Transnational (Counter) Topographies"; Yeoh and Huang, "Transnational Domestic Workers."
35. Korfman and Raghuram, *Gendered Migrations.*
36. Beverley Mullings, "Neoliberalization, Social Reproduction and the Limits to Labour in Jamaica," *Singapore Journal of Tropical Geography* 30, no. 2 (2009): 178.
37. Ching Kwan Lee and Yelizavetta Kofman, "The Politics of Precarity: Views Beyond the United States," *Work and Occupations* 39, no. 4 (2012): 388–408.
38. Michael Ashby, "The Impact of Structural Adjustment Policies on Secondary Education in the Philippines," *Geography* 82, no. 4 (1997): 335–88; Joseph Lim and Manuel F. Montes, "The Structure of Employment and Structural Adjustment in the Philippines," *Journal of Development Studies* 36, no. 4 (2000): 149–81.
39. World Bank, "Personal Remittances, Received (% of GDP)," 2016, http://data.worldbank.org/indicator/BX.TRF.PWKR.DT.GD.ZS?locations=PH.
40. Bernadette Stiell and Kim England, "Domestic Distinctions: Constructing Difference among Paid Domestic Workers in Toronto," *Gender, Place & Culture* 4, no. 3 (1997): 339–60; Rhacel Salazar Parreñas, "Migrant Filipina

Domestic Workers and the International Division of Reproductive Labor," *Gender and Society* 14, no. 4 (2000): 560–80; Rhacel Salazar Parreñas, "The Reproductive Labour of Migrant Workers," *Global Networks* 12, no. 2 (2012): 269.

41. Yeoh and Huang, "Transnational Domestic Workers," 220.
42. Linda McDowell, "Life without Father and Ford: The New Gender Order of Post-Fordism," *Transactions of the Institute of British Geographers* 16, no. 4 (1991): 400–19; Stiell and England, "Domestic Distinctions."
43. Stiell and England, "Domestic Distinctions"; Anderson, *Doing the Dirty Work?*; Linda McDowell, "Father and Ford Revisited: Gender, Class and Employment Change in the New Millennium," *Transactions of the Institute of British Geographers* 26, no. 4 (2001): 448–64; Mignon Duffy, *Making Care Count: A Century of Gender, Race, and Paid Care Work* (New Brunswick, NJ: Rutgers University Press, 2011); Duffy, "Doing the Dirty Work"; Parreñas, "Migrant Filipina Domestic Workers."
44. Federici, *Revolution at Point Zero*, 100.
45. Ibid.
46. Federici, "Precarious Labour."
47. Stiell and England, "Domestic Distinctions."
48. Brenda Cossman and Judy Fudge, eds., *Privatization, Law, and the Challenge to Feminism* (Toronto: University of Toronto Press, 2002).
49. Makeda Silvera, *Silenced: Makeda Silvera Talks with Working Class West Indian Women about Their Lives and Struggles as Domestic Workers in Canada* (Toronto, ON: Williams-Wallace, 1983); Wenona Mary Giles and Sedef Arat-Koç, eds., *Maid in the Market: Women's Paid Domestic Labour* (Halifax, NS: Fernwood Publishing, 1994); Abigail B. Bakan and Daiva K. Stasiulis, "Making the Match: Domestic Placement Agencies and the Racialization of Women's Household Work," *Signs* 20, no. 2 (1995): 303–35; Daiva Stasiulis and Abigail B. Bakan, "Negotiating Citizenship: The Case of Foreign Domestic Workers in Canada," *Feminist Review* 57, no. 1 (1997): 112; Arat-Koç, *Caregivers Break the Silence*; Glenda Lynna Anne Tibe Bonifacio, "I Care for You, Who Cares for Me? Transitional Services of Filipino Live-in Caregivers in Canada," *Asian Women* 24, no. 1 (2008): 25–50; Geraldine Pratt, "Stereotypes and Ambivalence: The Construction of Domestic Workers in Vancouver, British Columbia," *Gender, Place & Culture* 4, no. 2 (1997): 159–78; Geraldine Pratt, *Working Feminism* (Philadelphia: Temple University Press, 2004).
50. Stasiulis and Bakan, "Negotiating Citizenship," 306.
51. Government of Canada, Citizenship and Immigration Canada, "Become a Permanent Resident—Live-in Caregivers," 2015, http://www.cic.gc.ca/english/work/caregiver/permanent_resident.asp.
52. Philip Kelly, Stella Park, Conely de Leon, and Jeff Priest, "Profile of Live-In Caregiver Immigrants to Canada, 1993-2009," Toronto Immigrant Employment Data Initiative (TIEDI) Analytical Report 18, 2011, http://www.yorku.ca/tiedi/doc/AnalyticalReport18.pdf, 11.

53. T.R. Balakrishnan, Zenaida R. Ravanera, and Teresa Abada, "Spatial Residential Patterns and Socio-Economic Integration of Filipinos in Canada," *Canadian Ethnic Studies* 37, no. 2 (2005): 67.
54. Federici, "Precarious Labour."
55. Smith and Winders, "Whose Lives, Which Work?"; Katharyne Mitchell, Sallie A. Marston, and Cindi Katz, eds., *Life's Work: Geographies of Social Reproduction* (Oxford: Blackwell Publishing, 2004).
56. Mitchell, Marston, and Katz, eds., *Life's Work*, 15.
57. Smith and Winders, "Whose Lives, Which Work?" 103.
58. Ibid.
59. In the province of Quebec, Canada, domestic workers employed by individual households are included under labor standards (e.g., minimum wage, overtime, vacation pay) but excluded from workers' compensation. In contrast, domestic workers who work for agencies in Quebec are covered by workers' compensation. In Quebec, workers' compensation and labor standards fall under the umbrella of La Commission des normes, de l'équité, de la santé et de la sécurité du travail (CNESST). The CNESST defines *domestic worker* (*domestique*) as a person hired for paid work who performs tasks in the dwelling of an individual in the form of housework, or as a person residing in a dwelling who is taking care of a child or someone who is sick, disabled, or (CNESST, "Glossaire: Domestique," 2016, http://www.csst.qc.ca/glossaire/Pages/domestique.aspx). This definition was translated from French by the author.
60. Philip Crang, "It's Showtime: On the Workplace Geographies of Display in a Restaurant in Southeast England," *Environment and Planning D: Society and Space* 12, no. 6 (1994): 675–704; Jennifer Claire Olmsted, "Telling Palestinian Women's Economic Stories," *Feminist Economics,* Feminist Economics, 3, no. 2 (1997): 141–51; Marieme Soda Lo, "Senegalese Immigrant Families' 'Regroupement' in France and the Im/possibility of Reconstituting Family across Multiple Temporalities and Spatialities," *Ethnic and Racial Studies* 38, no. 15 (2015): 2672–87.
61. Claude Turcotte, "Les Travailleuses Domestiques Veulent être Couvertes Par La CSST Comme Les Autres Travailleurs," *Le Devoir,* February 23, 2009, http://www.ledevoir.com/politique/quebec/235521/les-travailleuses-domestiques-veulent-etre-couvertes-par-la-csst-comme-les-autres-travailleurs.
62. Balakrishnan, Ravanera, and Abada, "Spatial Residential Patterns."
63. Stiell and England, "Domestic Distinctions"; Anderson, *Doing the Dirty Work?*; Blackett, "Regulating Decent Work for Domestic Workers"; Peggie R. Smith, "The Pitfalls of Home: Protecting the Health and Safety of Paid Domestic Workers," *Canadian Journal of Women and the Law* 23, no. 1 (2011): 309–39; PINAY and McGill School of Social Work, "Warning! Domestic Work Can Be Hazardous to Your Immigration Status, Health and Safety and Wallet," Google Doc, 2008, https://docs.google.com/file/d/1PINzXgoxDvSX3ZP9Ua44M6Zoy_bIrwfgzd-UFHocwLjJxsmGsUo2wEQBRwj6/edit?hl=en; Elsa Galerand, Martin Gallié, Jeanne Ollivier

Gobeil, PINAY, and le Service aux collectivités de l'UQAM, "Travail Domestique et Exploitation: Le Cas Des Travailleuses Domestiques Philippines Au Canada (PAFR)," 2015, https://www.mcgill.ca/lldrl/files/lldrl/15.01.09_rapport_fr_vu2.5.11_0.pdf.

64. PINAY and McGill School of Social Work, "Warning!," 16–17.
65. Federici, "Precarious Labour"; Federici, *Revolution at Point Zero.*
66. Federici, *Revolution at Point Zero*, 100.
67. Bonifacio, "I Care for You," 33.
68. Ibid., 33.
69. Ibid., 39.
70. Doreen B. Massey, *Space, Place, and Gender* (Minneapolis: University of Minnesota Press, 1994), 166–67.
71. Blackett, "Regulating Decent Work for Domestic Workers"; Blackett, "The Decent Work for Domestic Workers Convention"; Glenn, "From Servitude to Service Work."
72. Federici, "Precarious Labour."
73. Smith and Winders, "Whose Lives, Which Work?"
74. Sarah Dyer, Linda McDowell, and Adina Batnitzky, "Migrant Work, Precarious Work–Life Balance: What the Experiences of Migrant Workers in the Service Sector in Greater London Tell Us about the Adult Worker Model," *Gender, Place and Culture* 18, no. 5 (2011): 685–700.
75. Michèle Vatz Laaroussi, "Du Maghreb Au Québec: Accommodements et Stratégies," *Travail, Genre et Sociétés* 20, no. 2 (2008): 47.
76. Katz, "On the Grounds of Globalization"; Katz, "Vagabond Capitalism."
77. Katz, "Vagabond Capitalism," 1228.
78. Katz, "On the Grounds of Globalization," 1229.
79. Ibid., 1231.

CHAPTER 8: PENSIONS AND SOCIAL REPRODUCTION

1. "The possessor of money does find such a special commodity on the market: the capacity for labour [*Arbeitsvermögen*], in other words labour-power [*Arbeitskraft*]. We mean by labour-power, or labour-capacity, the aggregate of those mental and physical capabilities existing in the physical form, the living personality, of a human being, capabilities which he sets in motion whenever he produces a use-value of any kind." Karl Marx, *Capital*, vol. I, translated by Ben Fowkes (London: Penguin, 1990).
2. K. Marx, *Wage Labour and Capital Plus Wages, Price and Profit* (London: Bookmarks, 1996).
3. B. Fine, "Exploitation and Surplus Value," in *The Elgar Companion to Marxist Economics*, edited by B. Fine and A. Saad-Filho (London: Edward Elgar, 2012), 118–24.
4. B. Fine, "Financialisation, the Value of Labour Power, the Degree of Separation, and Exploitation by Banking." *Mimeo* (2009), https://eprints.soas.ac.uk/7480.

5. K. Marx, *Critique of the Gotha Programme* (Moscow: Progress Publishers, 1978).
6. S. Gill and I. Bakker (eds.), *Power, Production and Social Reproduction* (Basingstoke, UK: Palgrave Macmillan, 2003).
7. R. Blackburn, *Banking on Death: Or, Investing in Life; the History and Future of Pensions* (London: Verso, 2002).
8. B. Fine, "Financialization from a Marxist Perspective," *International Journal of Political Economy* 42, no. 4 (2013): 47–66.
9. "It should not be forgotten here that this capital's money value, as represented by this papers in the banker's safe, is completely fictitious even in so far as they are drafts on certain assured revenues (as with government securities) or ownership titles to real capital (as with shares), their money value being *determined differently* from the value of actual capital that they at least partially represent: or, where they represent only a claim to revenue and not capital at all, the claim to the same revenue is expressed in a constantly changing fictitious money capital " (K. Marx, *Capital*, vol. III, translated by D. Fernbach, London: Penguin, 1991, 600, emphasis added).
10. Blackburn, *Banking on Death.*
11. T. Akpinar, "Türk Sosyal Güvenlik Sisteminin Ekonomi Politiği: Kuruluş Süreci," *Calisma ve Toplum* 42, no. 3 (2014), http://www.calismatoplum.org/sayi42/akpinar.pdf.
12. M. Pilch and V. Wood, *Pension Schemes: A Guide to Principles and Practice* (Farnham, England: Gower Press, 1979).
13. S. Gokbayrak, *Refah Devletinin Donusumu ve Ozel Emeklilik Programlari* (Ankara: Siyasal Kitabevi, 2010).
14. L. Kreiser, "A Short History of the Economic Development and Accounting Treatment of Pension Plans," *Accounting Historians Journal* 3, no. 1/4 (1976): 56–62. In *Banking on Death* (2002), Blackburn ranks the underlying reasons behind the first public pension schemes as follows: to attract or retain favored or strategic civil servants (for example, in 1598, Elizabeth's Parliament voted for a pension for soldiers who had fought for the Queen); to smooth down the discontent and restiveness that accompanied the spread of precapitalist social relations (for example, the Elizabethan Poor Law of 1601 as a response to the need for social protection against the disruptive new regime that was transforming rural existence); and to obtain a surety of good service by institutions (for example, Louis XIV's naval minister established a pension system for naval officers, master mariners, and administrators to boost the French navy in 1673).
15. Blackburn, *Banking on Death*; Thomas Paine, *The Rights of Man* (London: J.M. Dent, 1951).
16. Pilch and Wood, *Pension Schemes.*
17. Kreiser, "Short History."
18. Blackburn, *Banking on Death.* For a popular historical figure, see Charles Booth, who was a social campaigner for pensions in the UK; his efforts

were influential during the end of the nineteenth century (Pilch and Wood, *Pension Schemes*).

19. Blackburn, *Banking on Death.*
20. B. Gilbert, *The Evolution of National Insurance in Great Britain* (Farnborough, UK: Gregg Revivals, 1966).
21. Gokbayrak, *Refah Devletinin Donusumu*, 90.
22. Akpinar, "Türk Sosyal Güvenlik Sisteminin Ekonomi Politiği."
23. E. Perotti and A. Schwienbacher, "The Political Origin of Pension Funding," *Journal of Financial Intermediation* 18, no. 3 (2009): 384–404.
24. Blackburn, *Banking on Death.*
25. W. Asbjørn, *The Rise and Fall of the Welfare State* (London: Pluto Press, 2011), 22.
26. Perotti and Schwienbacher, "The Political Origin of Pension Funding."
27. W.H.B. Beveridge, *Social Insurance and Allied Services* (London: H.M.S.O., 1942).
28. T. Cutler and B. Waine, "Social Insecurity and the Retreat from Social Democracy: Occupational Welfare in the Long Boom and Financialization," *Review of International Political Economy* 8, no. 1 (2001): 96–118.
29. Akpinar, "Türk Sosyal Güvenlik Sisteminin Ekonomi Politiği."
30. "The welfare state is defined as a set of legal entitlements providing citizens with claims to transfer payments from compulsory social security schemes as well as to state organized services (such as health and education) for a wide variety of defined cases of need and contingencies" (C. Offe, "Competitive Party Democracy and the Keynesian Welfare State: Factors of Stability and Disorganization," *Policy Sciences* 15, no. 2, 1982: 225–46).
31. In order to understand their position, we should first reveal their position in the state discussions. The Marxian approaches to the nature of the state can be divided into three lines: Marxist, neo-Marxist, and post-Marxist. The advocates of the first line, the so-called "instrumentalist view," argue that the state is an instrument in the hands of the ruling class and that the ruling class uses the state in order to enforce the class structure and defend its own interests. The second view, neo-Marxist, is referred to as "structuralist" because it locates the function of the state as protector and reproducer of the structure of capitalist societies against inherent crises, with which capitalist society is pregnant, originating from three different sources: the economy, class struggle, and uneven development. The last Marxist state approach comprises of two subsections: The systems-analytic approach (post-Marxism I) and the organizational realist approach (post-Marxism II) (C.W. Barrow, *Critical Theories of the State: Marxist, Neo-Marxist, Post-Marxist*, Madison: University of Wisconsin Press, 1993). In addition to these, there is the "derivationist" approach, which emerged as a response to the debate between instrumentalists (Miliband) and structuralists (Poulantzas) during the 1970s. According to derivationists, the state is derived from the requirements of capital accumulation and the welfare state is the result of the class struggle and capitalism's own tendencies (ibid.). The derivationist Gough defines the

welfare state as "the use of state power to modify the reproduction of labour power and to maintain the nonworking population in capitalist societies" (I. Gough, *The Political Economy of the Welfare State*, London: Macmillan, 1979, 44).

32. J. Quadagno, "Theories of Welfare State," *Annual Review of Sociology* 13 (1987): 109–28.
33. Offe, "Competitive Party Democracy."
34. J. Myles and J. Quadagno, "Political Theories of the Welfare State," *Social Service Review* 76, no. 1 (2002): 34–57.
35. W. Korpi and J. Palme, "New Politics and Class Politics in the Context of Austerity and Globalization: Welfare State Regress in 18 Countries, 1975–95," *American Political Science Review* 97, no. 3 (2003): 425–46.
36. "The role of pressure from subordinate classes and other organized pressure groups associated with them is of recognized importance in explaining the introduction of welfare measures. Bismarck's social insurance schemes of 1880s, Lloyd George's unemployment insurance scheme of 1911, the improvement and extension of Italian social security benefits in 1969, the introduction of the National Health Service or of comprehensive schooling in Britain, all represent in varying ways the pressure of the working class and allied groups" (I. Gough, *The Political Economy of the Welfare State*, London: Macmillan, 1982, 58).
37. B. Fine, *The Continuing Enigmas of Social Policy*, WB 2014-10 No. 10, UNRISD, 2014, http://www.unrisd.org/80256B3C005BCCF9/search/30B153EE73F52ABFC1257D0200420A61?OpenDocument.
38. For instance, in the case of a funded scheme, monthly contributions below a certain level might give insignificant financial returns, which would render low-income groups vulnerable in terms of pension income. Another example is the PAYG schemes, which distribute pensions not only intragenerationally, but also intergenerationally. Therefore, pension levels vary across different income groups within a generation, as well as between different cohorts with changing economic and social factors, such as baby booms, and high or low productivity and employment.
39. Marx, *Capital*, vol. I; Marx, *Wage-Labour and Capital.* In this sense, labor power is not the same as labor. By pointing at this crucial difference, Marx elucidates the origin of surplus value under the capitalist mode of production. Accordingly, labor power has a dual value: its use value is producing value, whereas its exchange value is the value of those commodities necessary to reproduce labor power. The difference between its use value and its exchange value is the origin of surplus value, which is appropriated by the capitalist. Thus, the reproduction of labor power is one of the determinants of the exploitation level, as it costs less; *ceteris paribus*, surplus value is higher (Fine, "Exploitation and Surplus Value"). This is the reason the value of labor power is crucial for understanding exploitation.
40. Gough, *Political Economy of the Welfare State*; Marx, *Capital*, vol. I.

41. B. Fine, *Labour Market Theory: A Constructive Reassessment* (New York: Routledge, 2002), 8–9. (Emphasis added.)
42. "1. Biological reproduction of the species, and specifically the conditions and social constructions of motherhood in different societies. 2. The reproduction of the labor force, which involves not only subsistence but also education and training. 3. The reproduction of provisioning and caring needs that may be wholly privatized within families, or socialized or, indeed, provided through a combination of the two" (Gill and Bakker, eds., *Power, Production and Social Reproduction*, 32).
43. "This aspect of social reproduction was the focus of a great deal of debate within Marxist Feminist Political Economy in the 1970s and formed part of the 'domestic labor debates.' The object of these debates was to specify women's contribution through their unpaid labor (hence 'exploited' labor) to the functioning of capitalism and the perpetuation of patriarchy within the family, in other words, to uncover the material conditions of women's oppression. More recent accounts link questions of the reproduction of the labor force to the systemic contradiction between capitalist accumulation and the necessary reproduction of different strata of labor power and consumers. Here the focus is on the changing conditions of both women's and men's contribution to the reproduction of labor power and the mediating relationship of the state via the social wage" (ibid., 77).
44. This aspect of Marx's theory is often criticized for referring to Malthusian population theory: see B. Rowthorn, *Capitalism, Conflict and Inflation: Essays in Political Economy* (London: Lawrence and Wishart, 1980). However, this is not a fair critique. Malthusian theory is an equilibrium theory which Marx severely criticizes. Malthus argues that if the population increases more than the food supply does, food would be scarce; then the population would again decrease. Thus Malthus argues that population increase, especially for the masses, should be kept under control. This is understood as a "natural selection of society" approach and is rightly criticized for using nature as a limit to the rules of capitalist relations. See Thomas Malthus, "An Essay on the Principle of Population," 1798, https://www.marxists.org/reference/subject/economics/malthus.
45. Marx, *Capital*, vol. I.
46. Gill and Bakker, eds., *Power, Production and Social Reproduction*. An important issue here is elder care activities, which become more significant with the increasing number of retirees across the world. Pension income is essential for retirees as, in the absence of a pension, either the family, the state, or society must provide a certain level of material living standard. Pension scheme is a systematic way of socializing the costs of elderly care. When these schemes are eroded or inadequate, a need emerges for individual responsibility on the part of family members. Mostly it is female workers who drop out of the labor market to take care of elderly family members (G. Peri, A. Romiti, and M. Rossi, "Immigrants, Domestic Labor and Women's Retirement Decisions," *Labour Economics* 36, 2015: 18–34).

In relation, the wage level must sustain unemployed women's and elderly family members' financial needs.

47. Marx, *Critique of the Gotha Programme*; E.D. Motta e Albuquerque, "Visible Seeds of Socialism and Metamorphoses of Capitalism: Socialism after Rosdolsky," *Cambridge Journal of Economics* 39, no. 3 (2014): 783–805.
48. The manuscript was sent to the Gotha Unity Congress of the German Social Democratic Party in 1875. Here, Marx severely criticizes Lassallean understanding of labor struggle while also highlighting how to understand social democratic reforms from a revolutionary point of view.
49. Marx, *Critique of the Gotha Programme*, 15. (Emphasis added.)
50. I. Gough, "State Expenditure in Advanced Capitalism," *New Left Review* 92 (1975): 53–92; G. Esping-Andersen, *The Three Worlds of Welfare Capitalism* (Princeton, NJ: Princeton University Press, 1990).
51. Gough, *Political Economy of the Welfare State.*
52. B. Fine and L. Harris, "'State Expenditure in Advanced Capitalism': A Critique," *New Left Review* I, no. 98 (1976): 97–112.
53. Gough, *Political Economy of the Welfare State.*
54. "In Marx's value analysis, a tax on wages cannot effect a redistribution of values toward capital, for wage revenues equal the value of labor power and the net value of wages cannot be permanently depressed below it. The imposition of a tax on wages (or wage goods) must lead to a rise in gross wages; it is, therefore, in fact a tax on capital which is collected through the wage mechanism. In Marx's value analysis, therefore, *all taxes are taxes on capital and the source of all tax revenue is surplus value.* Moreover, for Marx this is not merely some simplified abstract proposition, it is the normal state of affairs in reality. While taxes on labor may *temporarily* redistribute from labor to capital, the normal situation will be for a restoration of the (net) value of wages to the value of labor power. Fine and L. Harris, "'State Expenditure in Advanced Capitalism,'" 106 (emphasis added).
55. Esping-Andersen, *Three Worlds of Welfare Capitalism.*
56. "To understand the concept, decommodification should not be confused with the complete eradication of labor as a commodity; it is not an issue of all or nothing. Rather, the concept refers to the degree to which individuals, or families, can uphold a socially acceptable standard of living independently of market participation. In the history of social policy, conflicts have mainly revolved around what degree of market immunity would lie permissible; i.e., the strength, scope, and quality of social rights. When work approaches free choice rather than necessity, de-commodification may amount to de-proletarianization" (ibid., 37).
57. For instance, for Esping-Andersen, if a pension provision is universal and equally distributed to the society at levels that enable people to live without working, that is a decommodifying service. However, this is not in fact what capitalist relations require, for obvious reasons: it needs workers to need to sell their labor power for a living. Without going to the orthodox

literature on welfare economics, which focuses on what level of social provision would not harm the labor supply, let us show how this contradicts with the Marxist understanding of the value of labor power. That is why the value of labor power cannot be simply reduced to the sum of wages and social benefits an individual worker gets during or after the working period; it is a standard of living for the whole working class, though this standard varies across different groups of the proletariat as well as across times and places.

58. R.L. Madrid, *Retiring the State: The Politics of Pension Privatization in Latin America and Beyond* (Stanford, CA: Stanford University Press, 2003).
59. K. Muller, *Privatising Old-Age Security: Latin America and Eastern Europe Compared* (London: Edward Elgar, 2003).
60. World Bank, *Averting the Old Age Crisis: Policies to Protect Old and Promote Growth*, Policy Research Report). (Washington, DC: World Bank, 1994), http://www-wds.worldbank.org/servlet/WDSContentServer/IW3P/IB/1994/09/01/000009265_3970311123336/Rendered/PDF/multi_page.pdf.
61. M.A. Orenstein, *Privatizing Pensions: The Transnational Campaign for Social Security Reform* (Princeton, NJ: Princeton University Press, 2008).
62. S. Sumaria, *Social Insecurity: The Financialisation of Healthcare and Pensions in Developing Countries,* Bretton Woods Project Report, 2010, http://ssreform.treasury.gov.za/Publications/Social%20Insecurity-%20The%20Finanacialisation%20of%20Healthcare%20and%20Pensions%20in%20Developing%20Countries%20%28Sumaria,%202010%29.pdf.
63. Indexation rule determines the pension benefit increase every year and this rule is advantageous for the retiree as long as it covers the inflation increase. Otherwise, retiree's pension income would melt year by year in the face of price level increase. Replacement rate refers to the success of the pension scheme in terms of replacing the career income level. If this rate lowers, it indicates that pension benefit becomes increasingly inadequate to sustain the career-term living standards of the pensioner.
64. Blackburn, *Banking on Death.*
65. Sumaria, *Social Insecurity.*
66. Organisation for Economic Co-operation and Development (OECD), *Reforming Public Pensions: Sharing the Experiences of Transition and OECD Countries* (Paris: OECD Publishing, 2004).
67. Fine, *Continuing Enigmas.*
68. G.R. Krippner, "The Financialization of the American Economy," *Socio-Economic Review* 3, no. 2 (2005): 173–208; C. Lapavitsas, *Profiting Without Producing: How Finance Exploits Us All* (London: Verso, 2013); O. Orhangazi, "Financialisation and Capital Accumulation in the Non-Financial Corporate Sector: A Theoretical and Empirical Investigation on the US Economy: 1973–2003," *Cambridge Journal of Economics* 32, no. 6 (2008): 863–86.
69. Fine, "Financialization from a Marxist Perspective," 55.

70. C. Lapavitsas, "Financialised Capitalism: Crisis and Financial Expropriation," *Historical Materialism* 17, no. 2 (2009): 114–48.
71. D. Yaffe, *The State and the Capitalist Crisis* (London: Revolutionary Communist Group, 1978).
72. R. Blackburn, *Age Shock: How Finance Is Failing Us* (New York: Verso, 2006).
73. "No direct or indirect wage hikes (pensions); instead, consumer credit and the push for stock market investment (pension funds, private insurance). No right to housing; instead, real estate loans" (M. Lazzarato, *The Making of the Indebted Man: An Essay on the Neoliberal Condition*, Los Angeles: Semiotext(e), 2012, 110).
74. J.D. Deken, "Towards an Index of Private Pension Provision," *Journal of European Social Policy* 23, no. 3 (2013): 275.
75. International Labour Organisation. *Turkiye Cumhuriyeti Sosyal Guvenlik Nihai Rapor* (Geneva: International Labour Organisation, 1996). In order to compensate for these people's old-age income, the recent reforms suggest "safety nets," a low basic income granted on the basis of need. In other words, although these people contribute to the social product and constitute an important fraction of the working class, their position in terms of production relations is completely ignored. Rather, they are presented as "losers" of the working class who did not even succeed in becoming entitled to old-age income. This is again a distortion of the relation between social reproduction and pensions as a component of the working class's means of consumption.
76. A.Y. Elveren, "Assessing Gender Inequality in the Turkish Pension System," *International Social Security Review*, 61, no. 2 (2008): 39–58.
77. S. Dedeoglu, "Eşitlik mi Ayrımcılık mı? Türkiye'de Sosyal Devlet, Cinsiyet Eşitliği Politikaları ve Kadın İstihdamı," *Calisma ve Toplum* 2 (2009): 41–54; A.Y. Elveren, and S. Hsu, *Gender Gaps in the Individual Pension System in Turkey*. University of Utah, Department of Economics, no. 2007-06, 2007, http://www.econstor.eu/bitstream/10419/64431/1/572640889.pdf.
78. P. Townsend, *The Right to Social Security and National Development: Lessons from OECD Experience for Low-Income Countries* (Geneva: International Labour Organisation, 2007).
79. Lazzarato, *Making of the Indebted Man.*
80. Blackburn, *Banking on Death.*
81. R.J. Shiller, "Democratize Wall Street, for Social Good," *New York Times*, April 7, 2012, http://www.nytimes.com/2012/04/08/business/democratize-wall-street-for-social-good.html.
82. C. Belfrage and M. Ryner, "Renegotiating the Swedish Social Democratic Settlement: From Pension Fund Socialism to Neoliberalization," *Politics and Society* 37, no. 2 (2009): 257–87.
83. M. Aglietta, "Shareholder Value and Corporate Governance: Some Tricky Questions," *Economy and Society* 29, no. 1 (2000): 146–59; W. Lazonick

and M. O'Sullivan, "Maximizing Shareholder Value: A New Ideology for Corporate Governance," *Economy and Society* 29, no. 1 (2000): 13–35.

84. J. Toporowski, *The End of Finance: Capital Market Inflation, Financial Derivatives and Pension Fund Capitalism* (London: Routledge, 2000).
85. E. Engelen, "The Logic of Funding European Pension Restructuring and the Dangers of Financialisation," *Environment and Planning A* 35, no. 8(2003): 1357–72.
86. F. Macheda, "The Role of Pension Funds in the Financialisation of the Icelandic Economy," *Capital and Class* 36, no. 3 (2012): 433–73.
87. T. Theurillat, J. Corpataux, and O. Crevoisier, "Property Sector Financialization: The Case of Swiss Pension Funds (1992–2005)," *European Planning Studies* 18, no. 2 (2010): 189–212.
88. C. Belfrage, "Towards 'Universal Financialisation' in Sweden?" *Contemporary Politics* 14, no. 3 (2008): 277–96.
89. R. Boyer, "Is a Finance-Led Growth Regime a Viable Alternative to Fordism? A Preliminary Analysis," *Economy and Society* 29, no. 1 (2000): 111–45.
90. Fine, *Continuing Enigmas.*
91. Marx, *Capital*, vol. I.
92. Esping-Andersen, *Three Worlds of Welfare Capitalism*; Gough, *Political Economy of the Welfare State.*
93. World Bank, *Averting the Old Age Crisis.*
94. Ibid.

CHAPTER 9: BODY POLITICS

1. Breanne Fahs, "'Freedom To' and 'Freedom From': A New Vision for Sex-Positive Politics," *Sexualities* 17, no. 3 (2014): 267–90.
2. Lauren Berlant and Michael Warner, "Sex in Public," *Critical Inquiry* 24, no. 2 (winter 1998): 548.
3. Jeffrey Weeks, *Sexuality*, 2nd ed. (London: Routledge, 2003), 4.
4. Jonathan Ned Katz, *The Invention of Heterosexuality* (New York: Plume, 1995), 182.
5. Ibid., 181.
6. Michel Foucault, *The History of Sexuality*, vol. 1 (New York: Random House, 1980), 26.
7. Ibid., 143–45.
8. Gayle Rubin, *Deviations: A Gayle Rubin Reader* (Durham: Duke University Press, 2011), 89.
9. Katz, *Invention of Heterosexuality.*
10. John D'Emilio, "Capitalism and Gay Identity," in *Making Trouble* (New York: Routledge, 1992), 8.
11. Peter Drucker, *Warped: Gay Normality and Queer Anti-Capitalism* (Leiden, Netherlands: Brill, 2015), 41.
12. Ibid., 60.

13. Eric Wolf, *Europe and the People Without History* (Berkeley: University of California Press, 1982).
14. Karl Marx, *Capital*, Vol. I (New York: Vintage, 1977), 273.
15. Ibid., 875.
16. Ibid., 876.
17. Ibid., 899.
18. Geoff Bailey, "Accumulation by Dispossession," *International Socialist Review* 95 (2015), http://isreview.org/issue/95/accumulation-dispossession.
19. Silvia Federici, *Caliban and the Witch* (New York: Autonomedia, 2004), 12–13.
20. Ibid., 12.
21. Ibid., 12.
22. Rosemary Hennessey, *Fires on the Border: The Passionate Politics of Labor Organizing on the Mexican Frontera* (Minneapolis: University of Minnesota Press, 2013), 131.
23. Ibid., 129.
24. Wallace Clement and John Myles, *Relations of Ruling: Class and Gender in Postindustrial Societies* (Montreal: McGill-Queen's University Press, 1994), 175.
25. Alan Sears, "Sexuality in the Social Reproduction Frame," *Historical Materialism* 24, no. 2 (2016): 138–63.
26. Angela Y. Davis, *Women, Race and Class* (New York: Random House, 1981), 5.
27. Roderick Ferguson, *Aberrations in Black: Toward a Queer of Color Critique* (Minneapolis: University of Minnesota Press, 2004), 86.
28. Johanna Brenner, *Women and the Politics of Class* (New York: Monthly Review Press, 2000), 2.
29. Lise Vogel, *Marxism and the Oppression of Women: Toward a Unitary Theory* (New Brunswick, NJ: Rutgers University Press, 1983), 139.
30. Marx, *Capital*, Vol. I, 284.
31. Karl Marx, *Economic and Political Manuscripts* (Moscow: Progress Press, 1969), 74.
32. Karl Marx and Friedrich Engels, *The German Ideology* (Moscow: Progress Press, 1976), 48.
33. Ibid., 73.
34. Marx, *Capital*, Vol. I, 283.
35. Ibid., 283.
36. Richard Levins and Richard Lewontin, *The Dialectical Biologist* (Cambridge, MA: Harvard University Press, 1985), 4.
37. Ibid., 257.
38. Marx and Engels, *German Ideology*, 48–49.
39. Marx, *Economic and Political Manuscripts*, 73.
40. Ibid., 71.
41. Ibid., 71.
42. Lisa Duggan, "The New Homonormativity: The Sexual Politics of Neoliberalism," in *Materializing Democracy: Toward a Revitalized Cultural*

Politics, edited by Russ Castronovo and Dana D. Nelson (Durham, NC: Duke University Press, 2002), 175–94.

43. I am focusing specifically on sexual assault against women by men here, given the preponderance and specificity of these forms of coercion and violence. There are other forms of sexual assault and gendered violence that I will not be able to approach within the confines of this article.
44. Nicola Gavey, *Just Sex? The Cultural Scaffolding of Rape* (London: Routledge, 2005), 2.
45. Ibid., 3.
46. Ibid., 222.
47. Ibid., 223.
48. Wayne Lewchuk, "Men and Monotony: Fraternalism as a Management Strategy at the Ford Motor Company," *Journal of Economic History* 534 (1993): 824–56.
49. Carolyn Steedman, "Prisonhouses," *Feminist Review* 20 (Summer 1985): 18.
50. Dorothy Smith, *The Conceptual Practices of Power* (Toronto: University of Toronto Press, 1990), 18.
51. Gavey, *Just Sex?* 124.
52. Ibid., 139.
53. Ibid., 139.
54. Ibid., 139.
55. Tithi Bhattacharya, "Explaining Gender Violence in the Neoliberal Era," *International Socialist Review* 91 (2014), http://isreview.org/issue/91/explaining-gender-violence-neoliberal-era.
56. Ibid.
57. Davis, *Women, Race and Class*, 175.
58. Ibid., 175.
59. Ibid., 177.
60. Ibid., 177.
61. Yoshimi Yoshiaki, *Comfort Women: Sexual Slavery in the Japanese Military During World War II* (New York: Columbia University Press, 2002), 190–91.
62. Nahla Abdo, *Captive Revolution: Palestinian Women's Anti-Colonial Struggle Within the Israeli Prison System* (London: Pluto, 2014), 208.
63. Kimberlé Crenshaw, "Mapping the Margins: Intersectionality, Identity Politics and Violence against Women of Color," *Stanford Law Review* 43, no. 6 (1991): 1250.
64. Carole Pateman, "Women and Consent," *Political Theory* 8, no. 2 (1980): 164.
65. Evgeny B. Pashukanis, *Law and Marxism: A General Theory* (London: Pluto, 1978), 110.
66. Bhattacharya, "Explaining Gender Violence."
67. Monica Shaw and Mave Mundy, "Complexities of Class and Gender Relations: Recollections of Women Active in the 1984–5 Miners' Strike," *Capital and Class* 87 (2005): 155.

68. Ibid., 165.
69. Mandi Gray, "An Open Letter to York University," March 2, 2015, http://www.academia.edu/11203878/an_open_letter_to_york_university_re_york_university_policy_on_sexual_assault_awareness_prevention_and_response; Sophie Allard, "Dénonciations à l'UQAM: l'origine de la colère," *La Presse* (Montréal), December 21, 2014, http://www.lapresse.ca/actualites/education/201412/20/01-4829963-denonciations-a-luqam-lorigine-de-la-colere.php.
70. Stephen Meyer, "Rough Manhood: The Aggressive and Confrontational Shop Culture of US Auto Workers during World War II," *Journal of Social History* 36, no. 1 (2002): 127.
71. Linda Briskin, "Feminisms, Feminization and Democratization in Canadian Unions," *Feminist Success Stories/Célébrons Nos Réussites Féministes*, edited by Karen A. Blackford, Marie-Lucie Garceau, and Sandra Kirby (Ottawa: University of Ottawa Press, 1999), 82.
72. Anne Forrest, "Connecting Women with Unions: What Are the Issues?" *Relations Industrielles* 56, no. 4 (2001): 647–75.
73. Jacquelyn Dowd Hall, "Disorderly Women: Gender and Labor Militancy in the Appalachian South," *Journal of American History* 73, no. 2 (1986): 372.
74. Ibid., 375.

CHAPTER 10: FROM SOCIAL REPRODUCTION FEMINISM TO THE WOMEN'S STRIKE

1. It is important to point out that the number of white women who voted for Trump is very small compared to the total number of white women of voting age in the United States.
2. Leslie McCall, "Men Against Women, or the Top 20 Percent Against the Bottom 80? How Does Growing Economic Inequality Affect Traditional Patterns of Gender Inequality?" *Council on Contemporary Families*, October 16, 2013, https://contemporaryfamilies.org/top-20-percent-against-bottom-80/.
3. Katha Pollitt, "Actually, Not Everything Is a Feminist Issue. And That's OK," *Nation*, March 23, 2017, https://www.thenation.com/article/actually-not-everything-is-a-feminist-issue.

Index